Diary of a Tuscan Chef

Diary of a Tuscan Chef

Tuscan Chef

RECIPES & MEMORIES OF GOOD TIMES AND GREAT FOOD

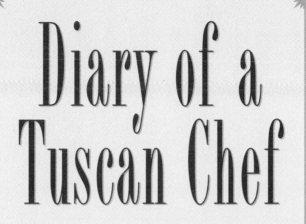

by Cesare Casella
&
Eileen Daspin

Doubleday

NEW YORK LONDON TORONTO SYDNEY AUCKLAND

PUBLISHED BY DOUBLEDAY

a division of Bantam Doubleday Dell Publishing Group, Inc.
1540 Broadway, New York, New York 10036

DOUBLEDAY and the portrayal of an anchor with a dolphin are
trademarks of Doubleday, a division of Bantam Doubleday Dell
Publishing Group, Inc.

BOOK DESIGN BY RENATO STANISIC

Photograph opposite title page: Mama, Papa, and me in front of Vipore, 1991;
photo by Art Streiber. Photo of food on title page by Guido Mannucci.

Library of Congress Cataloging-in-Publication Data
Casella, Cesare.
    Diary of a Tuscan chef : recipes and memories of good times and
great food / Cesare Casella and Eileen Daspin. — 1st ed.
      p.   cm.
    Includes Index.
     1. Cookery, Italian—Tuscan style.   2. Menus.   3. Casella, Cesare.
I. Daspin, Eileen.   II. Title.
TX723.2.T86C37   1998
641.59455—dc21   97-27743
                                                         CIP

ISBN 0-385-48547-6
Copyright © 1998 by Cesare Casella and Eileen Daspin
All Rights Reserved
Printed in the United States of America
April 1998
First Edition
10 9 8 7 6 5 4 3 2 1

Dedication

This book is dedicated, with great amore, to our parents,
Rosa and Pietro Casella
and Sara and Michael Daspin.

Cesare Di ore

Acknowledgments

. . . .

Thanking everyone who helped bring this cookbook to life would almost be impossible for us. The recipes and stories are the reflection of dozens and dozens of friendships, innumerable meals, and the accumulated experience of a lifetime. Some of the recipes are the result of a chance exchange at a favorite greengrocer's of Cesare's in the countryside, others evolved organically, after years of his adjusting, dabbling, traveling, and tasting other chefs' ideas.

A list of all the people who helped make Cesare who he is today would start with his parents, Rosa and Pietro, who taught him not only about food, but about life, and who set him on his journey as a chef. They also include his Aunt Anna, who helped out at Vipore and in remembering many details that went into the stories of this book, and his cousin, Paolo, whose friendship and assistance have been invaluable during the course of this project.

We would also like to thank everyone who worked with us during the past two years, starting with David Kratz, our friend and agent; Judy Kern, our editor; Sara Daspin, whose patience with *buccellato* deserves a mention of its own, and whose advice, skill, and assistance were invaluable in completing this book; Michael Daspin, whose taste buds were as crucial as his unflagging support.

Finally, we'd like to thank Fairchild Publications for sending Eileen to Italy; Julian and Lisa Niccolini for their friendship; Annie Brody, for encouraging Cesare to write a book; Augusto Marchini and the Italian Trade Commission; Giorgio Onesti, Faith Willinger, Gualtiero DiPuccio, Oliviero Prunas, Bill Flower, Kevin Garcia, Luca Belli, Walter Sodano, Peter Soerke, Matthew Gavzie, Renzo Menesini, Elsa Haft, David Colman, Janet Ungless, and all of our friends who helped taste and evaluate our efforts and listened to months and months of gastronomic and personal adventures. We couldn't have done it without you. All that's left is to enjoy. *Buon appetito.*

Contents

....

Introduction

Spring

Summer

EDUARDO FORNACIARI

Fall

Winter

Index

Introduction

．．．．．．．．．．．．．．．．．．．．

I *don't know where I was conceived exactly, but if I had to guess, I'd say it was in the kitchen, among dusty rounds of pecorino put up for the winter, tins of salted anchovies to eat with bread, jars of preserved shallots, and liters upon liters of* vino delle colline Lucchesi, *the house wine for natives of Pieve Santo Stefano, the tiny Tuscan town where I spent my youth.*

That's not to suggest that my mother, Rosa, twenty-seven at the time, and father, Pietro, also twenty-seven, had an improper tryst in my grandmother Maria's pantry. But by the time they met—introduced by the husband of Erminia, a friend of Mama's—Rosa was already working in the kitchen of a prominent Lucchese family and Pietro was running the restaurant owned by Zio Francesco, who later took off for Canada.

Their first date was on New Year's Eve, for dinner in Altopascio. They courted in modest countryside trattorie, *saving money for the day they would marry. When Papa popped the question, he treated Rosa to dinner at Solferino, a restaurant that used tablecloths, just down the street from where I would grow up.*

Their first dream as a couple was to own their own restaurant. I remember, when I was three, riding on a Vespa, wedged between Pietro and the handlebars, to the neighboring village of Pieve Santo Stefano. Actually, I was standing up; Mama was in the back with her arms stretched long around Papa. It took twenty minutes from Lucca, and until just a few years ago, still did, since the most direct road collapsed after a storm in the early seventies and wasn't repaired for almost two decades. We passed Solferino and went to look at a run-down country tavern, Il Vipore, which, I later learned, was best known for renting rooms upstairs by the hour, no questions asked. That was April. In August, Rosa and Pietro signed a lease. They spent two weeks cleaning and scrubbing, then we went into business.

PIETRO CASELLA AND ROSA POLIDORI ON THEIR WEDDING DAY, OCTOBER 17, 1959.

On opening night, I got my first taste of the famous local rosso, *red wine, from Forci. I don't remember that moment. Mama says I drained my cup, and no doubt I did, as I have many times since. It was the beginning of a long affair with the pleasures of wine and food.*

In the summer of 1993, I came to New York to be the executive chef for Coco Pazzo, a popular restaurant on the Upper East Side of Manhattan. It was often a "scene," packed with celebrities and loyal regulars. On a busy night, we did three seatings, ninety people at a clip. I then moved on, working in other restaurants, planning to open my own, and learning to live in a city with 8 million people. I discovered I could walk ten blocks and change worlds, from Chinatown to Little Italy to Little Korea.

I knew even before I got here that life in New York would be more stressful than in Pieve Santo Stefano, but I also knew there is no other city that would offer so many

**FROM LEFT, AUNT LANDA, COUSIN PIERO, PAPA (I'M ON HIS SHOULDERS), AND MAMA,
AT VIPORE JUST AFTER IT OPENED IN 1964.**

*opportunities. For an Italian that possibility is something incredible. For someone who
likes to compete and win as I do, New York is the perfect place to be, a daily challenge.*

Of course, no matter how long I live in this city, I will always be un ragazzo di
campagna, *a country kid, which is why I wanted to write* Diary of a Tuscan Chef.
*Yes, there are already dozens of Italian cookbooks on the market. But as far as I
know, no one has written a cookbook for the American public that presents Tuscan
food as it is—good, simple, and natural. The Tuscan table should be as easy to set
in New York as it is in Garfagnana, or in Rome, Georgia, for that matter.*

*Remarkably, I've seen Tuscan cookbooks whose recipes are so complicated, they
are practically French. I've seen books where they use tons of butter, which in Tuscany
is only used in the mountains, and I've seen books relying on exotic products. Maybe
because they produce dishes that photograph better. This is not the Tuscan cooking
I know.*

The way I learned to cook, the way my family ate as I was growing up, and the way I cook today, is Tuscan cooking. It is using what you have on hand—whether from the garden or cupboard—an important factor when the store is a long hour or more away. Tuscan cooking doesn't require a professionally equipped kitchen or a pantry stocked with every spice and condiment imaginable. Where I grew up, if you came home from work and all you had was canned tuna and spaghetti, that, with a few grinds of black pepper, good bread, and table wine, became dinner. You learned to be flexible and to experiment. If a recipe called for lemon thyme and all you had was mint, you went with it; if you wanted to flavor your seafood risotto with pancetta, you forged ahead.

Tuscan food has always been and still is a cuisine without rules. Some dishes, like a ragù, are more time-consuming than others, but almost everything is simple. You need only to know your ingredients and to improvise. I believe the most important tool for organizing a menu is the calendar, which is why I've arranged this book along seasonal lines. I've put together dozens of menus—both traditional and innovative—inspired by moments from my life, favorite meals, the vendemmia *(grape harvest), and at the* sbottaturra *(when new wine is transferred from barrels into bottles).*

Sometimes I digress and talk about Giacomo Puccini, a native of Lucca, as famous locally for his music as for his appetites, romantic and otherwise. Or I reminisce about my friend Lorenzo in Forte di Marmi, who makes the most incredible baby octopus "salami," or Romano, my friend in Viareggio, who makes the best prawns I've ever had. These stories are part of who I am.

Since the Italian cheeses, wines, and salame—*cured meats—are worlds unto themselves, I have also included tips to help the person cooking at home begin to understand them. With every menu, I suggest two Tuscan wines because they are the ones I know best and feel most comfortable recommending. (This, of course, is merely a guide. All of the wines might not be available in the United States, and they might not suit your taste. You can either rely on the type of grape named to select an alternative, or simply pick a wine you think will complement your meal.)*

Occasionally I will describe a salami I like or tell a story about one of my favorite cheeses. Tuscany, for example, is famous for its pecorino. There are dozens of differ-

ent pecorinos; they vary from frazione to frazione *(village to village) and farm to farm. Some are sold aged because the farmer lives far from the central market and only goes to town once a month; others are eaten fresh; some are spicy, others mild. Myself, I like pecorino best at the bar of Il Vipore, in the company of Piero "Penna Bianca" (the White Feather), my best friend Emilio, and Ernesto (a.k.a. Camay, because when he was young, he would steal bars of Camay soap to give to the local girls). On Sundays, we play* briscola, *an Italian card game, until very late. Everyone smokes, and as we insult each other, yell and pound the table, we consume slabs of cheese, washed back with Forci's best red wine.*

Eating in Italy is almost a full-time occupation. There is as much pleasure in anticipating a meal and reminiscing about it afterward as there is in the eating. That's because Italians love Italian food. I even know a few who carry pasta, olive oil, and espresso with them when they travel—for fear of going hungry. I've gotten over that, but what I do miss about eating in Italy is an attitude. Italian cooking isn't just recipes, it's a fusion of many cultures, and it's from the heart. It's simple, based on friendship, good whether you're dining on fagioli *(beans) or* caviale *(caviar). In fact, the best Tuscan dishes are simple, like* fettunta, *toasted bread with olive oil, or* acquacotta, *literally, cooked water, to which vegetables, a piece of meat, whatever is in the cupboard, are added.*

In opening my diary to you, I share my childhood, my life in New York, and my secrets from across the Atlantic. Sometimes, you'll find ingredients that don't exist in traditional Tuscan cooking. That's because when I came to the United States, I had to adapt and adjust and juggle to re-create the taste of Italy. I took my clues from the peasant's wife, the mother of Tuscan cooking. She works the fields all day, then returns home to put a meal on the table for her family. She doesn't run out to the supermarket for anything at all. She doesn't have to. She takes stock of her pantry and goes to work, more often than not producing love, and sometimes magic. I hope to help you do the same.

A SELECTION OF VIPORE'S SALUMI, LARD, PECORINO, AND PACKAGED PRODUCTS.

Spring Menus

1. AL MERCATO CON PAPÀ · **AT THE MARKET WITH DAD**

Antipasto dal Mercato · Roasted Market Vegetables

Penne con Favoli · Penne with Crab Meat

Filetto di San Pietro in Brodo di Lattuga e Finocchi · John Dory in Lettuce and Fennel Broth

Pannacotta con Salsa di Aranci · Flan with Orange Sauce

2. IL MIO PESTO · **MY PESTO**

Insalata di Fagiolini · Haricots Verts Salad

Pasta al Gusto dell'Arometo · Garden Fresh Pasta

Coniglio Marinato alle Erbe Aromatiche · Rabbit Marinated in Aromatic Herbs

Biscotti Misti · Mixed Cookie Plate

3. UNA PRIMAVERA SENZA POLLO · **A CHICKEN-FREE SPRING**

Insalata di Carciofini · Baby Artichoke Salad

Pasta con Verdure alla Griglia · Pasta with Grilled Vegetables

Osso Buco con Purè di Patate · Veal Shank with Mashed Potatoes

Frittelle di San Giuseppe · Father's Day Fritters

4. CAMPOCATINO · **ON MY MOUNTAIN**

Torta di Erbe della Lunigiana · Herb Pie, Lunigiana Style

Spaghetti con Pecorino · Spaghetti with Pecorino

Controfiletto di Maiale al Profumo di Rosmarino · Pork Chops Perfumed with Rosemary

La Torta co' Bischeri · Scalloped Pisa Pie

5. IL VIN ITALY · **THE COMPETITION**

Scarpaccia · Zucchini and Red Onion Scramble

Insalata di Coniglio e Radicchio · Rabbit and Radicchio Salad

Pollo Ripieno · Stuffed Roast Chicken

Torta di Marmellata · Marmalade Tart

AL MERCATO CON PAPÀ
At the Market with Dad

Antipasto dal Mercato	Roasted Market Vegetables
Penne con Favoli	Penne with Crab Meat
Filetto di San Pietro in Brodo di Lattuga	John Dory in Lettuce and
e Finocchi	Fennel Broth
Pannacotta con Salsa di Aranci	Flan with Orange Sauce

SUGGESTED WINES: VERNACCIA, GIANNINA (GRAPE: VERNACCIA); TERRE DI TUFI,
TERUZZI E PUTHOD (GRAPE: VERNACCIA, BARREL-AGED)

If you look in any guide book about Lucca, you'll find notes on the Piazza dell'Anfiteatro, a Roman amphitheater dating back to the second century. For tourists, the piazza is a curiosity, an oddly shaped public square ringed with stylish boutiques like Mamma Ró linens—like the Anna Magnani character in Pasolini's *Mamma Roma*—and Il Vecchio Funaio gift shop. But when I was growing up, the piazza was Lucca's busiest fruit and vegetable market, a lively link in the food chain. Piazza dell'Anfiteatro was where merchants, farmers, housewives, and restaurateurs congregated to buy and sell the earth's bounty, where Papa went three or four times a week to stock the restaurant.

The people who lived and worked in the piazza—we called them *piazzaioli* (people from the piazza)—sold an abundance of fresh vegetables and produce. So did the stalls of the farmers in the middle of the piazza, who came from the country, sometimes by foot, from as far away as twenty kilometers. Everyone seemed to have a half-dozen children—all as loud and boisterous as their parents—and everyone helped sell, whether from a shop, stand, cart, umbrella, basket, or whatever makeshift business operation the family could pull together.

Until 6:45 A.M., only vendors were allowed to pass into the square. Everyone else was kept outside. The crowd would grow and grow, and then at 6:45 sharp, a guard would ring a bell and open the gate. I remember the first time Papa asked me to go with him to Piazza dell'Anfiteatro. I was about twelve, and as we were swept into the middle with all the other shoppers, I thought I would lose Papa. There were so many people and sounds and smells, it made me dizzy. It was April, and there were asparagus and strawberries and green beans after long months of only oranges and broccoli rabe. There were women in black dresses with black kerchiefs on their heads and baskets on their arms. There were men in dark vests and rough linen shirts. Everyone was shouting over one another. They had such strong voices. *"La mia insalata e più bella di quella di Giovanna!"* (My lettuce is better than Giovanna's!) *"Tre limoni 50 lire!"* (Three lemons, 50 lire!) They yelled at my dad as we passed by, *"Biondo! Vieni qua!"* (Blondie! Come over here!) He talked to certain ladies, the prettiest ones, it seemed to me. After the second or third time I said, "Papa, Mama's at home, why are you talking to those women?" In answer, he gave me my first lesson in purchasing power, "I'm getting the best prices possible," he explained. "It always pays to be nice to the people with the best products."

Antipasto dal Mercato
Roasted Market Vegetables
(SERVES 4–6)

1 small eggplant, cut lengthwise into
$1/4$ inch slices

1 small zucchini, cut lengthwise into
$1/4$ inch slices

2 plum tomatoes, quartered lengthwise

$1/2$ medium head fennel, cut lengthwise
into $1/4$-inch slices

1 medium carrot, cut diagonally into
$1/4$-inch slices

$1/4$ pound shiitake mushrooms, cleaned
and sliced

4 scallions, cleaned

4 stalks asparagus, tough ends trimmed

1 head endive, cut into 4 lengthwise
pieces

1 head radicchio, cut into 8 lengthwise
pieces

$1/2$ yellow bell pepper, seeded and cut
into chunks

$1/2$ red bell pepper, seeded and cut into
chunks

4 tablespoons extra-virgin olive oil

4 tablespoons white wine

2 tablespoons water

1 teaspoon salt

$1/2$ teaspoon fresh ground black pepper

Turn on the broiler. Place all the vegetables in a roasting pan. In a bowl, whisk together the olive oil, wine, water, salt, and black pepper. Drizzle the olive oil mixture over the vegetables, and stir to coat them well. Place the pan under the broiler for 8 to 12 minutes, stirring occasionally, watching so the vegetables don't burn but become slightly grilled and tender.

Serve the vegetables on 4 separate plates or one big serving platter while still hot.

Penne con Favoli
Penne with Crab Meat

In Italy, it's difficult to get precooked crab meat, so for a recipe like this, we boil the crabs ourselves in vegetable broth and tomatoes, then remove the meat and add it to the tomato sauce. This makes a tastier sauce, but the procedure is such a headache, I suggest you start off with cooked jumbo lump or backfin crab meat.

(SERVES 4 AS AN APPETIZER)

3 quarts water

1 1/2 tablespoons salt, plus more to taste

1/2 pound penne pasta

1/4 cup extra-virgin olive oil

2 tablespoons chopped garlic

2 teaspoons fresh thyme leaves

1 1/2 teaspoons crushed red pepper flakes

1 1/4 cups crushed canned tomatoes

2 1/2 cups cooked jumbo lump or backfin crab meat, picked over to remove cartilage

1/4 teaspoon fresh ground black pepper

In a large pot, bring the water to a boil and add the 1 1/2 tablespoons of salt and the penne.

Place the olive oil, garlic, thyme, and red pepper flakes in a medium saucepan and sauté over medium heat for about 3 minutes. Stir in the crushed tomatoes, salt, and simmer for 15 minutes. Add the crab and cook another 5 minutes. When the penne is very *al dente*, drain and add it to the sauce. Cook for 5 minutes. Stir in the black pepper and serve.

Perfect Pasta

....

I remember hearing with disbelief that Americans tested spaghetti by throwing a strand against the wall; it was ready to eat if it stuck and didn't slip. I'd like to believe that story was apocryphal, but just in case, a few words about cooking and choosing pasta.

First of all, the pasta is the basis for your dish and is just as important as the sauce. It must be cooked in the right amount of water, with the right amount of salt, for the right amount of time. I suggest 3 quarts of water and 1½ tablespoons of salt for every ½ pound of pasta. (The salt will vary depending on the saltiness of the sauce.) Some insist that the salt be added before the water boils. Others, only after. The important thing is to remember the salt—preferably kosher—and to taste the pasta for doneness. That is the only failproof test. Pasta should be cooked al dente, so that it is still resilient when you bite it.

The other important thing about pasta is that certain shapes go better with certain sauces. A safe rule is, the thinner the pasta, the lighter the sauce. A heavy cheese sauce on capellini will result in a blob; olive oil and garlic on bucatini will be lost. Rotelle are good for "catching" tomato sauce, as are conchiglie. Use short pastas with chunky sauces; longer strands for "saucier" sauces.

Filetto di San Pietro in Brodo di Lattuga e Finocchi

John Dory in Lettuce and Fennel Broth

I invented this dish in a moment when I was trying to eat well, and light.

(SERVES 4)

3 quarts cold water

1 whole fennel bulb, sliced, fronds reserved

1 medium carrot, sliced

2 stalks celery, sliced

1 medium red onion, sliced

3 scallions, split lengthwise

4 cloves garlic, peeled and slightly crushed

4 sprigs fresh thyme

2 tablespoons sliced fresh ginger (optional)

2 tablespoons chopped lemongrass (optional)

4 John Dory fillets (sole works fine here, too)

2 plum tomatoes, quartered

18 fresh basil leaves

2 sprigs fresh Italian parsley

1 head baby Bibb or Boston lettuce

1 tablespoon salt

Crushed red pepper flakes, to taste

In a pot with the cold water, place the vegetables, garlic, thyme, ginger, and lemongrass. Bring to a boil, then reduce the heat and simmer for 2 hours, until the liquid is reduced by half.

Add the John Dory fillets and the tomato quarters. Cover the pot and cook the fish for 4 to 5 minutes. Add the basil, parsley, lettuce, salt, and red pepper flakes, and cook for 2 minutes more, covered.

Serve in wide bowls, starting with the fish. Arrange the vegetables on top, and add about a cup of broth. Garnish each bowl with some of the reserved fennel leaves.

Lemongrass

. . . .

After he helped me design the "Arometo," my extensive herb garden, Signor Lippi, the director of the Botanic Gardens of Lucca, gave me my first lemongrass plant. At the time, I didn't know what to do with it, so I just chewed the stalks as they were, papery covering and all. When Lippi asked me how I'd liked his gift, I was embarrassed and said I'd used it in a dish that sold out immediately and never even got to taste it. Then he brought me some more, and I started to experiment for real. I had to act fast, though. Mama thought it was like marijuana and would confiscate it from the kitchen. When I insisted the lemongrass was for cooking, she relented—and started to use it as rabbit feed. Lemongrass's sour lemon flavor nicely enhances clear broths.

Pannacotta con Salsa di Aranci
Flan with Orange Sauce

Though *pannacotta* and *crème brûlée* are often confused, there is a big difference between them: *pannacotta* is a cooked custard (literally, cooked cream), while *crème brûlée* is an egg custard that you dust with sugar and broil (literally, burned cream). The *crème brûlée* I like best is Le Cirque's, but my *pannacotta* holds its own.

(S E R V E S   4)

1 cup whole milk

1 cup heavy cream

½ cup sugar

1 vanilla bean, split; or ¼ teaspoon
    vanilla extract

2 gelatin sheets soaked in cold water, or
    2 teaspoons unflavored powdered
    gelatin sprinkled over 3 tablespoons
    cold water

Orange Sauce (recipe follows)

In a medium-size saucepan, heat the milk, cream, sugar, and vanilla over high heat. Whisk the mixture to dissolve the sugar and bring it to a quick boil. Remove the pan immediately from the stove. Continue to whisk the mixture to combine all the ingredients. Add the soaked gelatin sheets (or the dissolved powder) to the hot cream mixture. Whisk thoroughly and let the mixture cool for 10 minutes. (If the vanilla bean was used, discard it at this point.)

Ladle the mixture into individual ramekins or custard cups, filling them almost to the top. Cover each cup with plastic wrap to prevent a skin from forming on the top. Then place them on a sheet pan and refrigerate for at least 3 hours, or until set.

When you are ready to serve, spoon a little sauce on each plate. Remove the *pannacotta* from their cups and place one in the center of each plate, upside down. Place 3 or 4 orange sections around each custard. Decorate the plate with the orange zest.

Salsa di Aranci

Orange Sauce

2 navel oranges

1¼ cups water

¼ cup sugar

1½ tablespoons orange liqueur

½ tablespoon sambuca liqueur

With a sharp knife, remove the zest from the oranges and slice it into thin strips. Remove the remaining pith, cutting deep enough into the fruit to remove the thin outer membrane of the orange sections. Hold each orange in your hand, and carefully slice out the individual sections so that there is no membrane attached. Set the sections aside.

Place the sliced zest in a medium-size saucepan. Add the water, sugar, and the liqueurs. Bring the mixture to a boil over medium-high heat and cook for 20 minutes, until the sauce is reduced and slightly thickened. Remove from the heat and let it cool for 15 to 20 minutes, then add the reserved orange sections. Refrigerate until serving time.

IL MIO PESTO
My Pesto

Insalata di Fagiolini	Haricots Verts Salad
Pasta al Gusto dell'Arometo	Garden Fresh Pasta
Coniglio Marinato alle Erbe Aromatiche	Rabbit Marinated in Aromatic Herbs
Biscotti Misti	Mixed Cookie Plate

SUGGESTED WINES: VILLA BIANCO, ANTINORI (GRAPES: TREBBIANO, MALVASIA, CHARDONNAY); SPARTITO, CASTELLARE (GRAPE: SAUVIGNON BLANC)

I'd been to Recco, a small town outside Genoa, which, like all of Liguria, is famous for silky, emerald pesto, redolent with garlic and basil, and cool Ligurian breezes. The Genovese turn a plate of *trenette al pesto*, a simple *primo* or first course, into a perfect, well-rounded meal by adding green beans and potatoes. I had an astounding plate of this at a Genovese restaurant called Manuelina with my friend Giorgio Onesti and on the way home became obsessed with creating a Tuscan pesto.

Literally, *pesto* means "crushed." In Liguria, recipes specify crushing the basil by hand in a marble mortar with a pestle "of good wood." In Pieve Santo Stefano, I had in my garden forty-seven herbs I could crush. I started to experiment.

It took me a month to find the right combination and proportion of herbs. I didn't want to take a bite and be able to discern a little marjoram, a little thyme, a little mint. What I wanted was for all the herbs to fuse into one flavor. I started chopping herbs and letting them macerate in olive oil for a week at a time until I got the taste I was looking for. A journalist I know, Domenico Acconci, dubbed the results *"l'Arometo,"* which means "the place where aromas come from"—just as *frutta* (fruit) comes from a *frutteto*, olives come from an *oliveto*, and grapevines come from a *vigneto*.

Insalata di Fagiolini

Haricots Verts Salad

(SERVES 4)

1 pound fresh haricots verts, ends
trimmed

2 teaspoons salt, plus extra to taste

2 tablespoons extra virgin olive oil
(truffle oil works well, too)

1 teaspoon red wine vinegar

1 teaspoon fresh-squeezed lemon juice

Fresh ground black pepper, to taste

1 cup well-washed arugula

1/8 pound pecorino Toscano cheese,
shaved into thin slices

Bring a saucepan of water to a boil and add the haricots verts and 2 teaspoons of salt. Simmer for 5 or 6 minutes, until tender but still crisp. Drain the beans and chill.

In a small bowl, mix the oil with the vinegar and lemon juice. Add salt and pepper. Toss the arugula with 1 tablespoon of the dressing, and the haricots verts with the remaining dressing.

Divide the beans among 4 plates and top each pile with a few arugula leaves. Finish each salad with some of the shaved pecorino and serve.

Parmigiano-Reggiano

Papa and I used to go once a week to Civago near Modena to buy fresh Parmigiano-Reggiano. I loved the drive, passing the dairy cows in the fields, the great green pastures, the silos. That farmer, I remember, had the best Parmigiano—nutty and grainy at the same time—and butter better than Nonna Maria's. But the image that sticks most in my mind was when he'd tell Papa how he was planning to take the Parmigiano rounds "to the bank." I thought he was taking them to the center in Modena and depositing them in the Banca Popolare in exchange for money. In fact, he was taking the cheese "to the bank" to be aged.

Good Parmigiano is expensive, but you can't cook Italian food without it. Buy the cheese in a chunk, and store it in the refrigerator wrapped in a damp cloth or in an airtight container. For the freshest taste, grate the cheese just before eating. Look for the Parmigiano Reggiano stamped into the crust of the cheese. Some people prefer Grana Padano, which is more moist than Parmigiano-Reggiano and doesn't have as much bite. (Other substitutes are American Parmesan and Argentinean Reggianito.)

Pasta al Gusto dell'Arometo

Garden Fresh Pasta

When we made *arometo* sauce at Vipore, it was always enough to last a week or two. Since there was so much chopping to be done—it took 2 to 3 cases of herbs—the whole staff pitched in to do the work. Everyone would get their own *mezzaluna* (a knife with a curved blade), and as the chopping began, the restaurant would fill up with the most amazing aroma of fresh herbs.

(SERVES 4 AS AN APPETIZER)

3 quarts water

1$\frac{1}{2}$ tablespoons salt, plus extra to taste

1 cup tightly packed fresh mixed herbs
(use a combination of basil,
rosemary, thyme, Italian parsley,
marjoram, and oregano)—$\frac{1}{2}$ cup
finely minced

2 cloves garlic, finely minced

$\frac{1}{3}$–$\frac{1}{2}$ cup extra-virgin olive oil

$\frac{1}{2}$ pound linguine #8, spaghettini, or
angel hair pasta

4 tablespoons grated Parmigiano-
Reggiano cheese

Fresh ground black pepper, to taste

1 small tomato, peeled, seeded, and
diced small, for garnish

Bring the water to a boil in a large pot. Add 1$\frac{1}{2}$ tablespoons of salt.

In a bowl, combine the herbs, garlic, and olive oil and set aside. (This mixture will keep for 2 to 3 weeks in the refrigerator. It's best after 4 to 5 days.)

When the water boils, add the pasta and cook until it is *al dente*, then drain it and toss with the oil-herb-garlic combination. Stir in the Parmigiano-Reggiano and salt and pepper. Garnish the pasta with the diced tomato and serve immediately.

ME WITH A PLATE OF PASTA AL GUSTO DELL'AROMETO

Coniglio Marinato alle Erbe Aromatiche

Rabbit Marinated in Aromatic Herbs

This dish combines innovation, tradition, and the fact that even my Vipore clients wanted to eat "light." Our neighbor, Sodini, supplied us with the tastiest rabbit, and this dish became a big hit.

(S E R V E S   4)

3 tablespoons chopped fresh rosemary

3 tablespoons chopped fresh marjoram

3 tablespoons chopped fresh thyme

3 tablespoons chopped fresh savory

2 teaspoons crushed red pepper flakes

3 shallots, finely chopped

1 (3-pound) rabbit, cut in 8–10 pieces, rinsed and patted dry

Salt and fresh ground black pepper, to taste

3 tablespoons plus $\frac{1}{4}$ cup extra-virgin olive oil

1 tablespoon balsamic vinegar

3 bunches arugula, washed

In a small bowl, mix together the chopped herbs, red pepper flakes, and shallots. First rub the rabbit pieces with salt and pepper, then with the herb mixture. Cover the rabbit and refrigerate it overnight.

When you are ready to cook, preheat the oven to 450°. Place the rabbit on a sheet of aluminum foil and seal it closed to make an airtight pouch. Cook for 30 minutes. Insert a toothpick into the thigh. If the juice runs clear, the rabbit is done. If not, return it to the oven another 5 to 10 minutes.

Beat 3 tablespoons of the olive oil with the balsamic vinegar and use it to dress the arugula. Divide the salad among 4 plates. Place the rabbit pieces on top, drizzle with the remaining $\frac{1}{4}$ cup of olive oil, and serve.

PAPA PREPARING A RABBIT.

Winter Savory

*W*hen I first started using winter savory in a monkfish dish at Vipore,
I told my clients it was an aphrodisiac. Then one day all the winter savory I
had in the Arometo disappeared, just like that. So I started saying that stolen
winter savory would curse the user with a sexual hex. I didn't get my garden
replenished, but I got the satisfaction of a few furrowed brows. I love the
spicy, thyme-like taste, especially to flavor game dishes.

Biscotti Misti
Mixed Cookie Plate

Biscotti al Cioccolato
Chocolate Biscotti

(MAKES 40 COOKIES)

....

2 cups flour

6 tablespoons cocoa powder

$^1/_8$ teaspoon salt

$^1/_2$ teaspoon baking soda

$^3/_4$ teaspoon baking powder

3 eggs

1$^7/_8$ cups sugar

1 teaspoon vanilla extract

4 teaspoons brewed espresso

1$^1/_2$ cups blanched, toasted hazelnuts

Preheat the oven to 350° and line a baking sheet with parchment paper. In a large bowl, sift together the flour, cocoa powder, salt, baking soda, and baking powder.

In a separate bowl, beat together the eggs, sugar, vanilla, and espresso until the sugar dissolves. Set aside 3 tablespoons of the egg mixture and pour the rest into the dry ingredients. Stir until a dough forms. Work in the hazelnuts, then divide the dough in half and form 2 logs, each about 15 inches long. (The dough will be sticky. Wet your hands to make handling easier.)

Place the logs, at least 3 inches apart, on the baking sheet. Bake them for 10 minutes, then remove them from the oven and brush them with the reserved egg wash. Return them to the oven for another 10 minutes, then let the logs cool for 10 minutes.

Lower the oven temperature to 325°. With a spatula, transfer the logs to a cutting board and, with a sharp knife, cut them into $^1/_2$-inch-thick slices. Arrange the slices on their sides on the baking sheet and bake for another 5 minutes. Then turn the *biscotti* over and return them to the oven for a final 5 minutes. Cool the *biscotti* on wire racks and store them in an airtight container.

Biscotti di Noci Misti

Mixed Nut Biscotti

(MAKES 40 COOKIES)

....

½ cup sweet butter

¾ cup sugar

2 medium eggs, lightly beaten, plus 1
    egg beaten with 1 tablespoon water

¼ teaspoon vanilla extract

¼ teaspoon almond extract

Grated zest of ½ lemon

Grated zest of ½ orange

1¾ cups flour

½ teaspoon baking powder

½ teaspoon baking soda

¼ teaspoon salt

½ cup toasted almonds

½ cup toasted hazelnuts

½ cup toasted pistachios

Preheat the oven to 350° and line a baking sheet with parchment paper. In a large mixing bowl, cream together the butter and sugar. Add the 2 eggs and mix well. Add the vanilla and almond extracts and continue mixing. Mix in the lemon and orange zests.

In a separate bowl, combine the flour, baking powder, baking soda, and salt. Add this to the sugar-egg mixture and blend thoroughly. Add the toasted nuts and blend thoroughly.

Divide the dough into 2 parts. Wet your hands and form each portion into a 12-inch log. Place the logs on the baking sheet and bake for 20 to 25 minutes, or until the logs are golden brown. Remove them from the oven and brush them with the egg wash. Return the logs to the oven for 5 minutes more, then remove and cool the *biscotti* for 10 minutes.

Reduce the oven temperature to 250°. With a long metal spatula, remove the logs to a cutting board. Use a long sharp knife to cut the logs into 1-inch-thick slices. Stand the cookies up on the baking sheet, and bake for another 15 minutes. Cool on wire racks. Store in an airtight container.

Ricciarelli
Siena Cookies

(MAKES 20 COOKIES)

1 (8-ounce) can almond paste

1 cup plus 5 tablespoons confectioners' sugar

1 teaspoon Grand Marnier

2 egg whites

½ cup blanched almonds

Preheat the oven to 300° and line a sheet pan with parchment paper. Place the almond paste in a food processor and pulse until the paste is softened. It will take between 2 to 6 minutes, depending on the quality of the almond paste. Add 1 cup plus 2 tablespoons of the confectioners' sugar and blend, then add the Grand Marnier and blend again.

Beat the egg whites until they are stiff. Transfer the almond paste mixture to a separate bowl. Add the whites, a tablespoon at a time. You will only need 5 tablespoons. Mix until a very stiff dough forms. Fold in the almonds and mix well.

Pinch off heaping tablespoons of dough and shape them into little logs, about 2 inches long and ¾ inch wide. Place them on the sheet pan and bake until golden brown, 20 to 25 minutes. While the cookies are still hot, dust them lightly with the remaining 3 tablespoons of confectioners' sugar.

Una Primavera Senza Pollo

A Chicken-Free Spring

Insalata di Carciofini	Baby Artichoke Salad
Pasta con Verdure alla Griglia	Pasta with Grilled Vegetables
Osso Buco con Purè di Patate	Veal Shank with Mashed Potatoes
Frittelle di San Giuseppe	Father's Day Fritters

SUGGESTED WINES: CHIANTI DEI COLLI SENESI, ROMITORIO (GRAPES: SANGIOVESE, CANNAIOLO, TREBBIANO, MALVASIA); SANGIOVETO, BADIA A COLTIBUONO (GRAPE: SANGIOVETO)

·········

I was coming home in my yellow Fiat 500 one night when I grazed a fox that had darted out into the road. *Ganzo*, I thought, cool, a pet fox. I scooped her up, put her in the back seat, brought her home, and tied her on a short leash in the chicken coop. *"Sci pazzo?"* Papa blew up the next morning. "Are you crazy? Putting a fox in the chicken coop?"

Papa, I knew, wasn't going to be the one to get close enough to liberate *la volpe*, so I teased him for two days straight, and all the while, my new pet stayed put. She even left the chickens alone, though she wasn't too fond of me; every time I went to see her, she'd give me dead-fish eyes.

Then one morning she was gone, her rope gnawed through, the chickens unharmed. I was a little sorry to lose her, but secretly relieved she hadn't taken a chicken dinner with her. The relief was short-lived, however; within a day, *la volpe* returned, *alla grande*, in style. There were blood and feathers everywhere. Papa dubbed it a minimassacre and insisted on giving the victims a burial. If we couldn't serve the chickens to the customers, he said, at least we could use them as fertilizer. My

(continued on next page)

punishment was to clean the coop, bury the chickens, and restock with new ones. I went to *I Frati della Certosa*, a local order of monks who raised chickens. It's a hot place and smells awful. You have to pick the chicks one by one. I hated it. Then, for the whole spring, every time someone would ask for chicken, Papa would smirk, *"É colpa di Cesare, se non c'é il pollo."* If there's no chicken, it's Cesare's fault.

MAMA FEEDING THE CHICKENS, 1979.

Insalata di Carciofini
Baby Artichoke Salad

In Italy, artichokes are believed to have all kinds of restorative powers. Growing up at Vipore, we always fed the tough outer leaves to our rabbits because it helped them digest their food and made their meat more tender. I remember in the '50s and '60s, there was even a famous *amaro*, or bitter, named Cynar, which was made from an artichoke base. It's slogan was *"Bevi Cynar Contro il Logorio della vita Moderna"* (Drink Cynar to combat anxiety and the stress of modern life). The ad showed a radiantly calm man drinking Cynar in the middle of a traffic jam.

(S E R V E S   4)

16 baby artichokes

4 tablespoons fresh-squeezed lemon juice

¼ cup extra-virgin olive oil

Salt and fresh ground black pepper, to taste

1 teaspoon finely chopped fresh oregano

2 bunches arugula, well washed

2 ounces Parmigiano-Reggiano cheese

Peel the outer leaves from the artichokes until you reach the part where the leaves are mostly a creamy yellow. Cut the top inch off the artichoke and trim away the stem so that you are left with a golf-ball-size artichoke heart. If you aren't going to eat the salad right away, put the artichokes into a bowl of water with 3 tablespoons of the lemon juice. To prevent the artichokes from turning black, lay a paper towel on top of the water to keep air from getting to them. Refrigerate.

When you are ready to prepare the salad, drain the artichokes and slice them lengthwise as thin as possible. (If you have an electric slicer, that's ideal.) Place the

(continued on next page)

artichokes in a bowl. Add the remaining tablespoon of the lemon juice, the olive oil, salt and pepper, and oregano. Toss.

Divide the arugula among 4 plates. Top each plate with some artichoke mixture. Shave slices of Parmigiano-Reggiano over each salad and serve.

Artichokes

Artichokes are very reactive. They turn your hands black and turn black themselves if exposed to air too long. When I prepare artichokes, I always wear surgical gloves, a trick that's useful in handling any food that might stain your skin, like beets, or leave it smelling unholy, like Gorgonzola or garlic. When you work with artichokes, don't touch other foods, otherwise the artichokes will turn bitter. At the end, wash your hands with lemon juice.

Pasta con Verdure alla Griglia

Pasta with Grilled Vegetables

The first time I went to restaurants in Milan, I couldn't get over how many vegetarian entrees were on the menus; this was something rare in Tuscany, where vegetables were eaten as side dishes. But I liked the idea, so when I went back to Vipore, I raided our garden, and went to work in the kitchen. This was the result.

(S E R V E S 4 A S A N A P P E T I Z E R)

3 quarts water

1½ tablespoons salt, plus 2 teaspoons

1 teaspoon crushed red pepper flakes

4 tablespoons extra-virgin olive oil

1 small zucchini, ends trimmed, sliced into ¼-inch ovals

1 yellow bell pepper, seeded and quartered

1 small red onion, cut into ¼-inch-thick slices

2 scallions

¼ bulb fennel, fronds trimmed, cut into ¼-inch slices

2 plum tomatoes, sliced in half lengthwise

1 small eggplant, peeled and cut into ¼-inch slices

2 cloves garlic, chopped fine

½ pound short pasta, such as penne or fusilli

1 sprig fresh basil, chopped

1 sprig fresh oregano, chopped

1 sprig fresh thyme, chopped

4 tablespoons freshly grated Parmigiano-Reggiano cheese

Bring the water to a boil in a large pot. Add the 1½ tablespoons of salt.

Heat the outdoor grill or oven broiler. Sprinkle the vegetables with the remaining 2 teaspoons of salt and the red pepper flakes, then drizzle them with 2 tablespoons of the olive oil.

(continued on next page)

When the grill is very hot, add the vegetables, cooking them for 4 minutes on the first side, 3 on the second. (If you don't have a grill, you can broil the vegetables for 20 minutes, stirring occasionally, until they become soft and slightly browned.) When the vegetables are cooked, cut them into strips. In a large sauté pan, sauté the garlic in the remaining 2 tablespoons of olive oil until it colors slightly, about 5 minutes.

Add the pasta to the boiling water and cook until *al dente*.

Add the chopped herbs to the sauté pan, sauté for 1 minute, and add the vegetable strips. Cook the mixture for 10 minutes. Drain the pasta, toss it with the vegetables and the grated Parmigiano-Reggiano, and serve immediately.

MY SECOND-GRADE CLASS AT MONTE SAN QUIRICO, 1968. I'M SECOND FROM THE RIGHT IN THE MIDDLE ROW.

Osso Buco con Purè di Patate

Veal Shank with Mashed Potatoes

This dish is much more popular in America than it is in Italy.

(S E R V E S 4)

4 tablespoons chopped fresh rosemary

4 tablespoons chopped fresh sage

6 tablespoons chopped garlic

Salt and fresh ground black pepper, to taste

4 sections veal shank, each 2 inches
thick (5 pounds total)

1 cup flour

2/3 cup extra-virgin olive oil

2 cups white wine

1½ cups roughly chopped red onions

1 cup 1-inch-long carrot pieces

1 cup 1-inch-long celery pieces

3 cups crushed canned tomatoes
(or peeled, chopped fresh tomatoes)

4 cups water

Mashed Potatoes (recipe follows)

Preheat the oven to 350°. In a bowl, mix together the chopped herbs, garlic, and salt and pepper. Cut 2 or 3 slits in each veal shank and stuff them with the chopped herbs and garlic. Dredge the shanks on all sides, generously, in flour.

Pour the olive oil into a 4-quart ovenproof casserole or a large saucepan with a lid. Heat over high heat and add the shanks, browning them well on all sides. If there is still oil in the casserole, drain it, then add 1 cup of the wine, stirring to scrape up any bits that have stuck to the bottom of the casserole, and add the onions, carrots, and celery. Cover the casserole and reduce the heat to medium. Stir occasionally. After 8 to 10 minutes, add the second cup of wine. Add the crushed tomatoes and stir well. Re-cover. After another 10 minutes, add the water.

Cover the casserole and transfer it to the oven. Bake for 2 hours. The meat should be very tender.

Serve with the mashed potatoes.

Purè di Patate

Mashed Potatoes

....

4 Idaho potatoes, peeled and cubed

4 tablespoons sweet butter

Salt and fresh ground black pepper, to taste

½ cup milk

Put the potatoes in a pot and cover with cold water. Boil them until they are soft, 20 to 30 minutes. Drain them, and return them to the pot briefly, shaking to remove any excess moisture. Add the butter, salt and pepper, and milk and mash well. Cook another few minutes and serve.

Frittelle di San Giuseppe
Father's Day Fritters

When we first started to make these for the San Giuseppe holiday (Italian Father's Day, March 19), we didn't have an electric mixer, so Aunt Landa and Aunt Anna—*"La Spezina"*—were put to work beating the dough by hand. They were very relieved when I started taking the dough to the pastry shop of some friends, and I liked the new system, too. I'd dawdle and talk to customers, barely making it back in time to fry the fritters for dessert.

(MAKES 45–50 FRITTERS)

1 cup water

Pinch of salt

¾ cup sweet butter

1½ cups plus 2 tablespoons sifted flour

6 eggs, at room temperature

½ cup granulated sugar

Vegetable oil, for frying

¼ cup confectioners' sugar

Place the water, salt, and butter in a medium saucepan over medium heat. When the butter melts, add the flour all at once, and lower the heat. Mix the dough rapidly until a ball forms. It will be very stiff. Remove from the heat and let cool slightly.

Place the dough in the bowl of an electric mixer, and beat in the eggs, one at a time, until they are well incorporated. The batter should be thick, shiny, and smooth. Mix in 1 tablespoon of the granulated sugar. Stir the batter for 5 minutes.

Fill a large sauté or saucepan one third full with the vegetable oil and heat it to 375°. In batches, spoon scant tablespoons of the batter into the hot oil. Mix the *frittelle* regularly to help them puff up. When the *frittelle* are evenly browned, after 2 or 3 minutes, remove them with a slotted spoon and drain on paper towels.

Mix the remaining granulated sugar with the confectioners' sugar and dust the *frittelle*. These are great with Moscato, a sweet sparkling wine from Piedmont.

CAMPOCATINO
On My Mountain

Torta di Erbe della Lunigiana	Herb Pie, Lunigiana Style
Spaghetti con Pecorino	Spaghetti with Pecorino
Controfiletto di Maiale al Profumo di	Pork Chops Perfumed with
Rosmarino	Rosemary
La Torta co' Bischeri	Scalloped Pisa Pie

SUGGESTED WINES: PALEO BIANCO, LE MACCHIAIOLE (GRAPES: CHARDONNAY, SAUVIGNON BLANC, VERMENTINO); CARMIGNANO VILLA DI TREFIANO, CAPEZZANA (GRAPES: SANGIOVESE, CABERNET SAUVIGNON, CANAIOLO)

My grandfather, sometimes called *Il Gallo* (the rooster), was born in Upper Vagli and Grandma *(nonna)*, in Lower Vagli. Between Upper and Lower, there may have been one kilometer, but when *Il Gallo* and *nonna* got married, neither wanted to move to the other's village; it would have been like acceding to a foreign power. So they compromised and bought a house in Vagli, which was halfway between. I guess that was a good choice, seeing as how half of Lower Vagli is now under water. That happened about seventy years ago, when the local power authority moved all the villagers out of the center, flooded it, and built a dam. Now, the only time you can see all of Lower Vagli is the day the authority drains and cleans the dam. I used to go sometimes and watch, it was like the unveiling of our own Tuscan Atlantis.

But the real reason I liked visiting Lower Vagli was because it gave me an excuse to drag my friends to Campocatino, a nearby mountain valley where *Il Gallo* owned a few hectares of land. I loved thinking of my family as mountainowners and showing off the property. One year, my cousin Paolo and I brought a few friends with us, and boasted that after seeing Lower Vagli, we could picnic on "our family's mountain" in Campocatino.

What would have been a run-of-the-mill picnic turned into a pecorino feast when two local shepherds tried to charge us two thousand lire a person to enter the valley. I pointed out that as *Il Gallo*'s grandsons and heirs, Paolo and I would be entitled to a portion of any fees the shepherds might collect. That's all I needed to say. The shepherds apologized profusely, explaining that they were just trying to discourage campers, and sent us on our way.

Our group wasn't twenty minutes into our picnic when the taller of the shepherds reappeared at the edge of our blanket. I came to apologize again, he said, and lay a straw basket down in front of us. Inside there must have been three kilos of five different homemade pecorinos, fresh, studded with peppercorns, medium- and well-aged, and a slab of sweet ricotta. I nabbed the aged *cacio*, declaring I wanted to bring it to my parents, Rosa and Pietro. What I had in mind was grating it on a steaming bowl of spaghetti, with lots of fresh ground pepper, olive oil, and butter. I suspected it would be one of the best *spaghetti con pecorino* of my life, and I was right.

Torta di Erbe della Lunigiana

Herb Pie, Lunigiana Style

(SERVES 6–8)

....

Cornmeal for baking sheet

1 pound fresh Swiss chard

1 pound fresh spinach

½ pound mixed leafy greens, such as dandelion, watercress, and chicory

6 cups water

2 medium zucchini, sliced into ½-inch rounds

¼ cup extra-virgin olive oil

2 tablespoons chopped garlic

¼ teaspoon crushed red pepper flakes

⅓ cup chopped mixed fresh herbs, including savory, oregano, and marjoram

4 leeks, white parts only, well washed and chopped

Salt and fresh ground black pepper, to taste

½ cup chopped fresh Italian parsley

2 eggs

2 tablespoons freshly grated Parmigiano-Reggiano cheese

3 tablespoons freshly grated pecorino Romano cheese

5 tablespoons ricotta cheese

Pie Dough (recipe follows)

Preheat the oven to 350°, and sprinkle a baking sheet with cornmeal. Wash the Swiss chard well to remove the sand. Cut the leaves from the stalks and string any large stalks that look like celery. Wash the spinach and other greens very well. Bring the water to boil in a large stockpot. Add the Swiss chard, spinach, other greens, and zucchini. Cook for 5 to 7 minutes, then drain and cool. Squeeze as much liquid as possible out of the vegetables, chop them roughly, and set them aside.

In a large sauté pan, heat the olive oil, garlic, red pepper flakes, herbs, and leeks over medium until the leeks start to soften, about 5 minutes. Add the cooled vegetables and mix well, adding salt and pepper. Stir in the parsley and cool.

EDUARDO
FORNACIARI

Mix together the eggs, Parmigiano-Reggiano, pecorino, and ricotta, and stir into the vegetable mixture. Set it aside.

Divide the pie dough approximately in half, and roll each half into a circle $\frac{1}{8}$ inch thick. One circle will be larger, about 14 inches in diameter. Place the larger circle on the baking sheet. Spoon the filling onto the dough and lay the smaller circle, about 12 inches in diameter, on top. Pinch the edges together and bake for 40 to 45 minutes, until the pie is golden brown. Cool slightly, slice, and serve.

Pasta

Pie Dough

. . . .

2 cups all-purpose flour

Pinch of salt

$\frac{1}{4}$ cup extra-virgin olive oil

$\frac{1}{2}$–$\frac{2}{3}$ cup water

In a large bowl, blend the flour with the salt, then whisk together the olive oil and the smaller quantity of water and add them to the flour, stirring until a dough forms. Add more water if necessary. Knead the dough for 1 to 2 minutes.

Parsley

In Tuscany, Italian parsley, sage, and rosemary are the three predominant herbs, but I'd say Italian parsley has an edge over the other two. In fact, when someone is in the newspaper or on television too much, in Tuscany, we say he's like parsley. You can find parsley in everything from our soffritto, the sautéed vegetable mixture that serves as a base for many of our dishes, to anchovy marinade. I like using parsley stems, which have a celerylike flavor. Americans seem to have the idea that parsley is bland, an ingredient that adds color, but not taste, to a dish. Nothing could be farther from the truth. In fact, in medieval Italy, parsley was considered so strong and peppery, pregnant women were advised not to eat it.

Spaghetti con Pecorino
Spaghetti with Pecorino

When I have a few leftover pieces of pecorino and am feeling lazy, this is the first dish
that comes to my mind.

(SERVES 4 AS AN APPETIZER)

3 quarts water

1½ tablespoons salt

½ pound spaghetti

10–12 tablespoons freshly grated
   pecorino cheeses (the more types of
   pecorino you have here, the better,
   try Sardo and Toscano, but don't use
   just pecorino Romano)

Salt and fresh ground black pepper, to
   taste

2 teaspoons sweet butter

2 teaspoons extra-virgin olive oil

Bring the water to a boil in a large pot. Add the salt and spaghetti. When the pasta
is *al dente*, reserve ¼ cup of the pasta water and drain the spaghetti.

Toss the pasta with the reserved water, the cheese, salt, lots of fresh black pepper,
butter, and olive oil. Let the spaghetti sit a minute or two to melt the cheese. Serve
with one last grating of cheese on top.

Pecorino Toscano

....

In Tuscany, every village has its own version of pecorino, sheep's milk cheese, ranging from fresh ricotta to hard, aged cheeses. We used to buy our pecorino from Franco, the local shepherd. He was a friend, and by far the best cheese man in Tuscany, but he only made two to three forms a day, and they were so much in demand, there was always a line outside his front door. One of Franco's idiosyncrasies was that he only sold his cheese to people he liked. Sometimes you could get to the head of the line, be given a sad nod, non c'é più—*we're all out—then see the guy who'd been behind you get a nice two-kilo round. It wasn't fair, of course, but luckily Franco liked us, so we always got the cheese we needed.*

Finding pecorino Toscano in the States can be as tricky as getting a round from Franco. There are some specialty stores that carry one or two types. In New York, Todaro Brothers has a good selection. If you can't find a pecorino Toscano you like, experiment with other sheep's milk cheeses such as Caciotta or Manchego.

Controfiletto di Maiale al Profumo di Rosmarino

Pork Chops Perfumed with Rosemary

(S E R V E S 4)

5 tablespoons extra-virgin olive oil

16 large shallots, cut into uniform pieces

Salt and fresh ground black pepper, to
    taste

$2^2/_3$ pounds center-cut loin pork chops

2 sprigs fresh rosemary

$1/_2$ cup white wine

$1/_4$–$1/_2$ cup homemade beef stock (if you
    don't have stock on hand, use water)

Place the olive oil and shallots in a large, heavy-bottomed frying pan and cook over medium heat until the shallots become translucent, 7 to 10 minutes. Salt and pepper the pork chops, and add them to the pan along with the rosemary. Brown the pork, about 4 minutes on each side, then add the wine. When the wine has reduced completely, after about 3 minutes, flip the chops, then cook them for another 3 minutes.

Transfer the pork to a platter, add the stock to the frying pan, and stir. Cook for about 2 minutes, until the stock has reduced and formed a gravy. Pour the gravy over the pork chops and serve.

La Torta co' Bischeri
Scalloped Pisa Pie

This pie is a specialty of Lucca and Pisa. Locals will tell you it was invented by a witch with a sweet tooth who longed for the best dessert in the world. It was one of Byron's favorite sweets during his stay in Pisa.

(S E R V E S   8)

La Pasta
THE CRUST:

2½ cups sifted all-purpose flour

2 teaspoons sifted baking powder

1 stick (½ cup) sweet butter

½ cup sugar

1 egg plus 1 yolk

1 teaspoon vanilla extract

Grated zest of 1 lemon

2 tablespoons rum or sambuca liqueur

Il Ripieno
THE FILLING:

1¾ cups milk

½ cup arborio rice

3 tablespoons sugar

¼ cup toasted pine nuts

3 tablespoons finely chopped candied
  citron

2 eggs, beaten

Grated zest of 1 orange

2½ ounces semisweet chocolate, grated

2 tablespoons rum or sambuca liqueur

For the crust: In a large bowl, combine the flour and baking powder. In the bowl of an electric mixer, cream together the butter and sugar until light and fluffy. Beat in the egg and the extra yolk, the vanilla, lemon zest, and rum or sambuca. Slowly beat in the dry ingredients. Chill the dough for about 1 hour.

Meanwhile, prepare the filling: In a heavy saucepan, combine the milk and rice. Bring to a simmer over high heat, then turn to low, cover tightly, and cook for 20 to

25 minutes, stirring occasionally to make sure the rice isn't sticking. When the rice is tender but firm, remove from the heat and stir in the sugar. Let the rice cool, then add the pine nuts, candied citron, eggs, orange zest, grated chocolate, and the rum or sambuca. Let this mixture sit for an hour.

Preheat the oven to 325° and butter an 8-inch pie pan.

Divide the dough into two pieces, one slightly larger than the other. Roll the smaller portion on a lightly floured surface to form a ⅛-inch-thick circle about 12 inches in diameter. Transfer the dough to the pan, leaving a 1-inch overhang. Pour the rice mixture into the piecrust. With a knife, trim the overhang into scallops and fold it over the filling. Roll the remaining portion of the dough ⅛ inch thick and cut it into pieces. Arrange the pieces, as if for a cobbler, on top of the pie filling.

Bake the pie until the crust is golden brown, 50 to 60 minutes. It is done when a toothpick inserted in the center comes out clean. Cool before serving.

IL VIN ITALY

The Competition

Scarpaccia

Insalata di Coniglio e Radicchio

Pollo Ripieno

Torta di Marmellata

Zucchini and Red Onion Scramble

Rabbit and Radicchio Salad

Stuffed Roast Chicken

Marmalade Tart

**SUGGESTED WINES: COL VENTO, TENUTA DEL TERRICCIO (GRAPE: SAUVIGNON BLANC);
GRIFI, AVIGNONESI (GRAPES: PRUGNOLO, CABERNET SAUVIGNON)**

....

The first food competition I ever entered was Vin Italy, an annual wine exhibition in Verona. I was just twenty-four, the youngest of the seventy participating chefs, and very nervous. Giuliano Taccetti, one of my mentors, had helped me develop my entry—a whole stuffed boneless chicken served with radicchio and rabbit salad—and had been very supportive of my debut. But as the day of the competition neared, I still hadn't worked out the final details of my peacock centerpiece, which, according to the Vin Italy rules, had to be made entirely from edible ingredients. A peacock body molded from butter with a tail from asparagus was as far as I'd gotten. I was stuck on what would make good body feathers.

Driving to Verona, I was so exhausted by anxiety, I fell asleep at the wheel. Luckily I wasn't hurt, but *Tutto il male non viene per nuocere,* we say. Bad things don't happen for nothing. I woke up in a ditch with a tree branch in my face and a vision of my peacock covered in sage leaves. My centerpiece was complete. It wasn't until an hour later that my anxiety returned. Pulling into the Vin Italy pavilion, I noticed one after another of Italy's most famous chefs, flanked by their sous chefs, unloading trucks of supplies, statues, and fancy cooking gear. I was by myself. All I had was my little peacock and what I had squeezed into my Cinquecento. I panicked and called Giuliano. There was no way I could win, I told him. I wanted to pull out.

"You have to participate, and you have to win," was all he said before hanging up. I downed a glass of red wine and went to work. All around me I could see these huge, complicated structures going up. When a friend showed up and invited me out to dinner, I saw my chance to escape. I approached Renato Ramponi, the president of the chef's association, and excused myself. I wouldn't be able to make the awards dinner, I had another engagement, I explained. Impossible, he said, you're a finalist. You have to be here. I was shocked, and even more so when they announced the winners: I'd split first place with two other chefs.

MY WINNING ENTRY AT VIN ITALY.

Scarpaccia

Zucchini and Red Onion Scramble

A *scarpaccia* in Italian is an ugly old shoe, but this *scarpaccia*—which should be as thin as the sole of an old shoe—is a delicious cross between a zucchini pancake and an omelet. It's nice to make when you can get zucchini blossoms. I use five per person and add them when I add the zucchini.

(S E R V E S   4 – 6)

6 tablespoons extra-virgin olive oil

1 tablespoon chopped garlic

1 tablespoon *each* chopped fresh
    oregano, mint, and thyme

1/2 teaspoon crushed red pepper flakes

1 1/2 cups thinly sliced red onions

4 cups thinly sliced zucchini

2 eggs

4 tablespoons flour

4 tablespoons water

4 tablespoons chopped fresh Italian parsley

Salt and fresh ground black pepper, to taste

2 tablespoons freshly grated
    Parmigiano-Reggiano cheese

2 tablespoons freshly grated pecorino
    Romano cheese

*Diary of a
Tuscan Chef*
42

Preheat the oven to 400°. In a medium sauté pan, heat 4 tablespoons of the olive oil, the garlic, oregano, mint, thyme, and red pepper flakes over medium for about 3 minutes. Add the onions and continue cooking, stirring occasionally, for 5 minutes. Add the zucchini and cook for another 7 to 10 minutes, stirring occasionally, until the onions and zucchini are almost translucent. Remove the pan from the heat and cool.

In a bowl, beat together the eggs, flour, water, parsley, salt and pepper, and the cheeses. Mix in the zucchini and onions.

Pour the remaining 2 tablespoons of olive oil into two 10-inch pie pans and heat it in the oven a few minutes. Remove the pans, swirl the olive oil around, and pour ½ the zucchini mixture into each. Bake for 15 to 20 minutes, then put the two *scarpaccia* under the broiler for 1 or 2 minutes to brown the top. The *scarpaccia* is done when it's lightly browned and has the consistency of a soft omelet. Remove, slice, and serve.

Pecorino Romano

I never used pecorino Romano until I got to New York, and that was only because I couldn't get pecorino Toscano. The two are not at all interchangeable: Romano is harder, sharper, and saltier, a cheese that's primarily used in the south of Italy the way the north uses Parmigiano-Reggiano. In fact, if you mix grated Romano with grated Parmigiano, you get something approximating pecorino Toscano.

Insalata di Coniglio e Radicchio
Rabbit and Radicchio Salad
(SERVES 2–3 AS AN APPETIZER)

1 rabbit loin (or half a rabbit)

Salt and fresh ground black pepper, to taste

½ cup extra-virgin olive oil

4 cloves garlic, peeled and crushed

2 sprigs fresh rosemary

¼ teaspoon crushed red pepper flakes

⅓ cup white wine

⅔ cup homemade chicken stock or water

1 tablespoon red wine vinegar

1½ cups shredded radicchio

Rub the flesh of the rabbit with salt and pepper. In a large sauté pan, place ¼ cup of the olive oil, the garlic, rosemary, and red pepper flakes, and sauté over medium heat. When the olive oil starts to sizzle, after about 3 minutes, reduce the heat to medium-low, add the rabbit, and brown it on all sides, 15 to 20 minutes.

Add the wine and cook until it reduces completely, about 6 minutes, then add the chicken stock or water. Continue cooking for another 9 to 10 minutes, until the rabbit is tender. Remove the rabbit from the pan and turn the heat to high. Reduce the pan juices for 4 or 5 minutes and set them aside.

When the rabbit is cool enough to handle, bone it. Whisk the red wine vinegar together with salt and pepper. Whisk in the remaining ¼ cup of olive oil. Add 2 tablespoons of the pan drippings. Toss the rabbit with the radicchio and the dressing and serve.

Pollo Ripieno
Stuffed Roast Chicken

My winning recipe was for a whole, stuffed boneless chicken, but since there aren't too many people who have the patience or time to learn how to bone a whole chicken, I've adapted the stuffing to use with a regular fryer. Of course, if you want, you can get a boneless chicken from your butcher and try it my way. With the chicken boned, all of the stuffing will fit inside.

(SERVES 4–6)

¼ cup extra-virgin olive oil

½ cup chopped red onion

½ cup chopped celery

¼ cup chopped carrot

1 tablespoon chopped garlic

2 teaspoons chopped fresh thyme

2 teaspoons chopped fresh sage

½ pound Italian sweet sausage

2 cups cubed, day-old Italian bread

¼ pound prosciutto, chopped

⅓ cup pistachio nuts

¼ cup chopped fresh Italian parsley

2 eggs, beaten

Salt and fresh ground black pepper, to taste

6 tablespoons homemade chicken stock (or water), plus more as needed

1 (4–5-pound) chicken, rinsed and patted dry

¼ cup white wine

¼ cup flour

Preheat the oven to 450°. Place the olive oil, the onion, celery, carrot, garlic, thyme, and sage in a medium frying pan and sauté over medium heat until the mixture is softened but not browned, about 10 minutes. Transfer the vegetables to a large mixing bowl.

Break the sausage out of its casing, add it to the frying pan, and raise the heat to

(continued on next page)

medium-high. Cook, breaking up the sausage with a spoon until the pieces are lightly browned, about 10 minutes. Add the sausage, bread cubes, prosciutto, pistachio nuts, parsley, eggs, and black pepper to the vegetables. Mix well. Add approximately 6 tablespoons of chicken stock. If the mixture still seems dry, add a little more.

Rub the chicken, including the cavity, with salt and pepper. Use 1 to 2 cups of the stuffing to fill the chicken cavity. It should be loosely filled. Place the rest in an oiled, covered baking dish. To keep the chicken moist, cover the breast with a piece of cheesecloth soaked in butter or vegetable oil. Place the chicken on a rack, in a roasting pan, put it in the oven and immediately reduce the temperature to 350°. Roast for 20 minutes per pound, basting it, from time to time, with the pan drippings. (Bake the extra stuffing along with the chicken.) Remove the chicken from the oven, splash it with the wine, and return it to the oven for another 20 minutes. The juices should run clear.

We don't use gravy in Italy, but if you want to make it, scrape the juices and fat from the roasting pan into a small saucepan. Blend this with the flour and heat over medium-low. Stir in enough chicken stock to make 2 cups of gravy. Raise the heat to medium, bring to a simmer, and cook for 5 minutes. Add salt and pepper to taste. Let the bird rest for 5 minutes. Remove the stuffing, carve, and serve.

Torta di Marmellata

Marmalade Tart

(SERVES 8)

½ cup plus 1 tablespoon sweet butter

½ cup plus 1 tablespoon sugar

½ teaspoon salt

2 eggs, plus 1 beaten egg

2¼ cups flour

Grated zest of 1 lemon

2 teaspoons ground cinnamon

2 teaspoons kirsch

½ cup plus 1 tablespoon toasted well-chopped almonds

1¾ cups marmalade of your choice

Preheat the oven to 350°. Generously butter a 9-inch tart pan. With an electric mixer, cream together the butter, sugar, and salt. Beat in the 2 eggs, flour, lemon zest, cinnamon, kirsch, and almonds until well blended.

Press two-thirds of the dough into the bottom of the tart pan. Refrigerate both portions of the dough for an hour.

Spread the marmalade over the piecrust. On a floured surface, roll out the remaining portion of dough into a ⅛-inch-thick circle. (The nuts will make the rolling bumpy, but the dough can be easily pinched back together if it breaks.)

Cut the dough into long strips, about ¾ inch wide. Create a lattice by laying half the strips across the marmalade, about ½ inch apart. Lay the other half across at a diagonal and seal the strips to the rim with the beaten egg. Brush all the pastry with the beaten egg and bake for 35 to 45 minutes, until golden brown. Cool and serve.

6

La Zuppa dei Sommozzatori in Diretta

SCUBA Soup, Live!

Calamari Ripieni	Stuffed Squid
Fettuccine dell'Ortolano	Greengrocer Fettuccine
Cacciucco	Tuscan Fish Stew
Torta di Riso alla Carrarina	Carrara Rice Pie

SUGGESTED WINES: VIGNA BELLARIA, AMA (GRAPE: PINOT GRIGIO); GUADO AL TASSO, ANTINORI (GRAPES: CABERNET SAUVIGNON, MERLOT)

Diary of a Tuscan Chef
48

On any given Sunday in Italy, there are probably as many households glued to *"Domenica In,"* the six-hour-long variety extravaganza, as there are families who attend mass. The show is wildly successful, partially because of its scantily dressed chorines, but also because the host, Pippo Baudo, a suave Jerry Lewis type, gets the most popular comedians, singers, and politicians week after week. For a while, Baudo sponsored regional cook-offs and showcased the contestants on *"Domenica In."* When the show called me to represent Tuscany in a contest with Le Marche and Lombardy, I felt as if I'd been knighted Chef Laureate. It was far better than being elected secretary of the Associazioni Cuochi di Provincia di Lucca (ACPL), which I had already experienced, and almost as exciting as cooking for Henry Kissinger, which I would do later.

The basic rules were this: The presentation had to be made from regional products, it had to represent regional cooking, and everything in the presentation had to be edible. After talking to Giuliano Taccetti, the president of ACPL, I decided to make a mixed fish soup, with a centerpiece honoring the Sommozzatori Artiglio, Viareggio's courageous World War Two SCUBA commando. The centerpiece itself would feature two SCUBA divers and a huge octopus crawling on a reef—all made from reduced ox fat—and tide pool made with blue gelatin, and live crabs.

ME ON "DOMENICA IN."

Just rendering the three hundred kilos of ox fat into a claylike substance took three weeks, and it smelled so bad that after the first week Mama barred me from using Vipore's kitchen. The soup itself took weeks to develop; Mama's friend Maria Giustina made seashell-shape bowls to serve it in, and Nicola, an artist I knew, helped me sculpt the divers and the rocks.

Finally, the day of the broadcast arrived and I drove to Rome, where *"Domenica In"* was produced. By coincidence, it was Easter Sunday, a day when everyone in Italy stays home and *Domenica's* ratings score higher than the soccer finals. I was understandably nervous. More than 30 million people would see me. Only the fact that Giovanni Spadolini, Italy's very serious ex–prime minister, would precede me gave me solace. Next to him, I would come off great.

When the stagehand started his countdown for me to prepare to wheel out my creation, I was ready. I took the live crabs from my pocket and let them loose over the ox-fat reef. Spadolini, however, wasn't giving up the spotlight so easily. He kept talking, and I had to retrieve the crabs. This happened twice; but after the third false start, one of the crabs jumped off my reef onto the stage and started crawling toward Spadolini. I unfortunately jumped after him with a little too much spring, right onto the stage. Spadolini got his first laughs ever, I think. When I finally got the chance to roll my masterpiece out, the applause was wild. Whether it was for my handiwork or my sprint work, I'll never know.

Calamari Ripieni
Stuffed Squid
(SERVES 6)

2 medium potatoes, sliced fine

1 small red onion, sliced thin

5 tablespoons extra-virgin olive oil

Salt and fresh ground black pepper, to
taste

2 tablespoons water

4 tablespoons white wine

2 tablespoons chopped fresh thyme

1 tablespoon chopped garlic

1/8 teaspoon crushed red pepper flakes

2 cups finely chopped zucchini

2 slices Tuscan bread, crusts removed,
soaked in water and squeezed dry
(about 1 cup)

1 pound raw cleaned squid, a third of it
tentacles

6 medium raw shrimp, shelled and
deveined

10 cherry tomatoes, halved

Paprika, to taste

1/4 cup chopped fresh basil

Preheat the oven to 350°. In a large bowl, toss the potatoes and onions together with 1 1/2 tablespoons of the olive oil and the salt and pepper. Place the mixture in a 9-×-11-inch baking dish and sprinkle with the water and 2 tablespoons of white wine. Cover the pan with aluminum foil and bake for 20 minutes.

Meanwhile, place 2 tablespoons of the remaining olive oil in a large frying pan with the chopped thyme, garlic, and red pepper flakes. Heat the mixture over medium until the garlic starts to color, 3 to 4 minutes. Add the zucchini and cook for another 2 to 3 minutes, then add the remaining 2 tablespoons of white wine and let it reduce completely, about 1 minute.

Mix in the soaked bread, making sure it is well blended. Remove the pan from the heat and season with salt and pepper. Rinse the bodies and tentacles. Chop the squid tentacles and the shrimp and stir them into the zucchini mixture. Stuff the squid bodies with the mixture.

Remove the potatoes from the oven and lower the heat to 325°. Arrange the squid and cherry tomato halves on top of the potatoes and onions. (If you have any leftover stuffing, form it into small balls and add them to the dish.) Drizzle the remaining $1\frac{1}{2}$ tablespoons of olive oil over the squid and sprinkle them with the paprika. Cover the baking dish with the aluminum foil and bake for 15 minutes. Then remove the foil and bake for another 15 minutes. Turn the heat to broil and let the squid color slightly, about 3 minutes. Test the potatoes to make sure they are tender. The dish is ready. Sprinkle with the basil and serve.

Fettuccine dell'Ortolano

Greengrocer Fettuccine

In Pieve Santo Stefano, we call greengrocers, or anyone who travels the country roads and sells their vegetables out of the back of their truck, *l'ortolano*. This pasta is in honor of our *ortolani*.

(SERVES 4 AS AN APPETIZER)

3 tablespoons extra-virgin olive oil

2 teaspoons finely chopped garlic

2 teaspoons finely chopped fresh
  rosemary

1/2 tablespoon finely chopped fresh
  oregano

1/2 teaspoon crushed red pepper flakes

2 1/2 tablespoons white wine

1 small eggplant, chopped fine

2 shallots, chopped fine

1 medium zucchini, chopped fine

1 small carrot, chopped fine

1 small onion, chopped fine

1 small stalk celery, chopped fine

Salt and fresh ground black pepper, to
  taste

1 (14-ounce) can Italian tomatoes

1 tablespoon finely chopped fresh Italian
  parsley

3 quarts water

1/2 pound fettuccine

4 tablespoons freshly grated
  Parmigiano-Reggiano cheese

In a large saucepan, put the olive oil, garlic, rosemary, oregano, and red pepper flakes and sauté over medium heat until the garlic starts to color, about 5 minutes. Add the wine and continue cooking until it reduces completely, about 5 minutes.

In a bowl, mix together the eggplant, shallots, zucchini, carrot, onion, and celery and season them with salt and pepper. Add the vegetables to the saucepan and cook the mixture for 15 minutes, stirring occasionally. Add the tomatoes and their juices and cook for another 20 to 25 minutes, stirring occasionally. (If the sauce gets too dense, you can thin it with a little water or vegetable stock.) Taste for salt and pepper, add the parsley, and cook for another 5 minutes.

Meanwhile, bring the water to a boil in a large pot and add 1½ tablespoons of salt. Cook the fettuccine until *al dente*, drain, then mix with the sauce and the grated Parmigiano-Reggiano; and serve.

**MAKING PIZZA IN
THE WOOD-BURNING
STOVE.**

Cacciucco
Tuscan Fish Stew
(S E R V E S 6)

2 sprigs fresh rosemary, leaves coarsely
  chopped

1 sprig fresh sage, leaves coarsely
  chopped

1 teaspoon crushed red pepper flakes

1 medium red onion, chopped

20 cloves garlic, peeled and crushed

¼ cup extra-virgin olive oil

1½ cups white wine

½ pound raw baby octopus, cleaned
  and cut into chunks

8 raw squid, cleaned and cut into 4
  pieces each

2 dozen raw mussels, well scrubbed
  (don't beard the mussels until you
  are ready to cook them)

2 dozen raw clams, cleaned (see Box)

1 pound plum tomatoes, pureed

3 cups water or fish stock

4 large raw shrimp, shelled and cleaned

¾ pound cleaned boneless fish
  (monkfish, salmon, tuna, grouper, or
  halibut)

Salt and fresh ground black pepper, to
  taste

4 slices Tuscan bread, toasted and
  rubbed with a cut clove of garlic

In a large soup pot, sauté the rosemary, sage, red pepper flakes, onion, and crushed garlic in the olive oil over medium heat. When the onion becomes translucent, after about 5 minutes, add the wine and cover the pot. Cook until the wine is reduced completely, about 7 minutes. Add the octopus and cook for 10 minutes; add the squid and cook for 10 minutes; add the mussels and the clams and cook for 8 minutes; add the tomatoes and the water or stock and cook for 15 minutes; add the shrimp, fish and salt and pepper, and cook for 8 minutes. The soup is ready when the calamari are tender. Discard any clams or mussels that don't open. When ready to serve, spoon the stew into bowls and top each serving with a slice of toasted bread.

To Clean Clams

At your fishmonger's, check that the clams you buy are still alive. To do this, tap the shell with your finger. If they are alive, they will open slightly. When you get the clams home, take a very large bowl, and put a plate inside it, upside down. Place the clams on top and cover them with water and a little salt. This way, the clams continue to live and will kick out the sand that has settled in their shells. The sand will sift under the plate. Leave the clams in the bowl for two hours, stirring occasionally. Lift the clams out of the bowl, being careful not to jog the plate and disturb the sand. The clams are ready to cook.

Torta di Riso alla Carrarina

Carrara Rice Pie

Michelangelo got his best marble from Carrara, so it's likely he got a taste or two of Carrara's renowned rice pie. The proportion of rice to milk and eggs may seem odd, but don't change it. The quantities are exactly as they should be. When this pie is just right, you'll have a layer of custard over a layer of rice. If you want to experiment, add aniseed or a little anisette to the custard.

(SERVES 6)

1½ cups water

¼ teaspoon salt, plus a pinch

½ cup arborio rice

Sweet butter, for the pan

1 tablespoon flour

7 eggs

1¼ cups sugar

¼ cup rum or brandy

Grated zest of 3 lemons

1 teaspoon vanilla extract

2 cups milk, at room temperature

In a heavy saucepan, bring the water to a boil and add the ¼ teaspoon of salt. Stir in the rice. Cover the pan tightly and cook over low heat for about 25 minutes, until the rice is light and fluffy. Set the rice aside.

About 15 minutes before the rice is done, preheat the oven to 350°. Butter a deep-dish 9-inch pie pan and dust it with flour, shaking off any excess.

In a large bowl, beat the eggs with the sugar, rum, grated zest, vanilla, and a pinch of salt. Mix well and stir in the milk.

With the back of a wet spoon, press the rice into the bottom of the prepared pan, then pour in the milk mixture. Bake for 50 to 60 minutes, until the top of the pie is golden brown. Cool, and serve at room temperature.

7

Cesare Va in Dieta

Cesare Goes on a Diet

Insalata di Sette Vegetali	Seven-Vegetable Salad
Minestra Chiara Componibile	Do-It-Yourself Vegetable Soup
Pollo al Cartoccio	Chicken in Paper
Spumini	Meringue Cookies

Suggested Wines: Podere Fontarca, Fattoria di Manzano (Grapes: Chardonnay, Viognier); Pergole Torte, Montevertine (Grape: Sangioveto)

In the winter in Pieve Santo Stefano, there was never much work, especially when it was very cold. For the farmers, there was little to do, and for the locals who maintained the villas of *"I Signori,"* our name for the rich weekenders, even less. To pass the time, everyone came to Vipore, and by early December the bar metamorphosed into a winter piazza. Emilio, Camay, Pietro the butcher, Renzo the barber, and Papa played cards, drank, had coffee. I remember one particularly bad winter when the *Signori* never came, and the restaurant was deserted well into March. For me, it was the perfect moment to experiment in the kitchen.

We had a lot of pork that year because we'd slaughtered more than ever before. Every day I would try a variation on a favorite pork recipe. My first attempts were with pork cheeks, boiled and mixed with beans, sea salt, and olive oil. Then I turned to *Pentolaccia*, the dish we make during the slaughter, which uses the less noble parts of the pig, like the tails and hooves. All of these dishes were very fatty—and very tasty. I started to feel it around my waistline. That had happened before, my growing a seasonal size. But this particular winter, I outdid myself. By the time March rolled around, I'd gained twenty-seven pounds.

(continued on next page)

ME, PAPA, ANDREW, AND CAMAY PLAYING CARDS IN THE BAR.

Dieting isn't easy for anyone, but for me it's especially difficult. My job is to be with food, and if I'm cooking just for myself, I can't do it. But that year, I had a brainstorm. I'd do a spa menu for Vipore. That way, even if I didn't sell any dishes to the clients, I'd still be able to eat low fat.

The surprise was that our clients actually liked the spa dishes. They were very Tuscan in concept, and flavorful, full of herbs and spices. Plus, we started putting bottles of olive oil on the tables so that customers could drizzle or douse their orders in as much oil as they pleased.

In less than two months, I not only sold our customers on the idea of spa cuisine, I lost all twenty-seven pounds. Then, when I wanted to get rid of the low-fat items, Papa balked. "They're selling," he declared. "They stay on the menu." I didn't really mind, it was just that after dieting so strictly, I wanted to splurge, and splurge for my clients, too. More to the point, I didn't want word getting out that I'd been on a diet. In Italy, no one trusts a skinny chef.

Insalata di Sette Vegetali
Seven-Vegetable Salad
(SERVES 4)

2 small carrots, peeled and halved

2 stalks asparagus, trimmed and halved

1/3 cup cauliflower florets

1 medium zucchini, diced

2 baby artichokes, outer leaves peeled
and stems pared, sliced paper thin
(see page 23 for instructions)

2 tablespoons minced red onion

1/3 cup cleaned, chopped cremini
mushrooms

3/4 cup washed and chopped mixed
salad greens

3 tablespoons red wine vinegar

Salt and fresh ground black pepper, to
taste

1/4 cup extra-virgin olive oil

1 cup cooked cannellini beans (optional)

In a pot of boiling water, separately blanche the carrots, asparagus, and cauliflower for 1 minute. Plunge them into cold water to stop the cooking, then chop them into medium dice. Mix them with the other vegetables in a salad bowl.

Whisk together the vinegar and salt and pepper, then whisk in the olive oil and dress the salad. (The beans provide a nice contrast if you have them ready and want to fold them in here.) Spoon the salad onto plates and serve.

Minestra Chiara Componibile

Do-It-Yourself Vegetable Soup

Don't worry about rounding up every ingredient here. Be creative. Substitutions, additions, and deletions are acceptable. Just choose the freshest, most readily available vegetables.

(S E R V E S   8 – 1 0)

4 cups water

4 cups homemade vegetable broth

3 tablespoons chopped lemongrass

1 small potato, diced

¼ pound green beans, trimmed

1 small carrot, diced

1 very small turnip, cut into chunks

⅓ cup diced onion

⅓ bulb fennel, trimmed and sliced lengthwise

1 small leek, well rinsed, dark leaves trimmed, cut into thick slices

⅓ yellow bell pepper, seeded and sliced into 1-inch strips

⅓ red bell pepper, seeded and sliced into 1-inch strips

⅓ stalk celery, diced

1 cup shredded cabbage

3 Brussels sprouts, trimmed and quartered

1 cup small cauliflower florets

1 scallion, chopped fine

1 small zucchini, chopped

⅓ cup broccoli rabe (leaves, stems, and florets), cut into 1-inch pieces

⅓ cup broccoli florets

3 stalks asparagus, bottoms trimmed, cut into 1-inch pieces

1 (28-ounce) can Italian tomatoes, including their liquid

⅓ bunch watercress, trimmed of stalks

12 fresh basil leaves, chopped

2 teaspoons fresh thyme leaves

1 teaspoon fresh grated ginger

1 teaspoon minced garlic

Salt and fresh ground black pepper, to taste

Optional:

½ pound chicken, cut into chunks

OR

½ pound red snapper or codfish

OR

½ pound raw shrimp, shelled and
  cleaned

In a large stockpot, combine the water, and vegetable broth and add the lemon-grass. Bring the liquid to a boil. Add the longer-cooking vegetables—the potato, green beans, carrot, and turnip. Cook for 20 minutes. Add the remaining vegetables, the basil, thyme, ginger, garlic, and salt and pepper. Lower the heat to a medium boil and continue cooking for 3 to 5 minutes more. Add the chicken, fish, and seafood if using it, and cook through, 7 to 10 minutes. Spoon the soup into bowls and serve.

Pollo al Cartoccio

Chicken in Paper

(S E R V E S 4)

2 large red bell peppers, seeded and cut
  into pieces

2 large yellow bell peppers, seeded and
  cut into pieces

12 scallions, sliced lengthwise

1–2 fresh chili peppers (red chili or
  jalapeño), minced fine

2 large ripe tomatoes, cut into 5 pieces

1 tablespoon finely chopped fresh
  rosemary

Salt and fresh ground black pepper, to
  taste

1 (2½-pound) free-range chicken, cut
  into pieces

½ teaspoon *each* ground cinnamon,
  ground cloves, and grated nutmeg

½ cup white wine

Extra-virgin olive oil (optional)

Preheat the oven to 450° and line an ovenproof baking dish with aluminum foil.

In a bowl, mix together the red and yellow peppers, scallions, chili peppers, tomatoes, rosemary, and salt and pepper. Place the mixture in the baking dish.

Season the chicken with salt and pepper and the ground spices. Arrange the pieces on top of the vegetables. Cover the dish with aluminum foil and seal it. Bake for 40 minutes.

Sprinkle the chicken with the wine, then return it, uncovered, to the oven for 10 minutes. (If the chicken hasn't browned, you might want to put it under the broiler for 5 to 10 minutes to give the skin a nicer color.) When you are ready to serve, drizzling a little olive oil on top will give a richer taste to the dish, but it isn't necessary.

Spumini

Meringue Cookies

(MAKES 20 COOKIES)

3 egg whites

1 cup sugar

Grated rind of ¹/₂ lemon

Preheat the oven to 225°. Line a sheet pan with parchment paper.

In the bowl of an electric mixer, beat the egg whites on medium-low until frothy. Continue beating while adding the sugar in a slow, steady stream. Stir in the lemon rind. Turn the speed to high and beat for 5 minutes, until the mixture has tripled in volume and has become quite stiff, dense, and glossy. Drop spoonfuls of the meringue onto the sheet pan and bake for 1 hour and 10 minutes. The cookies should be dry and crisp all the way through. Cool, then store them in an airtight container. They will keep for up to a month.

8

Un Granchio Fuori d'Acqua
A Crab Out of Water

Granchi Teneri Fritti	Deep-Fried Soft-Shell Crabs
Granchi Teneri Sauté	Sautéed Soft-Shell Crabs
Risotto di Granchi Teneri	Soft-Shell Crab Risotto
Zuccotto	Tuscan Parfait

SUGGESTED WINES: BRUT, FRESCOBALDI (GRAPES: CHARDONNAY, PINOT NERO, SPUMANTE);

LE GRANCE, CAPARZO (GRAPES: CHARDONNAY, SAUVIGNON BLANC, TRAMINER)

When I first started working at Coco Pazzo, I came into the kitchen and noticed two crates of crabs sitting in a corner. They didn't look like any crabs I'd ever seen, and I was a little hesitant to ask what they were. Then Kevin, my sous chef, asked me how he should prepare the soft-shell crabs, and I played *furbo* (sly). "Make them the way you always do, and I'll tell you if you make any mistakes," I instructed, watching him closely. After work, I pulled out a few of the books I'd brought with me from home and looked up soft-shell crabs.

What I discovered was that at the turn of the century, soft-shell crabs, called *granchi teneri* or "tender crabs," were a popular delicacy in Tuscan cooking. In Sesto Fiorentino, a small town northwest of Florence, there was even a professional association of soft-shell crab fishermen. During the molting season, the fishermen would place crabs in stacked terra-cotta boxes made by Sesto Fiorentino craftsmen. Every day they would pour well water into the top box, and it would drain down, from one container to the next, washing over the crabs. After a period of days, when the crabs molted, they would be transferred to containers lined with damp grape leaves. Then the fishermen would take to the streets shouting *"Granchi teneri!"*

Armed with this information, I showed up for work the next day with a dozen ideas for soft-shell crab recipes. Here are a few of them.

Granchi Teneri Fritti
Deep-Fried Soft-Shell Crabs

The traditional way to fry soft-shell crabs, back when they were plentiful, was to place the crabs (while they were alive) in a bath of beaten egg. The crabs would eat the egg and plump up. Then the chef would clean them, dip them in flour, and toss them into hot oil. This version is a little lighter.

(SERVES 4)

8 soft-shell crabs, cleaned

1 1/2 cups milk

Salt and fresh ground black pepper, to taste

1/2 cup coarse cornmeal

1/2 cup flour

Peanut oil, for frying

4 cloves crushed garlic, papery covering intact

4 sprigs fresh rosemary

4 sprigs fresh thyme

2 lemons, quartered

Rinse the crabs under cold water. In a bowl, season the milk with salt and pepper, then soak the crabs in the milk for 30 minutes.

Mix together the cornmeal, flour, and salt and pepper. Fill a large saucepan one third full with the peanut oil. (It should be at least 3 inches deep.) While the oil is heating, coat the crabs lightly in the cornmeal-flour mixture.

When the oil reaches 375°, drop in the garlic, rosemary, and thyme. Then drop in the crabs, 2 or 3 at a time, and let them cook until they are golden and crispy, about 3 minutes. Remove the crabs and drain them on paper towels. Serve the crabs accompanied by a fried garlic clove, a sprig of rosemary, a sprig of thyme, and 2 lemon wedges.

Granchi Teneri Sauté
Sautéed Soft-Shell Crabs
(SERVES 4)

....

8 soft-shell crabs, cleaned

Salt and fresh ground black pepper, to
    taste

2 sprigs fresh rosemary, leaves only

2 sprigs fresh thyme, leaves only

6 tablespoons extra-virgin olive oil

5 cloves garlic, chopped

½ cup chopped fresh Italian parsley

1 teaspoon crushed red pepper flakes

1½ cups chopped red onions

½ cup white wine

2½–3 cups chopped tomatoes

3 tablespoons drained capers

¼ cup flour (optional)

Rinse the crabs in cold water. Salt and pepper both sides of the crabs, and sprinkle them with the leaves of 1 sprig of rosemary and 1 sprig of thyme. Refrigerate them, covered, for 1 hour.

Place the remaining rosemary and thyme, 3 tablespoons of the olive oil, the garlic, parsley, red pepper flakes, and onions in a large sauté pan. Heat over medium until the onions turn translucent, about 8 minutes. Add the wine and let it reduce completely, about 3 minutes. Add the tomatoes and capers and cook for 20 minutes more. Remove the sauce from the heat and keep it warm.

If you want, dust the crabs with flour, then heat the remaining 3 tablespoons of olive oil over high in a large sauté pan. Add the crabs, top side down, and cook for 1½ minutes. Turn the crabs over, lower the heat to medium, and sauté until they're browned on the bottom and cooked through, 3 or 4 minutes. Place 2 crabs on a plate, spoon some of the sauce on top, and serve.

Risotto di Granchi Teneri

Soft-Shell Crab Risotto

(SERVES 6 AS AN APPETIZER)

....

½ cup extra-virgin olive oil

4 scallions, sliced

1 teaspoon crushed red pepper flakes

1 teaspoon chopped fresh thyme

1 tablespoon chopped fresh rosemary

2 tablespoons chopped fresh basil

3 tablespoons white wine

8 small soft-shell crabs, cleaned

1 pound asparagus, tough stems
   removed, sliced into 1-inch lengths

5 cups homemade vegetable stock

½ cup finely chopped red onion

2 cups arborio rice

½ cup chopped tomato

3 tablespoons chopped fresh Italian
   parsley

2 tablespoons butter

In a large sauté pan, place ¼ cup of the olive oil, the scallions, red pepper flakes, thyme, rosemary, and 1 tablespoon of the chopped basil. Sauté over medium heat until the scallions start to soften, about 5 minutes. Add the white wine and let it reduce completely, about 3 minutes. Add the crabs, top side down, and sauté for 2 minutes. Turn the crabs over, and continue sautéing until they are browned on the bottom and cooked through, 3 or 4 minutes. Remove the crabs from the heat, cut them in quarters, and set aside.

In a pot, steam the asparagus for 4 minutes and set them aside. Add the cooking liquid to the vegetable stock and bring it to a simmer.

In a heavy-bottomed saucepan, sauté the red onion in the remaining ¼ cup of olive oil until the onion softens, about 5 minutes. Add the rice and stir until it is thoroughly coated, sautéing for 2 minutes. Add ½ cup of the simmering broth and stir while cooking until the rice absorbs the liquid. When the rice dries out, add another

(continued on next page)

½ cup of the liquid and continue stirring. Make sure to loosen any rice that may attach to the bottom of the casserole. Continue adding liquid by the ½ cup as the rice dries out.

The entire risotto process should take about 20 minutes. When there is just ½ cup of liquid remaining, add the cooked soft-shell crabs and the asparagus. Add the remaining liquid and the tomato. Cook for another few minutes. The rice should be firm, and the risotto slightly soupy. Remove it from the heat, stir in the parsley, the remaining basil, and the butter, and serve.

Zuccotto
Tuscan Parfait

A *zucchetto* in Italian is a skullcap. This dessert is called *zuccotto* because it's shaped like the Duomo in Florence, but you can also make the parfait in layers in a cake pan. The ingredients are similar to those found in *semifreddo:* In fact, *zuccotto* was probably the first *semifreddo*, a precursor of *gelato*. Though Catherine de Médicis is credited with bringing sorbet with her to France, what she probably served was *semifreddo*.

(SERVES 4 – 6)

½ (12-ounce) sponge cake, cut into
½-inch-thick slices (any spongy,
non-frosted cake will do here)

1⅛ cups heavy cream

1⅛ cups fresh ricotta

½ cup chopped toasted hazelnuts

½ cup chopped toasted almonds

¼ cup chopped candied fruit

6–8 tablespoons sugar, or more to taste

3 tablespoons sweet liqueur
(Bénédictine, framboise, Grand
Marnier)

1½ ounces bittersweet chocolate,
chopped fine

2½ teaspoons unsweetened cocoa
powder

Completely line a deep, 1½-quart bowl with the sponge cake. With an electric mixer, beat the cream on medium-high until it begins to thicken, then lower the speed and continue beating until it is thick and glossy. In a separate bowl, mix the ricotta on medium speed for 3 minutes, until it is smooth. Combine the whipped cream with the ricotta. Incorporate half the chopped nuts and all of the candied fruit, blending well. Add sugar to taste and mix well.

(continued on next page)

Drizzle the liqueur over the sponge cake. Spread half the whipped cream and ricotta mixture in a 2-inch-thick layer over all of the sponge cake. There will be a well in the middle.

Mix the remaining whipped cream ricotta mixture with the chopped chocolate and the cocoa powder until it is well blended. Spoon the chocolate whipped cream ricotta mixture into the center of the *zuccotto* and sprinkle the top with the remaining chopped nuts. Place the *zuccotto* in the freezer until it is firm, about 6 hours.

Fifteen minutes before serving the *zuccotto*, remove it from the freezer. Invert the bowl onto a plate so the *zuccotto* drops out. Cut it into wedges and serve.

LA BUSINESS CLASS
Traveling Business Class

Sardine Gratinate	Sardines with Bread Crumbs
Zuppa di Fagioli, Cozze, Vongole,	Bean, Mussel, Clam, and Black Truffle
e Tartufo Nero	Soup
Piccione Ripieno	Stuffed Squab
Spumone al Miele	Honey Mousse

**SUGGESTED WINES: CHARDONNAY, ROMITORIO (GRAPE: CHARDONNAY); MORMORETO,
FRESCOBALDI (GRAPES: CABERNET SAUVIGNON, CABERNET FRANC)**

. . ..

About six months after I started at Coco Pazzo, the owner, Pino Luongo, came into the kitchen and told me that we had been invited to participate in a gourmet weekend at the Highlands Inn in Carmel, California. Lots of famous chefs would be there and Pino would go as my assistant. I was thrilled—I was still in my honeymoon period with my new boss—and started working on a menu right away. The day of our trip, there were delays and setbacks at the airport too dreary to describe—Pino and I passed the time playing *briscola* (trump) in the passenger lounge—but we finally made it to San Francisco, rented a car, and drove up the coast to the hotel. It was so beautiful, it made up for the day of snafus. My room was huge, had a Jacuzzi, and looked out over the ocean (Pino, since he had come as my assistant, had a smaller room with a partial view, blocked by a tree). Since I couldn't sleep, I roamed the grounds listening to the waves, the birds, watching the sunrise, and waiting until morning, when the work would start.

First thing the next day, Pino took me into the kitchen and introduced me to the other chefs: Patrick Clark, who was at the Hay Adams Hotel in Washington, Dean

(continued on next page)

COOKING WITH PINO (SECOND FROM LEFT) AT THE HIGHLANDS INN.

Fearing from the Mansion at Turtle Creek in Dallas, Todd English from Olives and Figs Pizzeria in Martha's Vineyard, and John Joho of Everest in Chicago. I met Brian Whitmer, the executive chef of the Highlands Inn, and David Fink, the inn's general manager. It was all amazing and perfect. Even Pino as an assistant was great. The first day, he cleaned 85 pigeons and stuffed them with herbs. He cleaned 375 mussels. He helped make the soup, the sardines, and helped serve the dishes. But I think the work got to him because our *luna di miele* (honeymoon) was obviously over. For the trip home, Pino bought two tickets, one business class, one economy. The boss traveled business.

Sardine Gratinate

Sardines with Bread Crumbs

Americans aren't used to eating fresh sardines and anchovies, which is a shame. These fresh items taste completely different from the kind preserved in oil that sit on grocery-store shelves collecting dust. In seaside towns like Viareggio and Pisa, sardines are a staple on restaurant menus: They're delicate, subtle, and, best of all, plentiful and cheap. Monterey has some of the best sardines in the United States, which is why I included them on my Carmel menu. In most parts of the country, they are admittedly hard to find. Ask your fishmonger to order some.

(S E R V E S 4)

2 pounds (16 whole) fresh sardines, cleaned and filleted

²/₃ cup freshly squeezed lemon juice

1¹/₁ cups extra-virgin olive oil

4 tablespoons chopped fresh Italian parsley

4 tablespoons chopped fresh oregano

Pinch of crushed red pepper flakes

Salt and fresh ground black pepper, to taste

¹/₂ cup thinly sliced red onion

1¹/₂ tablespoons bread crumbs

1 cup washed, mixed salad greens

¹/₂ cup chopped tomato

Have your fishmonger clean and fillet the sardines, unless you want to try it yourself. If so, using a sharp knife, slit the sardine open along the belly and, with a spoon, remove the innards. There will be about a teaspoon. Cut off the heads, then pry the fish open, catch the end of the tail bone under the tip of the knife, and pull up. (This is easiest done under running water.) I also cut out the fin, which is in the back. Wash

(continued on next page)

the fillets and, if you have time, marinate them for 24 hours in the lemon juice. (If you are in a hurry, an hour or two will do.)

Gently remove the sardines from the lemon juice and pat them dry (they are "cooked" and will break easily). In a dish large enough to hold all the sardines, combine the olive oil, parsley, oregano, red pepper flakes, salt and pepper, and onion. Add the sardines, making sure they are all completely submerged in the oil. (They will keep in this preparation for 2 to 3 days.) Let them marinate for at least an hour.

You can eat the sardines like this, on a slice of toasted Tuscan bread with a little of the onion and herbs spooned on top; they are delicious. Or you can remove them from the olive oil and lay them out in a broiler pan. Sprinkle them with bread crumbs, and broil them until golden brown, 3 to 4 minutes. Serve them on a bed of salad greens, garnished with the chopped tomato.

Zuppa di Fagioli, Cozze, Vongole, e Tartufo Nero
Bean, Mussel, Clam, and Black Truffle Soup

Truffles are expensive. If you prefer to keep costs down, garnish the dish with a sprig of parsley instead.

(S E R V E S   5)

1¼ cups dried cannellini beans

8–9 cups cold water

1 pork chop, cut into chunks

5 cloves garlic, peeled and crushed

2 small potatoes

1½ teaspoons salt

½ teaspoon fresh ground black pepper

3 tablespoons extra-virgin olive oil

1 strip bacon, chopped fine

1 slice pancetta, chopped fine (or omit this and double the bacon)

¼ medium onion, chopped fine

½ stalk celery, chopped fine

½ tablespoon finely chopped fresh rosemary

½ tablespoon finely chopped fresh sage

½ teaspoon crushed red pepper flakes

¼ cup canned plum tomatoes

1 tablespoon tomato paste

1 cup dry white wine

½ tablespoon chopped fresh Italian parsley

25 clams, well cleaned (see page 302)

25 mussels, well scrubbed (beard the mussels at cooking time)

25 thin slices black truffle

Rinse the beans, picking over them to remove any pebbles, and soak them overnight in 4 cups of cold water. Drain, and place them in a large stockpot with 4 or 5 cups of fresh cold water, the pork, 1 clove crushed garlic, and the potatoes.

(continued on next page)

Bring the beans to a boil, add the salt and pepper, then reduce the heat to a simmer and cook for 40 to 45 minutes, until the beans are soft. Discard the pork and the garlic.

In a large sauté pan, warm 1 tablespoon of the olive oil over low heat. Add the bacon, pancetta, onion, celery, 3 cloves of the garlic, the rosemary, sage, and red pepper flakes. Sauté the mixture until the onion and celery are transparent but not brown, about 15 minutes. Add the tomatoes and the tomato paste and cook for about 10 minutes more, stirring frequently.

Add the tomato mixture to the beans and cook the mixture approximately 15 minutes over low heat to warm it through. Puree the soup in a food processor and return it to the stockpot.

In another large stockpot, mix together the remaining 2 tablespoons of olive oil, the white wine, the remaining garlic clove, parsley, clams, and mussels. Bring the mixture to a boil and remove the shellfish as they open, placing them in a bowl. Remove the clams and the mussels from their shells, discarding those that do not open on their own, and add the meats to the pureed soup. Spoon the bean mixture into soup bowls and garnish it with the slices of black truffle. Serve immediately.

Piccione Ripieno

Stuffed Squab

If you make an extra squab or two, you can have an easy risotto or pasta. Just debone the bird (or, if you're lazy, cut it in pieces and let people eat the meat off the bone, which can be fun). Mix the meat of one squab into a risotto (for 2 people) halfway through the cooking time (to make a risotto, see page 218); or dress up a plate of spaghetti with the squab, a little olive oil, some chopped parsley, and fresh ground black pepper.

(S E R V E S   4)

4 squab

Salt and fresh ground black pepper, to taste

2 sprigs fresh rosemary

4 sprigs fresh thyme

4 bay leaves

12 juniper berries

12 whole cloves

4 sticks cinnamon

4 cloves garlic, peeled, plus 3 cloves garlic, peeled and chopped

1 onion, quartered, plus 1/2 cup roughly chopped onion

1/2 cup plus 3 tablespoons extra-virgin olive oil

2 tablespoons chopped fresh oregano

2 cups cleaned, sliced, mixed mushrooms (shiitake, oyster, cremini)

3/4 cup red wine

1 stalk celery, cut into 1/2-inch pieces

1 carrot, cut into 1/2-inch pieces

4 slices pancetta

Preheat the oven to 375°. Wash and dry the squab well, removing the giblets and reserving them for another use.

With your fingers, pull off the extra fat (don't use a knife, you might cut the skin, which keeps the bird moist). Salt and pepper the flesh and cavities of the squab. Divide the rosemary, thyme, bay leaves, juniper berries, cloves, cinnamon, whole garlic cloves, and onion quarters into 4 batches and use them to stuff the squab cavities.

(continued on next page)

To a medium sauté pan, add the 3 tablespoons of olive oil and the chopped garlic and heat over medium. When the garlic starts to color, after 3 or 4 minutes, add the oregano, mushrooms, and salt and pepper to taste. Cook the mushrooms for 7 to 8 minutes, lowering the heat if the garlic starts to burn. Set the mushrooms aside.

Meanwhile, pour the remaining ½ cup of olive oil into a large ovenproof sauté pan and heat over medium-high. When the olive oil is hot, add the squab and brown them on all sides. (Be careful, the oil will splatter.) Remove the pan from the heat and add the wine (again, being careful). Return the pan to the heat until the wine reduces completely, about 1 minute. Add the celery, carrot, and chopped onion, and stir.

Turn the squab breast side up and lay 1 slice of pancetta on top. Place the squab in the oven and cook them for 15 minutes. Turn and cook for another 10 minutes. Transfer the vegetables to a food processor and puree. Stir the reserved mushrooms into the puree and pour the mixture back into the pan. Lower the oven temperature to 300°. Return the pan to the oven and cook the squab for another 15 minutes or so, depending on their size. They are done when the juices run clear.

Bay Leaf

Bay leaf, what we call in Italian alloro, *is so common in Tuscany that it's used to make funeral wreaths, as hedges to divide neighboring properties, and to hide anything unsightly—even garbage dumps. I sometimes use bay leaf in boiled chestnuts, pork livers, or game dishes, but I never really appreciated* alloro *until I went to Arpege in Paris and ate Dover sole with fresh bay leaves stuffed between the flesh and the skin. It was one of the most memorable dishes of my life. It's difficult to find fresh bay leaf in the United States, and it is also expensive. Bay leaf is often available only in the dried form—either the California or Turkish variety. Both types taste different from the Tuscan* alloro *but add subtle flavor to everything from soups to vegetables.*

Spumone al Miele

Honey Mousse

(SERVES 8)

. . . .

¹/₄ cup water	¹/₃ cup sugar
¹/₂ cup honey	1 cup heavy cream
4 eggs, separated	

In the top of a double boiler over boiling water, bring the water to a boil and add the honey, mixing well until the honey is completely dissolved. In a bowl, beat the egg yolks and the sugar together, then pour the mixture into the honey-water syrup and mix well. Return the pan to the stove, and stir continuously over medium-low heat (don't let it boil) until the mixture starts to stick to the spoon, doesn't separate, and is a uniform golden color, 20 to 22 minutes.

Remove the pan from the stove, pour the mixture into a large bowl, and set it aside to cool, about 20 minutes. Meanwhile, beat the egg whites until they form stiff peaks, and fold them gently into the cooled honey mixture. Then whip the cream and fold that in, too. Cover the mousse with plastic wrap, and refrigerate it until serving time.

LE CENE
The Dinner Parties

Insalata di Funghi	Wild Mushroom Salad
Farfalle al Salmone e Asparagi	Bowties with Salmon and Asparagus
Pollo con Peperoni	Chicken with Peppers
Zuppa Inglese	"English Soup"

SUGGESTED WINES: BORRO LASTRICATO, SELVAPIANA (GRAPES: PINOT GRIGIO, PINOT BIANCO); COLTASSALA, VOLPAIA (GRAPES: SANGIOVESE, MAMMOLO)

. . . .

When I started writing this book, I had lived and worked in New York for three years but had never shopped in a New York grocery store or cooked in a New York home kitchen.

Two things I wanted to be sure of were that the ingredients I listed were available to the general public and that the dishes were simple enough to be made at home. So, instead of testing the recipes in a professional kitchen, Eileen and I decided to host dinner parties and invite our friends and colleagues to sample our goods. We agreed to shop only at local markets and to prepare all forty menus with the equipment she had in her own four foot by three foot kitchen (my own kitchen contained only a microwave, toaster, coffeepot, and an odd assortment of flatware and dishes).

One exception we made was for one of the first test dinners. Actually, we bent the rules only slightly by cooking in the country house of my old friends Benita and Kenny, near Rhinebeck. It was a rough initiation into life outside of New York City. First of all, the closest supermarket was forty-five minutes away. Then there was the stock itself; or rather, the lack of it. In the dairy department, the only "Italian" cheeses were American Parmesan, vacuum packed in geometrically correct bricks or pregrated in cardboard cylinders, and prefabricated mozzarella. As for the produce, most of it I wouldn't have even fed to our chickens at home. Luckily, Eileen had packed her own bunches of fresh sage, rosemary, and thyme, because the store had none. (If you can't find these herbs in your own supermarket, they should be readily available from a local greengrocer.) We were also saved by Benita's healthy supply of Lucchese olive oil.

I finally settled on a simple menu—a salad made with romaine lettuce, domestic mushrooms, and the Parmesan brick; penne with salmon and asparagus; and chicken with red and green peppers. For dessert, we made *zuppa inglese*, which translates as "English soup" but is actually Tuscan.

Aside from a major blow-out with Eileen over how to cut asparagus—she snaps off the tough ends by breaking the stem where it bends, I slice the vegetable on the diagonal and throw away the bottom—dinner was a success. At least Benita and Kenny seemed to think so; they invited friends over the next day to finish the leftovers and to sample my wildly generous mixed grill. Benita announced that if she closed her eyes, she was transported to the verandah at Viporc; she could feel Tuscany around her. I hope you all feel the same way.

Insalata di Funghi
Wild Mushroom Salad
(SERVES 4)

³/₄ pound mushrooms (porcini, oyster, cremini), cleaned

12 small leaves romaine lettuce, washed

¹/₄ pound Parmigiano-Reggiano cheese

Salt and fresh ground black pepper, to taste

Extra-virgin olive oil

Slice the mushrooms very fine, through the stem. To assemble the salad, arrange the lettuce leaves on 4 plates and pile them with mushrooms. Using a cheese slicer, shave Parmigiano Reggiano sheets over each salad. Season with salt and pepper, then drizzle a thin stream of olive oil over each salad. Serve immediately.

Farfalle al Salmone e Asparagi

Bowties with Salmon and Asparagus

(SERVES 4 AS AN APPETIZER)

2 tablespoons extra-virgin olive oil

2 cloves garlic, chopped

1/2 teaspoon crushed red pepper flakes

1 sprig fresh rosemary

1/2 pound asparagus, cut into 1-inch
  lengths, tips set aside

2 tablespoons finely chopped fresh
  Italian parsley

1/2 pound salmon fillet, cut into thin
  slices

1 medium tomato, peeled and chopped

Fresh ground black pepper, to taste

3 quarts water

1 1/2 tablespoons salt, plus extra to taste

1/2 pound bowties or other short pasta

Place the olive oil, garlic, red pepper flakes, rosemary, and asparagus stems (not the tips) in a large sauté pan and cook over medium-high heat, stirring, for approximately 5 minutes, until the garlic is golden and the asparagus is bright green. Add the parsley and stir. Add the salmon and cook for 2 to 3 minutes more. Add the tomato, along with salt and pepper, and the asparagus tips. Lower the heat to medium-low and cook for another 3 minutes. Set aside and keep warm.

Bring the water to a boil in a large pot. Add the 1 1/2 tablespoons of salt and the bowties and cook until the pasta is very *al dente.* Drain and add to the salmon. Cook for 2 or 3 minutes more. Serve. This is also nice served at room temperature as a salad.

Pollo con Peperoni

Chicken with Peppers

(SERVES 4)

....

½ cup extra-virgin olive oil

1½ teaspoons crushed red pepper flakes

8 fresh sage leaves

8 cloves garlic, peeled and crushed

6 sprigs fresh rosemary

1 (3-pound) chicken, cut into pieces

1 large onion, cut into chunks

1 *each* red, green, and yellow bell pepper, seeded and cut into pieces

Salt and fresh ground black pepper, to taste

½ cup white wine

1 (28-ounce) can Italian tomatoes, drained

Place ¼ cup of the olive oil, the red pepper flakes, sage leaves, 4 cloves of the garlic, and the rosemary in a large, heavy-bottomed sauté pan over medium heat. When the olive oil starts to sizzle, add the chicken, skin side down. Cook for 15 to 20 minutes, turning the pieces regularly so they brown evenly (you might have to lower the heat a little).

In a medium frying pan, place the remaining ¼ cup of olive oil, the remaining 4 cloves of garlic, and the onion. Cook over medium-high for 7 to 10 minutes, until the onion is slightly translucent, then add the bell peppers. Continue cooking until the peppers soften, about 15 minutes, then set the mixture aside.

Add salt and pepper and the white wine to the chicken. When the wine has completely reduced, 5 to 7 minutes, transfer the chicken to a plate and add the tomatoes to the sauté pan. Raise the heat to high and reduce the juices by half, 4 or 5 minutes. Add the pepper mixture and the chicken to the reduced tomatoes, lower the heat, and simmer, covered, for approximately 20 minutes. Uncover and cook for 5 minutes more. Serve.

Zuppa Inglese
"English Soup"
(SERVES 6)

½ pound ladyfingers

½ cup Alchermes (a sweet, red liqueur
of spices, flowers, and red
cochineal—if you can't find it,
substitute Vin Santo)

Pastry Cream (recipe follows)

1 recipe Chocolate Sauce (page 320)

Place half the ladyfingers in the bottom of an 8-inch square serving dish. Drizzle them with half the Alchermes. Spread a layer of the pastry cream over the cookies. Drizzle ½ the chocolate sauce over the cream. Follow this with another layer of ladyfingers, Alchermes, pastry cream, and chocolate. Refrigerate the *zuppa Inglese* at least an hour before serving.

ME WITH KENNY AND BENITA, 1987.

Crema Pasticcera

Pastry Cream

. . . .

2 cups milk

Grated zest of ¹/₂ lemon

1 large egg plus 2 large egg yolks

¹/₃ cup sugar

¹/₃ cup flour

1 teaspoon vanilla extract

In a small saucepan, bring the milk and lemon zest to a low boil. Remove the pan from the heat.

In a bowl, beat the egg, egg yolks, and sugar together until pale yellow. Continue beating, adding the flour, the vanilla, and the hot milk. Pour this custard back into the saucepan and heat over medium, stirring, until the mixture thickens, 2 to 3 minutes. It will be the consistency of yogurt. Spoon the warm pastry cream into a bowl, cover it with plastic, and refrigerate until just chilled, about 2 hours.

Summer Menus

AIUTANDO A FARE LA PASTA

Helping Make the Pasta

Panzanella	Tomato and Bread Salad
Tordelli con Ragù di Carne	Lucchese Ravioli with Meat Sauce
Agnello Arrosto con Aglio, Limone, e	Roasted Leg of Lamb with Garlic,
Spinaci Saltati	Lemon, and Sautéed Spinach
Torta di Ricotta con Salsa di Fragole	Ricotta Cheesecake with Fresh
Fresche	Strawberry Sauce

SUGGESTED WINES: CHIANTI CLASSICO, MONTEFILI (GRAPES: SANGIOVESE AND LOCAL VARIETALS); LE STANZE, POLIZIANO (GRAPE: CABERNET SAUVIGNON)

. . . .

A few years after my parents opened Vipore, my nonna Cesarina came to live with us. She helped in the kitchen, around the restaurant, and mostly, taking care of me. Since I had been born the same year her youngest son died, I was her favorite grandchild, which made her my favorite adult. Cesarina did everything for me, from brushing my hair to laying out my clothes in the morning—my shirt, pants, socks, and shoes. If I got scolded, I would console myself in Cesarina's skirts. If I had a secret, I shared it first with Cesarina. On Saturday afternoons, when Cesarina went to visit our cousins in San Concordio, I was her companion. That meant that on Saturday mornings, before our trips to San Concordio, Cesarina would make fresh *tordelli*—a ravioli typical of Lucca that is stuffed with ground beef, pork, and chicken—so that Mama and Papa wouldn't run out while we were gone. The *tordelli* were her secret recipe, and Cesarina was very territorial about who she allowed to help her with the task.

One morning, I went to watch Cesarina as she made the *tordelli*. I know this was the day I decided I would become a chef. I was thirteen, and Cesarina started to show me how to roll and cut the pasta. Her hands flew, tucking and pinching like a seamstress. My first tries were disastrous, but when Papa came in, he was so encouraging that I caught on quickly and was soon producing perfect, savory rectangles.

I went to see Mama to brag, but I think she barely heard me. Instead she grabbed my hand and took me with her to check on the lamb and potatoes, which were roasting in the outdoor oven. I've breathed that smell a million times since, but I'll always remember the air that day. It was overpowering, a smoky haze of sage, rosemary, oil, garlic, and lamb roasting over wood. I watched Mama pull out the pan, splash on red wine and lemon juice, and toss in a handful of salt. When we got back in the kitchen, I asked so many questions about the meat and roasting, the pasta and the ragu, that Mama told me to be quiet and stay in the corner and watch. She may have been impatient, but she was a good teacher. I never went to San Concordio again with Nonna. From then on, I spent my weekends learning in the kitchen.

Panzanella

Tomato and Bread Salad

(SERVES 5)

....

10 ounces day-old country bread

½ cup red wine vinegar

4 scallions, sliced into thin rounds

1 cucumber, peeled and sliced thin

1 yellow or red bell pepper, seeded and
   sliced into thin strips

3 tomatoes, seeded and sliced

20 basil leaves, julienned

8–12 anchovy fillets, rinsed and
   chopped (optional)

6 ounces Italian tuna (canned in oil),
   drained and flaked (optional)

6 tablespoons extra-virgin olive oil

1½ teaspoons salt

1½ teaspoons fresh ground black
   pepper

1 teaspoon chopped fresh marjoram

Soak the bread in 4 tablespoons of the vinegar mixed with enough water to cover. After 2 minutes, squeeze it dry and place it in a bowl with the vegetables, basil, anchovies, and tuna.

In another bowl, mix the olive oil, the remaining vinegar, salt, and pepper until it is well combined. Add the dressing to the vegetable mixture and toss. Let the *panzanella* sit for 30 minutes at room temperature. Remix and serve with marjoram sprinkled on top.

If you have trouble sleeping, you can use basil leaves, which are known to calm the nervous system, in an infusion, or you can cook the leaves in water with a little oil and grated Parmigiano-Reggiano for a soothing soup.

Mortadella

*T*his is actually a more refined cousin of what in America is known as bologna. Mortadella comes from the Latin phrase farcimen murtatum *which means a cooked sausage, spiced with myrtle. The best mortadella comes from Bologna, and whole ones can run the size of a small tree trunk. Mortadella is recognizable by the large chunks of lard that can be seen when it's sliced to eat. It's very pungent; a little bit goes a long way.*

GUIDO MANNUCCI

A SELECTION OF VIPORE'S SPECIALTIES: TOMATO AND BREAD SALAD (PANZANELLA; WILD BARLEY SOUP, GARFAGNANA STYLE (ZUPPA DI GRAN FARRO DELLA GARFAGNANA); STEAK FLORENTINE (BISTECCA ALLA FIORENTINA); FRESH GARDEN PASTA (PASTA AL GUSTO DELL'AROMETO); PORK CHOPS WITH ROSEMARY (CONTROFILETTO DI MAIALE AL PROFUMO DI ROSMARINO); ZUCCHINI POCKETS (FAGOTTINI DI ZUCCHINI).

Tordelli con Ragù di Carne

Lucchese Ravioli with Meat Sauce

(SERVES 10–12 AS AN APPETIZER)

Il Ripieno

Meat Filling

....

1½ pounds meat (beef, pork, rabbit, chicken, and/or turkey), cut into 3-×-3-inch cubes

Salt and fresh ground black pepper, to taste

¼ cup chopped fresh herbs (sage, marjoram, thyme, rosemary, and Italian parsley)

⅛ teaspoon grated nutmeg

⅛ teaspoon ground cinnamon

⅛ teaspoon ground cloves

¼ cup plus 3 tablespoons extra-virgin olive oil

½ pound Swiss chard, well washed and stemmed

½ cup day-old coarse bread crumbs

½ cup chopped cured meats (such as mortadella, salami, or prosciutto)

5 tablespoons freshly grated Parmigiano-Reggiano cheese

1 egg, beaten

Homemade Beef broth, as needed

Preheat the oven to 400°. Season the meat with salt, pepper, fresh herbs, spices, and ¼ cup of the olive oil. Place the mixture in a roasting pan and roast for 25 to 30 minutes, stirring occasionally, until the meat is well done.

While the meat is cooking, place the Swiss chard with the water still clinging to its leaves into a medium pot, cover, and heat it over medium-high, stirring occasionally. When the chard has wilted, after about 7 minutes, drain it, and squeeze out as much water as possible. Chop the chard roughly.

In a medium frying pan, heat the remaining 3 tablespoons of olive oil and add the chopped Swiss chard. Cook it for 2 minutes, then set it aside to cool.

When the meat is done, place it in the bowl of a food processor along with its roasting juices, the Swiss chard, bread crumbs, cured meat, Parmigiano-Reggiano, and egg. Pulse until everything is well blended. If the mixture is dry, add some beef broth, a tablespoon or so at a time. Adjust the seasoning and set the mixture aside, allowing it to cool before using it.

Pasta per Tordelli
Tordelli Dough

Making pasta by hand takes patience and time. After 2 or 3 tries, you'll get it right, and be happy you did.

. . . .

4½ cups unbleached white flour

4 large eggs plus 4 large egg yolks

2 tablespoons extra-virgin olive oil

½–¾ cup water

2 teaspoons salt

Mound the flour on a clean work surface and form a well in the center. Add the eggs and the egg yolks to the well and scramble them with your fingers or with a fork. Add in the olive oil, ½ cup of the water, and the salt. Use one hand to mix the eggs and the other to hold up the wall of the flour well from the outside. Gradually begin incorporating the flour from the inside wall of the well into the eggs.

When the eggs are no longer runny, push in the walls of the flour and work the mixture into a mound of soft crumbs. Gather the mass together and begin working it into a ball. (If it seems too dry here, add up to ¼ cup more water, a tablespoon at a time.) Once the dough has formed, knead it vigorously for 10 minutes, until it is elastic and smooth. Shape the dough into a flat oval. Cover it with a kitchen towel, and let it rest for an hour.

(continued on next page)

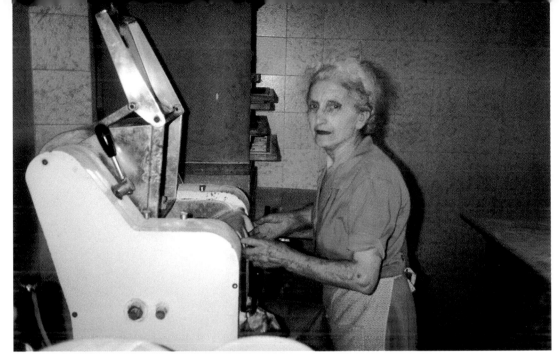

NONNA CESARINA MAKING TORDELLI AT VIPORE, 1983.

To make the *tordelli*, clean, then lightly flour your work surface. Pinch off a baseball size portion of dough and shape it into a flat oval. Begin rolling it out with a rolling pin into a rectangular sheet, no more than $1/8$ inch thick, preferably thinner. With a knife, trim the pasta into a long strip, approximately 3 inches wide.

You must work quickly so the dough does not dry out. Pinch off pieces of the meat filling and roll them to form small, marble-size balls, about $1/2$ inch in diameter. Center the balls, approximately 2 inches apart, in the middle of the strip of dough. Fold the pasta over the balls, pressing down on the pasta between each ball with your fingers to seal the dough. Cut out the *tordelli* by using a pastry wheel with a wavy edge to make half-moon shapes. Repeat the process with the rest of the filling and dough. Dry the *tordelli* on a flat screen until ready to use. If you are not going to use the *tordelli* within 24 hours, cover them lightly and refrigerate them. They will also keep frozen for 2 months. Thaw them in the refrigerator before using.

When ready to use, cook the *tordelli* for approximately 8 minutes (depending on the thickness of the pasta) in a pot of abundant boiling, salted water. Add a tablespoon or two of olive oil to the water to keep the *tordelli* from sticking to each other.

Ragù di Carne
Meat Sauce

(MAKES 10–12 CUPS)

....

1 large yellow onion, chopped fine

2 stalks celery, chopped fine

1 medium carrot, chopped fine

4 cloves garlic, chopped fine

1/4 cup extra-virgin olive oil

1/2 pound ground pork

1/2 pound ground beef

1/2 pound ground veal

4 thin slices pancetta, chopped

4 thin slices prosciutto, chopped

2 cups white or red wine

1 (28-ounce) can whole Italian
   tomatoes, drained

1 cup crushed canned tomatoes

1/2 cup water

1/2 teaspoon salt

1/2 teaspoon crushed red pepper flakes

1/4 teaspoon fresh ground black pepper

1/2 teaspoon ground allspice or a dash
   each of grated nutmeg, ground
   cloves, and ground cinnamon

In a large saucepan, sauté the onion, celery, carrot, and garlic in the olive oil over medium heat until the mixture is tender and translucent, about 15 minutes. Just before the mixture begins to color, add the pork, beef, veal, pancetta, and prosciutto. Continue cooking until the meat is browned, about 8 or 9 minutes.

Add the wine, and raise the heat to reduce the liquid. Cook for 5 to 10 minutes. Add the tomatoes and cook, covered, over medium-low heat for about 50 minutes. Add the water, salt, red pepper flakes, black pepper, and spices and cook for another 50 minutes, until the sauce is thick and flavorful. (Check occasionally to make sure the sauce isn't drying out. If it is, add a bit more water.)

Assembly:
Freshly grated Parmigiano-Reggiano cheese

Drain the cooked *tordelli*, mix them with the meat sauce, and serve with grated Parmigiano-Reggiano cheese.

Agnello Arrosto con Aglio, Limone, e Spinaci Saltati
Roast Leg of Lamb with Garlic, Lemon, and Sautéed Spinach

In Italy, we eat lamb very well done, but I've adapted my recipe for American tastes, which lean toward rare or medium meat.

(SERVES 6–8)

2 tablespoons chopped fresh rosemary

2 tablespoons chopped fresh sage

1 tablespoon minced garlic, plus 15 whole cloves, peeled and crushed (1 bulb)

2 teaspoons salt

1 teaspoon fresh ground black pepper

1 (4–5-pound) boneless leg of lamb

½ cup extra-virgin olive oil

Juice of 1 lemon

1½ cups white wine

Sautéed Spinach (recipe follows)

Preheat the oven to 400°. In a bowl, combine the chopped herbs, minced garlic, and salt and pepper. Make 20 or more deep slits around the lamb and stuff them with the herb mixture, rubbing the remaining mixture onto the outside of the meat. Place the lamb in a casserole just large enough to hold it, and pour the olive oil over the lamb, massaging the oil into the meat. There should be some extra that collects in the bottom of the casserole. Put the lamb in the oven. If the meat is very lean, you should check on it after 15 minutes to make sure it isn't cooking too fast.

Wait another 30 minutes, then pour the lemon juice and wine over the lamb, turn the lamb over, and add the crushed garlic cloves to the pan. Lower the heat to 350° and return the lamb to the oven. For rare meat, roast it another 5 to 10 minutes. Insert an instant reading thermometer. It should say 120° for rare. For medium-rare, roast another 20 to 25 minutes.

Let the lamb rest for 15 minutes before carving. Pour the juices into a gravy boat. Slice the meat, and serve with its juices and the Sautéed Spinach on the side.

Spinaci Saltati

Sautéed Spinach

If you can find tender, baby spinach, you can add it directly to the oil and garlic without precooking it.

(S E R V E S   6 – 8)

4 pounds spinach, well washed, tough
stems removed

6 tablespoons extra-virgin olive oil

4 cloves garlic, sliced

Salt and fresh ground black pepper, to
taste

Place the spinach, with the water still clinging to its leaves, in a pot large enough to hold it. Cover and cook it over medium heat, stirring occasionally, until the spinach just wilts, about 7 to 8 minutes. Drain the spinach well in a colander, pressing out the excess water with the back of a spoon.

Heat the olive oil and garlic in a medium sauté pan. When the garlic begins to color, after about 5 minutes, add the spinach and cook it briefly, about 2 minutes, adding salt and pepper.

Torta di Ricotta con Salsa di Fragole Fresche

Ricotta Cheesecake with Fresh Strawberry Sauce

(S E R V E S 8)

....

Il Ripieno

FILLING:

1³/₄ pounds ricotta cheese

1¹/₄ cups sifted confectioners' sugar

1¹/₄ tablespoons sifted cornstarch

1¹/₂ teaspoons vanilla extract

3 eggs

Grated rind of 1 lemon

La Pasta

CRUST:

6 tablespoons sweet butter, cubed

3 tablespoons sugar

1 small egg

1 teaspoon cold water

¹/₄ teaspoon salt

1¹/₂ cups sifted flour

Salsa di Fragole Fresche

FRESH STRAWBERRY SAUCE:

2 cups finely chopped strawberries

2 tablespoons sugar

To make the filling: Combine all the ingredients in listed order in the bowl of an electric mixer. Mix on medium-low speed for 15 minutes or until the mixture is smooth and well blended. Set aside in a cool place (not the refrigerator) while preparing the crust.

To make the crust: In a large bowl, cream the butter and the sugar until they are light and fluffy. Add the egg and the water and mix well. Add the salt, continuing to beat until the salt and sugar dissolve. Bring the mixture to the center of the bowl. Add the flour around the edge. Then slowly incorporate the flour into the butter-sugar mixture. Stir until it forms a dough and makes a ball. Sprinkle the dough with flour to prevent it from getting sticky, then refrigerate it for 1 hour.

Meanwhile, preheat the oven to 350°. Butter a 10-inch springform pan.

To assemble the cheesecake: On a lightly floured surface, roll out a ¹/₄-inch-thick,

11-inch circle of dough and fit it into the prepared pan. The crust should come up the sides of the pan slightly. Pour the cheese mixture into the pastry-lined pan.

Bake the cheesecake for 30 to 40 minutes, or until it has risen in the center and formed a skin on top. It should give like Jell-O when touched. Cool it at room temperature, then chill for 1 hour before serving.

To make the sauce: Mix the strawberries and the sugar together.

Spoon over cut slices of the chilled cheesecake.

Gigi il Maiale
Gigi the Pig

Fagottini di Zucchini	Zucchini Pockets
Garganelli con Tonno Fresco	Garganelli with Fresh Tuna
Controfiletto di Manzo alla Moda di Mezza Estate	Midsummer's Rib-eye Steak
Tiramisù	Tiramisù

SUGGESTED WINES: POMINO ROSSO, FRESCOBALDI (GRAPES: SANGIOVETO, CABERNET SAUVIGNON, MERLOT, PINOT NERO); ROMITO DEL ROMITORIO, ROMITORIO (GRAPES: SANGIOVESE, CABERNET SAUVIGNON)

Visiting my grandfather Beppe's farm was always a treat for me, especially when he let me play with his prized boar, Gigi. Gigi was huge and grizzly with a long snout covered with bristles. I called him Gigi the Stud, which wasn't poetic license, it was fact. Before my grandfather took Gigi to a neighboring farm to work, my job was to wash him and brush him and get him ready. In those days, Gigi was very much in demand in the neighborhood—so much so that he got two pigs every time he mated with a sow—and his prowess was a great source of pride for Grandpa Beppe. One year, Gigi brought home ninety pigs, giving new meaning to bringing home the bacon—or pancetta, as the case may be.

Eventually, technology intervened, and the demand for Gigi's services dropped off. If he'd been any other pig, we'd have butchered Gigi, but Gigi being Gigi, we let him live out his days in peace.

Toward the end, when Gigi started to lose his appetite, I remembered how he had once loved Grandma Maria's *conserva*, the tomato sauce she cooked and canned in huge batches every summer when tomatoes were at their peak. At the end of the day, she would slur the leftover pulpy skins and seeds into the pig trough, and Gigi would lap them up midair. With that in mind, I started stealing into Maria's pantry to sneak out a jar of *conserva* to mix into Gigi's feed. He loved it. Lucky for me, Beppe and Maria never found out, but I'm convinced it added months to his life.

MAMA AND ME IN FRONT OF UNCLE FRANCESCO'S BAR, DAL BIONDO, IN SAN PIETRO A VICO, 1963.

Fagottini di Zucchini
Zucchini Pockets

Sour cream isn't an ingredient you'd ever find in Tuscany, but it makes the pastry crust extra flaky. At Vipore, we make *fagottini* with homemade puff pastry, but it's complicated to prepare. You can cheat with frozen puff pastry.

(MAKES 12)

2 cups sifted flour

1 teaspoon salt, plus extra to taste

¾ cup vegetable shortening

2 tablespoons cold water

2 tablespoons sour cream

¼ cup extra-virgin olive oil

2⅔ cups finely chopped zucchini

⅔ cup finely chopped shallots

¼ cup white wine

4 teaspoons finely chopped fresh oregano

4 teaspoons finely chopped fresh parsley

2 teaspoons finely chopped fresh mint

2 teaspoons finely chopped fresh tarragon

Fresh ground black pepper, to taste

1 egg, beaten

In a bowl, combine the flour with the teaspoon of salt, then cut in the vegetable shortening. Sprinkle the water and the sour cream over the flour mixture and work the dough into a ball. Refrigerate for 20 minutes.

Preheat the oven to 350°. Place the oil, zucchini, and shallots in a medium-size sauté pan and cook over medium heat until the juices given off by the zucchini are nearly evaporated, about 7 minutes. Add the white wine, oregano, parsley, mint, and tarragon, and cook until the wine completely reduces, 8 to 10 minutes. The mixture should not be too dry. Add salt and pepper and let the mixture cool.

On a lightly floured surface, roll out the pastry to about a ⅛-inch thickness. With a glass or a cookie cutter, cut out circles about 4 inches in diameter. Spoon about 1 tablespoon of the zucchini mixture into the middle of each circle. Brush the edges of the circles with the beaten egg and fold the dough over to form a half moon. Press down around the edge with the tines of a fork to seal the dough shut. Place the *fagottini* on a cookie sheet and brush the tops with the beaten egg. Bake for 15 to 20 minutes, until golden brown. Serve.

There's hardly a mushroom, artichoke, or zucchini dish in Tuscany and Liguria that doesn't contain nepitella, *but unfortunately, you can't find that herb in any other region in the world. I've tried to reproduce the flavor here by mixing one-third fresh oregano, one-third fresh parsley, one-sixth fresh tarragon, and one-sixth fresh mint. I use it to flavor mushrooms, artichokes, and fish dishes.*

Garganelli con Tonno Fresco

Garganelli with Fresh Tuna

(SERVES 4 AS AN APPETIZER)

3 quarts water

1½ tablespoons salt plus extra to taste

½ pound garganelli or penne pasta

1½ tablespoons chopped garlic

2 tablespoons chopped fresh oregano

3 tablespoons extra-virgin olive oil

¾ pound tuna steak, cut into ½-inch
  chunks

⅓ cup white wine

1 cup chopped tomato

2 tablespoons chopped fresh Italian
  parsley

Fresh ground black pepper, to taste

Bring the water to a boil in a large pot. Add the 1½ tablespoons of salt and the garganelli.

Place the garlic, oregano, and olive oil in a large sauté pan and heat over medium until the garlic starts to color, about 5 minutes. Add the cut-up tuna and stir so the fish browns evenly, 3 or 4 minutes (depending on how well you like your tuna cooked).

When the pasta is *al dente*, drain it and keep warm.

Add the white wine to the tuna sauce and let it reduce, about 2 minutes. Then add the tomato and cook for another 2 minutes. Stir in the parsley and salt and pepper. Toss with the pasta and serve.

Controfiletto di Manzo alla Moda di Mezza Estate

Midsummer's Rib-eye Steak

(S E R V E S 4)

4 cups well-washed arugula

4 medium tomatoes, cut into bite-size
  chunks

2²/₃ tablespoons balsamic vinegar

Salt and fresh ground black pepper, to
  taste

2 (18–20-ounce) shell, New York,
  rib-eye, T-bone, or strip steak, with
  bone

2 tablespoons extra-virgin olive oil

Preheat the broiler. Arrange the arugula on 2 plates.

In a small bowl, mix the tomatoes with the balsamic vinegar, and add salt and pepper.

Salt and pepper the steak on both sides. Be especially generous with the pepper. Place the meat under the broiler. Cook for 5 or 6 minutes on each side, or to desired doneness. Remove from the oven and trim the meat. Arrange the tomatoes on top of the arugula. Cut the meat into ½-inch-thick slices and arrange on top of the salad. Drizzle each plate with olive oil and serve.

Tiramisù

Tiramisù

You can also layer the tiramisù in a rectangular serving dish, starting with a layer of ladyfingers, then mascarpone, then cocoa. Finish with cocoa sprinkled over the top.

(S E R V E S   8)

6 eggs, separated

7 tablespoons confectioners' sugar

1½ pounds mascarpone cheese

¼ cup grappa, brandy, or Vin Santo

1½ pounds ladyfingers

¾ cup cold espresso

3 tablespoons unsweetened cocoa powder, or 4 ounces bittersweet chocolate, grated

In one bowl, beat the egg yolks with the sugar, then fold in the mascarpone and the liqueur.

In the bowl of an electric mixer, beat the egg whites until they are stiff and form peaks. Fold the whites into the mascarpone mixture.

Dip the ladyfingers into the espresso and drop 2 into a wineglass. Spoon the mascarpone over the cookies and sprinkle cocoa powder or grated chocolate on top. Chill several hours before serving.

ALLA CONQUISTA DEL LETTO
In Search of a Bed

Insalata di Crescione e Fagioli	Watercress and Bean Salad
Pasta alla Moda di Mezza Estate	Midsummer-Style Pasta
Rosticciana di Maiale alla Griglia	Pork Ribs Grilled with Rosemary
Frutti di Bosco con Zabaglione	Summer Berries with Zabaglione

**SUGGESTED WINES: TORNIELLO, VOLPAIA (GRAPES: SAUVIGNON BLANC, SEMILLON);
NERO DEL TONDO, RUFFINO (GRAPE: PINOT NERO)**

. . . .

When Mama and Papa bought Vipore, it was an old inn, with three rooms and a restaurant upstairs, and a bar downstairs. Since we wanted more space for the restaurant, we converted the *stanzina della televisione*, "the small room with the TV" into an extra dining room. Six to fourteen could fit in the *stanzina* to eat, but if it was more than ten, we had to move the TV into my room, the *stanza del fuoco*, "the fire room," which was exactly above the kitchen, toasty warm in winter and burning hot in summer. But when Nonna Cesarina came to live with us, everything got moved around. Papa gave Cesarina the *stanza del fuoco;* I got a murphy bed and was moved into the *stanzina della televisione*.

Unfortunately, the *stanzina della televisione* always got booked up, especially on Friday and Saturday nights. It was small and intimate and everyone loved it for private parties. For me, that meant not being able to go to sleep until the people finished eating. I rarely lasted that long, and instead I would crawl into the space under the refrigerator where there were sacks of bread I could use as a pillow. In the summer, I liked the *capanna*, the shed where we made *tordelli* and stored the big vats of wine. It was cool, and there was Billy, our dog, as a pillow. Sometimes I used other places, which meant that after everyone had gone, Mama and Papa had to search high and low to find me to put me to bed.

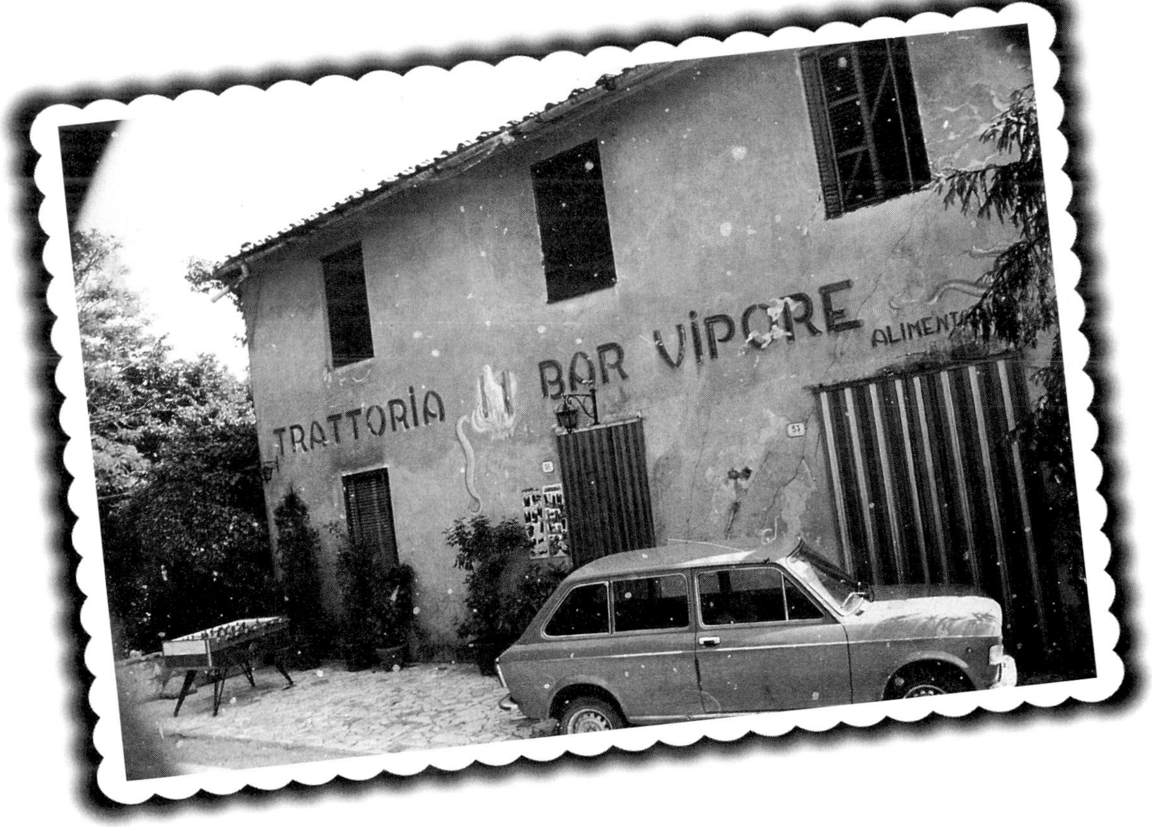
TRATTORIA
BAR VIPORE

Insalata di Crescione e Fagioli

Watercress and Bean Salad

(SERVES 4)

2¹/₂ tablespoons red wine vinegar

Salt and fresh ground black pepper, to
    taste

¹/₂ cup extra-virgin olive oil

¹/₄ cup cooked cannellini beans

¹/₂ cup chopped tomato

3 tablespoons chopped red onion

8 cups well-washed watercress

Croutons, for serving

In a small bowl, whisk together the vinegar and the salt and pepper. Whisk in the olive oil. Mix together the beans, tomato, red onion, and watercress, and toss with a few tablespoons of the dressing.

Divide the salad among 4 plates. Sprinkle with croutons and serve.

Pasta alla Moda di Mezza Estate
Midsummer-Style Pasta
(SERVES 4 AS AN APPETIZER)

4 medium, ripe tomatoes

1 tablespoon kosher salt

3 quarts water

1½ tablespoons plus 2 teaspoons salt

½ tablespoon *each* finely chopped fresh
    oregano, thyme, marjoram, and basil

½ bunch arugula, washed and chopped

½ teaspoon crushed red pepper flakes

2 small cloves garlic, peeled and crushed

3 tablespoons extra-virgin olive oil

½ pound fusilli or other short pasta

4 tablespoons freshly grated
    Parmigiano-Reggiano cheese

Chop the tomatoes and layer them in a colander. Sprinkle them with the kosher salt and let them sit for 2 hours, stirring occasionally. This will draw the extra water out of the tomatoes and make their flavor more intense.

In a large pot, bring the water to a boil, then add 1½ tablespoons of the salt. Transfer the tomatoes to a bowl large enough to hold all the ingredients, and add the remaining 2 teaspoons of salt, the herbs, arugula, red pepper flakes, garlic, and olive oil. Cook the pasta until it is *al dente*, then drain and toss it with the sauce and the grated Parmigiano-Reggiano. Serve. (This dish is also good served cold.)

Rosticciana di Maiale alla Griglia

Pork Ribs Grilled with Rosemary

(SERVES 5)

....

⅓ cup chopped fresh rosemary

8 cloves garlic, chopped

Salt and fresh ground black pepper, to
 taste

4½ pounds pork ribs, cut into separate
 ribs

1 cup white wine

Rub the rosemary, the garlic, and the salt and pepper into the ribs. Cover them and let them marinate at room temperature for 1 to 2 hours.

Heat an outdoor grill. When the grill is hot, cook the ribs approximately 20 minutes, turning them often. Remove the ribs to a platter, splash them with the wine, then return them to the fire and cook them for another 5 to 10 minutes. Then serve. If you don't have a grill, you can place the ribs in a broiler pan and broil in the oven instead.

Frutti di Bosco con Zabaglione
Summer Berries with Zabaglione
(SERVES 4)

4 egg yolks

¼ cup sugar

1¼ cups Vin Santo or dry Marsala

4 cups raspberries or other fresh berries

Place the egg yolks, sugar, and Vin Santo or Marsala in the top of a double boiler over simmering water, and beat with a wire whisk until the mixture becomes thick and creamy and doubles in volume. (The zabaglione must not be made over direct heat. If you don't have a double boiler, bring water to a simmer in a saucepan and beat the zabaglione in another pan, over the simmering water.) It will take about 5 minutes.

Spoon the berries into individual serving dishes, pour the zabaglione on top, and serve.

4

LE MERENDE DI ALDA
Alda's Snacks

Crostini di Pomodoro	Tomato Toasts
Bruschetta	Bruschetta
Risotto con Pesto, Funghi, e Gamberi	Pesto Risotto with Mushrooms and Shrimp
Manzo Cotto al Vapore di Pomodoro	Filet Mignon Baked Over Tomatoes
Torta con Frutti di Bosco	Mixed Berry Tart

SUGGESTED WINES: SERENA, BANFI (GRAPE: SAUVIGNON BLANC); VINO NOBILE DI MONTEPULCIANO, BINDELLA (GRAPES: PRUGNOLO GENTILE, CANAIOLO, MAMMOLO)

When I turned ten, Papa decided to send me to a private school in town, run by the Dorote nuns. The idea, I guess, was that I'd get a better education with the sisters than at the public school out at Pieve, in the country. I really couldn't say about that, but what did make an impression on me, from the first day, was *merenda*, the morning snack break.

In the country school, *merenda* meant thick slabs of crusty bread with prosciutto or pecorino. My friends and I would sit around with our sandwiches bragging about whose cow had given the most milk and whose chickens had laid the most eggs. At Dorote, the students talked about whose Papa had the nicest car and who had the newest toys. If they had snacks at all, they were Kit Kats, Bon Dí, or some other prepackaged sweet.

When I'd pull one of Rosa's meaty sandwiches out of my brown paper bag, I could feel all thirty pairs of eyes on me. Actually, they weren't on me, but on my sandwich, shiny and promising in its foil wrapping. If Mama had just slaughtered a pig, the sand-

(continued on next page)

wich would be thick with *soppressata* (salami) or *arrosto* (roast). If not, it was garlicky *fettunta* soaked in olive oil or *buccellato* dripping with marmalade. For me, *fettunta* (sliced, grilled bread with olive oil) or *buccellato* (Lucchese dessert bread) was actually disappointing. I liked the warm spiciness of the pork, but I wouldn't have traded even a *fettunta* for a Kit Kat, ever.

There was only one boy I knew who got *merende* as good as mine. That was Mauro, whose family lived down the road from us in Pieve Santo Stefano. Since Mauro didn't go to Dorote, it's not like he gave me any competition at school. But in the summer, I got the *merende* tables turned on me. That's because Mauro's mom, Alda, made the most heart-stopping *bruschetta* I've ever had, then or since.

Like the city boys at Dorote who envied my *soppressata* sandwiches from Rosa, I coveted Mauro's mom's *bruschetta*. What made her *bruschetta* so memorable, I've never quite figured out, because I never saw her do anything more than go into the garden, pick a tomato and slice it in half. Then she'd brush the cut side on warm toast, sprinkle it with olive oil and salt, and hand over the slices. I can still feel the toast crackling as I bit down, the flood of olive oil and salt and summer sun-warmed tomatoes. I would eat four or five without breathing in between.

Americans seem to think *bruschetta* is chopped tomato, garlic, basil, and olive oil on toast. I don't know why. For us, that's *crostini con pomodoro*. Real *bruschetta*, the way Alda made it, is the way I've just described. I have my own version, which is delicious, but it might not satisfy what I've concluded is an American craving for cubed tomatoes.

LINA PIERONI WITH TRAYS OF DRYING TORDELLI IN THE PASTA ROOM.

Crostini di Pomodoro

Tomato Toasts

(SERVES 4)

2 cups seeded and chopped plum
   tomatoes

2 tablespoons chopped shallot or Vidalia
   onion

1/4 cup finely chopped fresh basil

6 tablespoons extra-virgin olive oil

4 tablespoons balsamic vinegar (you can
   also use red wine vinegar, for a very
   different taste)

1/2 teaspoon fresh ground black pepper

1 1/2 teaspoons salt

4 slices Tuscan bread

In a bowl, combine the tomatoes, onion, and basil. Add all the other ingredients except the bread, and mix well.

Toast the bread until golden brown. Spoon the tomato mixture on top of the toast and serve immediately.

Bruschetta

Bruschetta

If you don't have a lot of fresh herbs, you can just use additional basil here; but the more herbs, the better.

(S E R V E S 4)

1 pound plum tomatoes, cored and
    quartered

¼ cup extra-virgin olive oil

1 clove garlic, peeled and crushed

1 scallion, sliced

½ teaspoon crushed red pepper flakes

½ teaspoon salt

1 teaspoon chopped fresh oregano

1 teaspoon chopped fresh tarragon

2 tablespoons chopped fresh basil, plus
    4 whole basil leaves

1 teaspoon chopped fresh marjoram

1 tablespoon balsamic vinegar

1½ teaspoons red wine vinegar

4 slices Tuscan bread, toasted

Place half of the tomatoes, the olive oil, garlic, scallion, red pepper flakes, salt, and herbs in a food processor. Pulse it on and off to make a sauce. It should be much chunkier than a puree. Add the remaining tomatoes and pulse a few more times. There should still be bite-size pieces of tomato visible. Add the vinegars and stir.

You can serve the *bruschetta* mixture in a bowl and allow your guests to make their own, or you can spoon the mixture onto the toast, garnish with the remaining basil leaves, and serve immediately.

Tarragon

. . . .

*T*he Italian word for tarragon is dragoncello. *I guess it's a reference to the fact that a dragon has a split tongue, just like the tarragon leaf. When I first discovered tarragon, I didn't like it. The aniselike flavor was overpowering, plus, I thought it was French. But as I started learning more about herbs, I discovered that the cooking of Siena relies heavily on tarragon, which changed everything for me. I embraced it. Now I use tarragon either very sparingly, or in large quantities.*

Risotto con Pesto, Funghi, e Gamberi

Pesto Risotto with Mushrooms and Shrimp

(SERVES 4 AS AN APPETIZER)

3 tablespoons chopped red onion

½ cup extra-virgin olive oil

1¼ cups arborio rice

¾ cup white wine

4 cups simmering homemade fish or
   vegetable stock

3 cloves garlic, peeled and crushed

1 cup cleaned, mixed mushrooms
   (chanterelles, shiitake, cremini)

1 dozen medium raw shrimp, shelled
   and cleaned

Salt to taste

Fresh ground black pepper, to taste

½ cup Pesto alla Cesare, more to taste
   (recipe follows)

1 tablespoon chopped fresh basil

In a medium saucepan, sauté the onion in ¼ cup of the olive oil over high heat until it begins to soften, about 5 minutes. Add the rice, stir to coat. Cook 2 minutes more, until the rice is lightly toasted. Remove from the heat and add ¼ cup of the white wine, then return the rice to the heat and let the wine reduce, about 1 minute. Add the simmering stock and continue cooking at a lively boil over high heat.

In a small sauté pan, heat 2 tablespoons of the remaining oil with 1 clove of the crushed garlic. Discard the garlic after 1 minute. Add the mushrooms and sauté over high, stirring constantly for 2 to 3 minutes. Add the mushrooms to the rice and stir. Over high, heat the remaining 2 tablespoons of the oil in the sauté pan with the remaining 2 crushed garlic cloves. Discard the garlic after 1 minute. Add the shrimp, salt, pepper, and the remaining ½ cup of wine (be careful, it will flame up). Cook for 2 minutes, then add to the rice mixture.

It will take about 15 minutes from the time the liquid is added for the rice to cook *al dente*. Taste it. If after 15 minutes it is still too hard, add a little more broth or water and continue cooking. The risotto should be slightly soupy and the rice firm to the bite. Add salt and pepper to taste. When it has reached this stage, remove the rice from the heat, add the pesto and chopped basil, stir well, and serve. (If you pour a thin layer of oil over the unused pesto, it will keep very well in the refrigerator for a week. You can use the leftover pesto to make pasta, drizzled over toasted tuscan bread, or as an addition to a vinaigrette to give your salad a light, basil taste.)

Pesto alla Cesare

Cesare's Pesto

(SERVES 6)

2 cups fresh basil leaves

½ cup fresh Italian parsley

¼ cup fresh chervil (or use all parsley)

1–1½ cups extra-virgin olive oil

5 tablespoons pine nuts

4–5 cloves garlic, peeled

Salt and fresh ground black pepper, to

    taste

5 anchovies, preserved in salt or olive oil

    (optional)

3 tablespoons freshly grated

    Parmigiano-Reggiano cheese

3 tablespoons freshly grated pecorino

    Romano cheese

Put the basil, parsley, chervil (if you don't use chervil, use more parsley), olive oil, pine nuts, garlic cloves, salt and pepper, and the anchovies in a food processor. Blend coarsely, stopping from time to time to scrape down the sides. When the ingredients are well blended, pour them into a bowl and add the grated cheeses. (If combining the pesto with pasta, add a tablespoon of the cooking water to the pesto to thin it out. This is unnecessary with risotto.)

Manzo Cotto al Vapore di Pomodoro

Filet Mignon Baked Over Tomatoes

(SERVES 4)

4 medium, ripe tomatoes

2 teaspoons kosher salt

4 pinches of sweet paprika

4 pinches of hot paprika

2 shallots, chopped fine

8 cremini mushrooms, cleaned and
 sliced thin

³/₄ cup loosely packed fresh basil

Salt and fresh ground black pepper, to
 taste

4 (6-ounce) filet mignons or strip steaks

4 tablespoons *Arometo* sauce (page 15;
 you can also use Pesto alla Cesare,
 page 123)

Extra-virgin olive oil (optional)

Preheat the oven to 475° Slice the tomatoes in half and place them, cut side up, in a deep, ovenproof skillet. Sprinkle them with the salt, paprikas, chopped shallots, and the mushrooms. Top with the basil (reserve a few leaves for the top of the steaks).

Salt and pepper the steaks and rub one side with the *Arometo* sauce. Place the steaks, sauced side down, on top of the tomatoes and garnish them with the reserved basil leaves. Seal the skillet with aluminum foil and bake for 35 to 40 minutes. If you want, it makes a nice presentation to open the foil at the table.

Transfer the steaks and tomatoes to a plate and spoon the juices from the skillet over them. If you want, drizzle a touch of olive oil on top and serve. You can make a bed of tomatoes and cook a large steak on top, too.

Torta con Frutti di Bosco

Mixed Berry Tart

(SERVES 6–8)

1 cup milk

1 teaspoon grated lemon zest

2 egg yolks

2²/₃ tablespoons granulated sugar

3¹/₂–4 tablespoons flour

¹/₂ teaspoon vanilla extract

1 cup heavy cream

2 tablespoons sifted confectioners' sugar, plus additional for dusting

1 Pastry Crust (recipe follows)

2 tablespoons Cointreau

¹/₂ cup fresh blackberries

¹/₂ cup fresh blueberries

¹/₂ cup fresh raspberries

Preheat the oven to 350°.

In a small saucepan, bring the milk and lemon zest to a low boil. Remove the pan from the heat. In a bowl, beat the egg yolks and granulated sugar together until pale yellow. Continue beating, adding the flour, vanilla, and hot milk. Pour this mixture back into the saucepan and heat over medium, stirring, until it thickens, 2 to 3 minutes. It will be the consistency of yogurt. Spoon the warm pastry cream into a bowl, drape it with plastic wrap so that no air is trapped between the wrap and the cream, and refrigerate until just chilled. The cream will be very stiff.

Meanwhile, in a bowl, whip the heavy cream to form stiff peaks, and add the 2 tablespoons of confectioners' sugar. Gently incorporate the whipped cream, a tablespoon at a time, into the chilled pastry cream, mixing well. Add only as much whipped cream as needed. The whipped cream/pastry cream mixture should be stiff, not runny. Spread it evenly over the cooled piecrust. Splash the Cointreau over the berries and mix. Arrange the berries in a pattern on the cream filling, or place them randomly. Dust with additional confectioners' sugar and serve.

Pasta Frolla

Pastry Crust

....

½ cup sugar	1¾ cups flour
1 stick (½ cup) sweet butter, cubed	1 teaspoon baking powder
1 large egg	¼ teaspoon salt
1 teaspoon vanilla extract	Dried beans or pie weights

Preheat the oven to 350°. In a bowl, cream together the sugar and butter. Add the egg and vanilla, and mix well.

In a separate bowl, combine the dry ingredients. Pour in the egg mixture and work into a smooth dough. Shape the dough into a ball, wrap it in plastic wrap, and chill it in the refrigerator for ¾ hour before using.

Roll out the dough on a lightly floured surface into a 10-inch circle, ⅛ inch thick. Transfer the pastry to a 9-inch pie plate and shape it to fit. Leave an inch overhang and fold it double around the edge to form a rim. Puncture the dough several times with the tines of a fork.

Completely cover the dough, including the rim, with a sheet of aluminum foil. Fill the pan with dried beans and bake for 25 to 30 minutes. Remove the crust from the oven, discard the beans, and take off the foil. If the shell is too white, return it to the oven, uncovered, for a few minutes. Remove and let it cool.

PESCANDO LE TROTE

Trout Fishing

Funghi Fritti	Fried Mushrooms
Pappa al Pomodoro	Bread and Tomato Soup
Trota Arrosto con Rosmarino	Roast Trout with Rosemary
Torta di Mele con Salsa di Sultana	Apple Cake with Raisin Sauce

SUGGESTED WINES: GHIAIE BIANCHE, COL'ORCIA (GRAPE: CHARDONNAY); SAN PIO,
MASTROIANNI (GRAPES: SANGIOVESE, CABERNET SAUVIGNON)

....

Il Lunedi, Monday, not Sunday, was always the day of rest for our family. We would close Vipore and set out on some adventure—a picnic on the beach in Viareggio, a drive to Torre del Lago, or an all-day game of *briscola* at Uncle Sergio's. In early and late summer, my favorite Mondays were always trips to the mountains to buy porcini. In the old days, we'd all go, the staff from Vipore, Mama, Papa, me, and always Mariano, the husband of our pasta cook. Mama insisted on Mariano because she was a picky eater. Mariano, on the other hand, was skinny but ate for two, so with him at her side, Mama could always clean her plate.

Usually, for porcini we went to Abetone, but one June I remember, Papa proposed a trip to Lucchio, a hilltop city famous for hens born with small sacks under their backsides. (It was said they used the sacks to store their eggs so they wouldn't roll downhill.) Papa wasn't interested in the hens; he wanted to stop in Lucchio to fish in the Lima River, which in summer brims with trout. The porcini, he promised, we'd buy on the way home.

We got to the Lima early, around 10 A.M. Some of our group went upstream, some down. I went with Papa in the car because he said he knew of a great spot. But after

an hour, I began to despair. We hadn't caught a single fish. Without a word, Papa motioned to me to join him in the car. In a few minutes, I understood. His "great spot" was a trout farm. The owner was wizened and weather-beaten, like a fish who'd seen one too many battles. Her eyes looked out in different directions, and she tried to sell us all the nicest trout, plump, with shiny scales. But Papa insisted on at least half ugly ones. Scrawny and ugly, too, he said, *magre e brutte, anche*, and picked out twelve.

By the time we reached Da Beppe, the restaurant where we'd arranged to meet for lunch, Mama, Adele, Camay, Onelia, and Mariano were already seated. I paraded our "catch" around the table; we had more than all their trout combined. Everyone was impressed and even a little envious. I felt as proud as if I'd actually caught the fish myself.

Until, that is, the *signora* from the trout farm appeared, carrying a crate of trout for Da Beppe. Spotting Papa across the room, she waved and called out, "*Eh, signore, ci sono altre brutte, vuole guardare?*" "I've got some more ugly ones, wanna have a look?" Mariano and Camay started in on us. Mama just shook her head. I was mortified, but not Papa. He laughed, because he almost got away with it. He even paid for everyone's lunch. "*Aspettate,*" "Just wait," he warned, indicating he'd get his revenge.

The bad news was that by the time we got to the porcini stand, the only ones left were as shriveled and unsightly as the trout we'd bought. That did make Papa mad. It meant he had to drive back the next day for some good ones.

(ABOVE) THE FAMILY AT TORRE DEL LAGO, 1965. I'M THE ONE ON THE RIGHT IN THE FIRST ROW.

Funghi Fritti

Fried Mushrooms

This recipe was written for fresh porcini, which are very hard to find in the United States, so I've substituted portobellos.

(SERVES 4)

Peanut oil, for deep frying

2 quarts water

3 tablespoons salt

1 cup flour

1 cup cornmeal

1½ pounds portobello mushrooms, cleaned, tough stems removed and caps quartered

4 cloves garlic, peeled

2 sprigs fresh oregano

Pour the peanut oil into a large frying pan, filling it one third full. Heat the oil to 375°.

Bring the water to a boil in a large pot and add the salt.

In a bowl, mix together the flour and cornmeal. When the water boils, remove it from the heat and add the mushrooms. Drain them after 1 minute. Quickly roll the mushrooms in the flour mixture, shaking off any excess.

When the oil has reached 375°, add the mushrooms, garlic, and oregano. Stir, cooking the mushrooms until they are golden brown and crispy, 3 to 4 minutes. Remove the mushrooms, garlic, and oregano from the oil with a slotted spoon and drain on paper towels. Serve immediately.

Pappa al Pomodoro
Bread and Tomato Soup

This is an extremely thick soup. You can add more water to make the dish soupier if you like.

(SERVES 4–6)

½ cup extra-virgin olive oil

1 leek, white part only, washed well and chopped

¼ cup chopped red onion

6 cloves garlic, chopped

1 cup white wine

½ cup fresh basil, cut into strips

1½ pounds ripe tomatoes, peeled and seeded (if you have time) and chopped

2½ cups water

1½ cups cubed day-old bread

Salt and fresh ground black pepper, to taste

½ cup freshly grated Parmigiano-Reggiano cheese

Place ¼ cup of the olive oil, the leek, onion, and garlic in a large pot and heat over medium. When the mixture starts to color, after 6 to 7 minutes, add the wine, and let it reduce completely, about 5 minutes. Reduce the heat to low and add ¼ cup of the basil, the tomatoes, and the water. Cook for 15 minutes. Add the bread, and stir occasionally for 20 minutes. Add salt and pepper, and cook for another 10 minutes. Then add the remaining ¼ cup of basil, and cook for a final 10 minutes. The soup is ready. It will be very thick.

Pour it into individual bowls and top each serving with a tablespoon of the remaining olive oil and 2 tablespoons of the cheese.

Trota Arrosto con Rosmarino
Roast Trout with Rosemary
(SERVES 4)

Salt and fresh ground black pepper, to taste

4 (1-pound) whole trout, cleaned, heads and tails left on

¼ cup finely chopped fresh Italian parsley

8 sprigs rosemary, leaves stripped, chopped fine

1 tablespoon finely chopped garlic, plus 3 whole cloves, peeled

½ cup extra-virgin olive oil

Juice of 1 lemon, plus 1 lemon cut in wedges

½ cup white wine

Preheat the oven to 425°. Salt and pepper the cavities of the trout. Mix together the parsley, rosemary, and the chopped garlic, then rub the mixture into the flesh of the fish (not on the scale side).

Place the olive oil and whole garlic cloves in a roasting pan and add the trout, turning them once to coat both sides in the olive oil. Bake the fish for 15 minutes. The trout goes from rare to well done in a matter of minutes. To see if it is the temperature you prefer, after the first 15 minutes of cooking time, cut a small slit near the spine of the fish. Douse the fish with the lemon juice and the white wine and continue baking for another 3 to 8 minutes. Remove the trout and serve it with lemon wedges.

THE DRIVEWAY LEADING TO THE HILL BEHIND VIPORE. THE HEDGES
ON THE RIGHT ARE ALL ROSEMARY.

Rosemary

. . . .

*R*osemary is my favorite herb, but since it is such a staple in Tuscan cooking, I think it is underappreciated. Whenever I have the chance, I try to promote rosemary. For black-tie functions, I always put a few sprigs in my tuxedo pocket; when I'm working, I mix it with other herbs and carry them in the pocket of my chef's jacket. I use rosemary as a bed to grill sea bass, as skewers for roasted meats and to garnish french fries. At Vipore I used to grow bushes of rosemary, some as big as trees. One year, I had almost a thousand, which were too many, even for me. When we cut them back, there were enough trimmings to fill a dump truck, so we decided to make a bonfire. As the rosemary was burning, we wet the fire so it would smoke. The whole countryside was filled with the scent of roasting rosemary.

Torta di Mele con Salsa di Sultana
Apple Cake with Raisin Sauce

(SERVES 6–8)

1 stick (¹/₂ cup) sweet butter

1 cup sugar

Grated rind of 1 lemon

¹/₂ teaspoon vanilla extract

4 eggs

2 cups flour

1 teaspoon baking powder

¹/₂–1 cup milk

2 pounds Golden Delicious or Rome
    apples, cored, peeled, and sliced
    (squeeze lemon over the cut apples
    to keep them from turning brown)

Salsa di Sultana (recipe follows)

Preheat the oven to 350°. Grease a 9-inch cake pan.

In a bowl, cream together the butter and ³/₄ cup of the sugar. Add the lemon rind and blend. Add the vanilla and the eggs and blend well. Add the flour and baking powder and ¹/₂ cup of the milk. If the batter is too sticky, add more milk, a little bit at a time. It should be like a thick cake batter. Fold in the apples, reserving a large handful to arrange on the top of the cake, and pour the batter into the cake pan. Arrange the remaining apples on top and sprinkle with the remaining ¹/₄ cup of sugar. Bake for 35 to 45 minutes, until golden brown. Cut in slices and spoon the sauce over each slice.

Salsa di Sultana
Raisin Sauce

....

1 cup milk

4 egg yolks

2 tablespoons sugar

2 teaspoons cornstarch

1/4 teaspoon vanilla extract

3 tablespoons white raisins, soaked in
warm, sweet white wine such as
Marsala or Vin Santo for an hour

3 tablespoons toasted chopped walnuts

Put the milk in a small saucepan and bring it to a boil. Remove from the heat and set aside.

In a bowl, beat together the egg yolks, sugar, cornstarch, and vanilla until the yolks turn lemony yellow, and pour into the top of a double boiler. Add the boiled milk, beating continuously until the mixture thickens. The sauce is ready when it coats the back of a spoon. Before serving, squeeze out the raisins and add them to the sauce. Then add the walnuts. Mix, and spoon over the apple cake.

LA MAGIA DI FORTE DEI MARMI

The Magic of Forte dei Marmi

Soppressata di Polpo con Salsa di Capperi ed Olive	Baby Octopus Salami with Caper and Olive Sauce
Spaghetti con Cozze	Spaghetti with Mussels
Rombo con Crosta di Patate	Turbot with Potato Crust
Croccante	Nut Brittle

SUGGESTED WINES: VIGNOLA, AVIGNONESI (GRAPE: SAUVIGNON BLANC); LE CACIAIE, CASTAGNOLI (GRAPES: CHARDONNAY, MULLER THURGAU, TREBBIANO)

....

Two of my parents' best friends were Silvana and Franco Guglielmi, who lived in Genoa but often came to eat at Vipore.

The Guglielmis had two daughters, Francesca, who was younger than I, and Alessandra, who was my age. I don't know this for sure, but I suspect Rosa and Pietro and Silvana and Franco thought Alessandra and I would make a great couple one day. That's why, I think, they decided to send me to spend summers with the Guglielmis at their vacation house in Forte dei Marmi. I was thirteen when it started, and living at the beach was fine with me, although there was as much chance of my one day marrying Alessandra as of my getting together with TV hostess Alba Parietti.

But that hardly put a damper on my summers, which were a country boy's fantasy. If you've never been to this part of Tuscany, you should try it. Imagine all the most chic and beautiful Italians you know, all in white linen and

ME IN FORTE DEI MARMI, 1965.

Ray · Ban sunglasses, sipping Campari in a two-mile-long, palm tree-lined, seaside café. That's Forte dei Marmi. And it's not just the presence of the Giorgio Armanis and Gianni Agnellis that give Forte its aura, it's everything: The endless stretch of *Stabilimenti Balneari*, the exclusive beach clubs; the oversize, candy-striped umbrellas; the pedalboats; the deck chairs. If you ask me, the sun is brighter, the water is warmer, and the sand whiter there than anywhere else in Italy.

I wasn't mingling with the Agnellis back then, but still, those summers for me were idyllic. On Sunday evenings, Franco and Silvana would pick me up in Pieve Santo Stefano. Sometimes Mama would come, too, then on Monday, Papa and some of his friends would drive over for the day and we'd all cook beach food together: baby octopus, spaghetti with mussels, and lots of sticky nut brittle. Tuesday morning, Mama and Papa would return to Vipore. I got to stay until Friday.

Those were the best times, after Mama and Papa had gone. As the favored houseguest, I had unlimited privileges. I didn't have to clean or do dishes; I came and went as I pleased. Every morning, I'd be up and out to meet my friends at the beach where we'd rent the *patini*, rowboats, build sandcastles, or knock down the ones of girls we liked. Every night, I'd be out at the movies, sneaking into the disco to be with the older kids, or biking up and down the *lungomare*, the seaside road, chasing my friends or being chased. We were always getting into the good kinds of trouble, coming home with great bruises we were proud of, too much sand in our pants, sticky from too much gelato. Believe me, it's not just the glow of memory. Life at Forte dei Marmi was magic.

Soppressata di Polpo con Salsa di Capperi ed Olive
Baby Octopus Salami with Caper and Olive Sauce

I first made this dish when I was at Coco Pazzo. I'd just come back from a vacation in Italy, where I'd had a similar dish at my friend Lorenzo's restaurant. Walter, my sous chef, and I came up with our own version. I especially like it in the afternoon as a "lite" snack.

(SERVES 8–10)

....

2 (1-pound) baby octopus, cleaned (see Note)

1 large red onion, quartered

3 cloves garlic, peeled

2 stalks celery

2 carrots

1 sprig *each* fresh rosemary, sage, thyme, and basil

8 cups well-washed arugula

Caper and Olive Sauce (recipe follows)

If you are using regular octopus, freeze it overnight, then defrost it before you start to cook. That will help tenderize the meat.

The day before you want to serve the *soppressata*, fill a large pot with water and add the octopus, onion, garlic, celery, carrots, and herbs. Bring the water to a boil, then simmer for approximately 1 hour, until the octopus is tender, not chewy.

NOTE: Most good fishmongers will sell octopus already cleaned, but if you want to try cleaning the octopus yourself, start by locating the valve (it almost looks like an eye) on the underbelly. Remove it with a sharp knife. Make a slit under the eyes and cut them out of the head. Use that opening to turn the octopus head inside out. Scrape off the brains and reverse the head to right side out. Rinse the octopus well. If you don't want your hands to smell, I suggest wearing surgical gloves to clean the octopus. Otherwise, you can rub your hands with lemon after you're done cleaning up.

For the next step, you'll need two 9-inch loaf pans or 2 small, deep containers one of which fits exactly into the second.

Drain the octopus and place it immediately in one of the containers. Make sure all the tentacles are inside, and force the second container on top of the octopus. Squeeze down as hard as possible so you are compressing the octopus into a small block.

Tape the 2 pans together with heavy-duty packing tape. Set the pans on a counter top and weigh them down with something very heavy. Once the octopus has cooled, after 1 or 2 hours, place the pans in the refrigerator, still weighted, overnight.

When you are ready to eat, untape the 2 pans. Insert a knife inside the rim of the top pan and run it around the edge to loosen the *soppressata*. Turn the inside pan upside down and bang it on the counter. It might take 2 or 3 tries, but eventually, the *soppressata* will pop out.

Arrange the arugula on individual plates. With a very sharp knife, cut slices of the *soppressata* as thin as possible. Lay 3 or 4 pieces on top of the salad and drizzle each serving with the caper and olive sauce.

*T*here are a few different types of soppressata *in Italy. One, found in both Emilia-Romagna in the north, and Puglia and Basilicata in the south, is a stuffed sausage made with cut instead of ground meat. It is aged, not cooked. Before machines, it took two people to make this type of* soppressata, *one to hold the sausage casing and one to stuff it with meat. The sausage had to be packed in tight—soppressata means super-pressed—to eliminate pockets of air where bacteria could grow.*

In Tuscany, soppressata *is a cross between paté and salami, made from all the poorest cuts of the pig: the head, ears, nose, cheeks, hooves, knuckles, and skin. They are first cooked, then either stuffed into a casing and cooked again, or stuffed into the skin from the head of the pig and cooked. When a butcher wants his clients to know he's got* soppressata, *he just leaves the pig's head on the counter and sells the "salami" by the slice. It goes in a flash.*

Salsa di Capperi ed Olive

Caper and Olive Sauce

....

2 tablespoons drained capers

2 tablespoons pitted and chopped
    imported black olives

1/4 teaspoon crushed red pepper flakes

1 tablespoon chopped fresh oregano

1 cup roughly chopped plum tomatoes

1 teaspoon chopped garlic

1 tablespoon chopped fresh Italian parsley

1 tablespoon chopped fresh basil

1 tablespoon red wine vinegar

1 tablespoon sherry vinegar

1 tablespoon red wine

1 tablespoon freshly squeezed lemon juice

1/4 teaspoon fresh ground black pepper

1 teaspoon salt

1/2 cup extra-virgin olive oil

Put the capers, olives, red pepper flakes, oregano, tomatoes, garlic, parsley, and basil in the bowl of a food processor and puree. Pour the mixture into a bowl and add the vinegars, red wine, lemon juice, black pepper, salt, and olive oil. Stir to combine.

Basil

....

There's more to basil than pesto: It was sacred to the Greeks, who called it "The King"; it was used as an embalming agent in ancient Egypt and to ward off dragons in medieval Europe. I think basil is best fresh, or cooked as little as possible. You can eat the whole leaves in a salad or with tomatoes. I love basil with lobster or a delicate white fish such as bass. Basil is easy to grow at home on a windowsill with lots of light. Please don't use dried basil.

Spaghetti con Cozze
Spaghetti with Mussels
(SERVES 4 AS AN APPETIZER)

3 quarts water

1½ tablespoons salt, plus extra to taste

3 tablespoons extra-virgin olive oil

2 teaspoons fresh thyme leaves

1 tablespoon finely sliced garlic

5 tablespoons chopped fresh Italian
   parsley

1 teaspoon crushed red pepper flakes

2 pounds mussels, cleaned (beard them
   just before cooking)

5 tablespoons white wine

½ pound plum tomatoes, chopped

Fresh ground black pepper, to taste

½ pound spaghetti

Bring the water to a boil in a large pot and add the 1½ tablespoons of salt.

In a large sauté pan, place the olive oil, thyme, garlic, 2½ tablespoons of the parsley, the red pepper flakes, and mussels. Heat over medium. When the mussel shells open and the garlic colors, after about 5 minutes, add the white wine and let it reduce completely, another 1 to 2 minutes. Add the tomatoes and salt and black pepper. Lower the heat to medium-low, cover, and cook for 5 minutes.

Add the spaghetti to the boiling water. When it is very firm, drain it, add it to the sauce, and cook uncovered for 5 more minutes, until *al dente*. Stir in the remaining 2½ tablespoons of parsley and serve.

Rombo con Crosta di Patate

Turbot with Potato Crust

(SERVES 4)

....

1 cup fresh basil leaves

1 cup plus 1 tablespoon extra-virgin
   olive oil

Salt and fresh ground black pepper, to
   taste

4 (⅓-pound) turbot fillets, skin intact
   (turbot is a type of flounder;
   mahimahi or sole can also be used)

6 cups spinach, well washed and
   stemmed

3 cloves garlic, peeled and crushed

1 Idaho potato

2 tablespoons flour

2 beefsteak tomatoes

1 lemon, sliced thin

In a blender, puree ½ cup of the basil with ½ cup of the olive oil and salt and pepper. Salt and pepper the flesh side of the fish fillets, then coat them with the basil mixture. Cover and refrigerate for 2 to 3 hours.

Place the spinach, with the water still clinging to the leaves, in a pot large enough to hold it. Cook over medium heat, covered, until the spinach is just wilted, about 7 minutes. Drain it well in a colander, pressing out the excess water with the back of a spoon.

Put ¼ cup of the olive oil and the garlic in a medium sauté pan and heat. When the garlic begins to color, in about 5 minutes, add the spinach and cook it briefly, about 2 minutes, adding salt and pepper to taste. Keep the spinach warm.

Preheat the oven to 350°. Peel the potato. If you don't have an electric slicer, it is probably easier to cut the potato in half lengthwise. Trim each half into a rectangle, then slice them crosswise. Coat the slices in 2 tablespoons of the olive oil to keep them from oxidizing (or keep them in a bowl of ice water). Arrange the potato slices on top of the basil mixture, so that they overlap and cover the fish fillets. (If you've kept the potato under ice water, you might want to drizzle a bit of olive oil on top to help the slices stick together while cooking.)

Pour 2 tablespoons of olive oil into a sauté pan and bring it to the smoking point. Dust the tops of the fish fillets with flour to keep them from sticking. Place the fillets in the pan, potato side down. When the potato side is brown and crispy, flip the fillets, transfer them to an ovenproof dish, and bake skin side down. The fillets will be ready in 5 to 8 minutes when the skin is crispy.

While the turbot is cooking, chop the tomatoes and the remaining basil. Toss to form a salad. Add salt and pepper to taste, and drizzle the salad with the remaining 1 tablespoon of oil. Remove the fish from the oven, remove the skin, and serve the fillets on beds of spinach, surrounded by the tomato-basil salad. Garnish the dish with lemon slices.

PAPA WITH FLICK AS A PUPPY.

Croccante

Nut Brittle

When I was little, I loved going to county fairs where there would be long tables selling every kind of nut brittle imaginable. The only thing I didn't like was that it made my fingers sticky. Lorenzo, my friend in Forte dei Marmi, was one of the first restaurateurs in Italy to serve *croccante* to his guests with coffee after dinner. Now many at the beach do.

(MAKES 2 POUNDS)

Hazelnut or other nut oil, for the pan

2 cups granulated sugar

1 cup brown sugar

$\frac{1}{2}$ cup light corn syrup

$\frac{1}{3}$ cup freshly squeezed orange juice

$\frac{1}{8}$ teaspoon salt

$1\frac{1}{2}$ cups whole toasted almonds, peanuts, hazelnuts, or pine nuts (rinsed and patted dry)

Generously grease a baking tin or cookie sheet with the nut oil.

Stirring constantly, bring the sugars, corn syrup, orange juice, and salt to a boil in a medium, non-reactive saucepan. When the mixture reaches 300° on a candy thermometer (or when a teaspoon of the liquid turns to a hard ball when dropped into cold water), add the nuts and stir well to keep the nuts from clumping together.

Remove the mixture from the heat, pour it onto the cookie sheet, and spread it about $\frac{1}{2}$ inch thick. Let it cool and harden.

When the *croccante* is hard, wipe off the excess oil from the surface with a dishcloth. With the point of a knife, break the candy into pieces. Put it on a plate and serve.

Store in an airtight container. The *croccante* will keep for a month, but it's best eaten fresh.

7

FURTI ESTIVI
Summer Fun

Insalata di Pomodori, Cipolle, Fagioli, *e Tonno*	Tomato, Onion, Bean, and Tuna Salad
Spaghetti del Babbo	Papa's Spaghetti
Maiale con Peperoni	Pork with Peppers
Budino di Cioccolato	Tuscan Bittersweet Chocolate Pudding

**SUGGESTED WINES: ROSSO DI MONTALCINO, MASTROIANNI (GRAPE: SANGIOVESE);
CASTELRAPINI ROSSO, MONTELLORI (GRAPES: SANGIOVESE, CABERNET SAUVIGNON)**

As I always imagined it, normal teenagers, or at least other Italian teenagers, passed their summer nights at the movies or in the disco. But in the country, for me and my friends, the height of summer fun was stealing fruits and vegetables from the local farmers. Conditions were ideal—the nights were long and there was no school in the morning—at least that was our reasoning.

I remember the night we did onions. There were about ten of us. During the day, each of us had gone around checking different farmers' crops to see how their onions were progressing. That night, we met at Vipore with our reports: who had the best, the biggest, the readiest, the most plentiful onions. I made spicy spaghetti and a salad of tuna, beans, tomato, and onions, and over dinner, we discussed strategy.

Usually our favorite targets for vegetables were Beppe del Lombardo, Leo del Micheli, and Sisto Colombini, because they cultivated the best of everything. But the idea was that no one farmer should suffer too much, and that we'd never drive anyone so crazy he'd stop growing a certain crop. That night, we set our goal at somewhere between forty and fifty onions.

(continued on next page)

As we talked, we knew our main obstacle would be lighting. In the dark, it would be difficult to tell the difference between onion and garlic stalks, and if we weren't careful, we'd end up with baskets of garlic. Also, the closer the garden was to the house, the more likely it was we'd be heard by the farmers and caught, which is why we decided to split up into teams.

That night, three squads went out, while I stayed at Vipore to work. Each team left at a different time, but all three came back with great onions, all the same size and color, really perfect. I thought, how odd that everyone in Pieve Santo Stefano is growing their onions the same way. But when my friends started talking, it turned out that the reason the onions all looked the same was that all three teams had raided the same farmer: Sisto. I felt so bad that the next day I went into Lucca, bought some young onions, and without letting myself be seen, left a basketful on Sisto's doorstep.

That night, Sisto showed up at Vipore. "*Ragazzi*," he said, "Boys, I already planted the onions once. What do you want, that I plant them again so you can rob me again? *Se volete mangiare le cipolle, ve le piantate da voi.*"

"If you want to eat onions, plant them yourselves."

LEO DEL MICHELI (LEFT), WHO GREW GREAT ONIONS. WHEN MY FRIENDS AND I RAIDED FARMERS' GARDENS, HIS WAS ALWAYS ONE OF OUR FIRST STOPS.

Insalata di Pomodori, Cipolle, Fagioli, e Tonno

Tomato, Onion, Bean, and Tuna Salad

(S E R V E S   4)

....

1¼ cups dried cannellini beans

9 cups cold water

1 tablespoon salt, plus extra to taste

2 medium tomatoes, cored and cut in
    bite-size pieces

½ sweet red onion, sliced thin

1 cup Italian tuna, canned in oil,
    drained, and flaked

⅛–¼ cup extra-virgin olive oil

2 tablespoons finely chopped fresh basil

Fresh ground black pepper, to taste

2–4 tablespoons red wine vinegar

Rinse the beans, picking them over to remove any pebbles. Soak them overnight in 4 cups of cold water. Drain them, add 5 cups of fresh water, and, in a medium saucepan, bring the beans to a simmer over medium heat. Add the tablespoon of salt and cook the beans until they are tender, 40 to 45 minutes. Drain and cool. Place the beans and the other ingredients in a serving bowl. Toss and serve.

Spaghetti del Babbo
Papa's Spaghetti

My father's specialty is grilling; beyond that the only two dishes he makes are *Frittata di Cipolle* and this pasta, which he invented. *Babbo*, in Tuscan dialect, means father.

(S E R V E S 4 A S A N A P P E T I Z E R)

2 tablespoons extra-virgin olive oil

2 cloves garlic, chopped or crushed

Pinch of crushed red pepper flakes

1/2 cup Italian black pitted olives

3 tablespoons chopped fresh Italian
    parsley

1/2 cup chopped walnut pieces

1/2 cup red wine

2 1/2 cups canned crushed tomatoes

1 tablespoon capers

1 1/2 tablespoons salt, plus extra to taste

3 quarts water

1/2 pound spaghetti

4 tablespoons freshly grated
    Parmigiano-Reggiano cheese

1/2 tablespoon chopped fresh basil

Place the olive oil, garlic, and red pepper flakes in a large frying pan and heat over medium until the garlic starts to color, about 5 minutes. Stir in the olives and 1 tablespoon of the parsley, and cook for 1 to 2 minutes. Rinse the chopped walnuts under water (to get rid of the walnut dust) and stir them into the sauce. Add the wine and let it reduce, about 5 minutes. If you've used crushed garlic, remove it here, then stir in the crushed tomatoes and capers. Add salt to taste and simmer for 20 minutes.

Bring the water to a boil in a large pot and add the 1 1/2 tablespoons of salt and the spaghetti. When the spaghetti is very *al dente*, drain it and add it to the tomato sauce. Cook for 5 minutes, then stir in the grated Parmigiano-Reggiano, the remaining 2 tablespoons of parsley, and the basil. Serve at once.

PAPA AT THE GRILL.

Maiale con Peperoni

Pork with Peppers

(SERVES 4)

2 tablespoons chopped fresh rosemary

2 tablespoons chopped fresh sage

½ teaspoon crushed red pepper flakes

4 boneless center-cut pork chops, each 1 inch thick

1 *each* red, yellow, and green bell peppers, halved and seeded

4 tablespoons extra-virgin olive oil

2 cloves garlic, crushed

½ medium red onion, sliced

1 tablespoon drained capers

Salt and fresh ground black pepper, to taste

⅓ cup white wine

Mix together half of the chopped herbs and the red pepper flakes and rub them into the pork chops. Wrap the meat in plastic wrap and refrigerate it for 48 hours. (If you don't have time to marinate the pork, the dish will be less flavorful, but still good.)

Preheat the broiler. Place the peppers, skin side up, on a broiler pan. Broil the peppers, watching them carefully. When the skin blackens, turn them over until they are black on both sides. It will take about ten minutes. Remove the peppers and place them in a closed plastic bag for 5 to 10 minutes. Rub off the skins and slice the peppers into thin strips.

Pour 2 tablespoons of the olive oil into a large frying pan. Add the garlic and the onion, and cook over medium heat until the mixture colors lightly, about 5 minutes. Add the other half of the herbs, the sliced peppers, and the capers. Season with salt and pepper and cook for 10 minutes. Remove from the heat, and keep warm.

In another large frying pan, add the remaining 2 tablespoons of oil and the pork chops. Sauté the chops over medium heat for 7 minutes on each side. Add salt and pepper and the white wine. Continue to cook until the wine reduces completely, about 5 minutes. Add the pepper mixture, warm through, and serve.

Budino di Cioccolato
Tuscan Bittersweet Chocolate Pudding
(SERVES 6)

4 egg yolks

¾ cup plus 1 tablespoon granulated
    sugar

1 package unflavored gelatin
    (2 teaspoons powdered gelatin)

¼ cup cold water

3 cups heavy cream

½ cup sifted unsweetened dark cocoa
    powder

1 teaspoon caramelized sugar (see Note)

2 tablespoons confectioners' sugar

1 cup fresh raspberries

In a medium-size bowl, combine the egg yolks and all the granulated sugar, beating until the yolks are pale, about 5 minutes. Set aside.

In a small saucepan, sprinkle the gelatin over the cold water. Let it stand for 1 minute, then stir it over low heat until the gelatin dissolves. (There will be 4 tablespoons of liquid gelatin.) Set aside.

Bring 2 cups of the cream to a boil in a heavy, medium-size saucepan. Remove it from the heat and add the cocoa powder, whisking constantly to break up any lumps. Whisk the egg mixture into the cream and continue whisking until the ingredients are all combined. The mixture should still be quite warm. Add the gelatin and mix well. Add the caramelized sugar and return the saucepan to medium-high heat for about 3 minutes, stirring until the mixture is smooth, thick, and dark.

Line a terrine with plastic wrap and pour in the chocolate pudding. (Or pour it into six individual ½-cup molds.) To prevent a skin from forming, drape plastic wrap over the pudding so the mixture is not exposed to the air. Refrigerate for 2 hours, or until it is set. While the pudding is setting, whip the remaining cup of heavy cream until it forms peaks, stir in the confectioners' sugar, and refrigerate.

When you are ready to serve the pudding, lift the plastic wrap off the top and in-

(continued on next page)

vert the mold onto a plate. Peel the plastic wrap off the bottom and cut the pudding into slices (or serve the individual molds as they are). Garnish with the whipped cream and berries.

NOTE: To caramelize sugar quickly, place a tablespoon of sugar in a microwave-proof pan with 2 teaspoons of water. Turn the microwave to high for $1^{3}/_{4}$ to 2 minutes, until the sugar melts and turns the color of straw. To caramelize sugar on the stove, mix two tablespoons of sugar with a tablespoon of water in a small pan. Heat over high, stirring constantly, until the sugar is the color of golden straw. It will take between two and three minutes. The caramelized sugar will harden if it cools, so this process has to be done just before you add the caramelized sugar to the cream mixture.

8

DUELLI IN CUCINA
Dueling Kitchens

Crostini al Pomodoro con Erbe Aromatiche	Tomato Toasts with Aromatic Herbs
Crostini con Peperoni	Red and Yellow Bell Pepper Toasts
Riso e Verdure	Rice and Vegetable Soup
Rovelline	Pan-Fried Veal Scallops in Tomato Sauce
Tortino di Ricotta	Country Ricotta Soufflés

SUGGESTED WINES: ROSSO DELLE COLLINE LUCCHESI, FATTORIA DI FORCI (GRAPES: SANGIOVESE, CANAIOLO, MALVASIA, TREBBIANO); TIGNANELLO, ANTINORI (GRAPES: SANGIOVESE, CABERNET SAUVIGNON, CABERNET FRANC)

....

After I moved to New York, I decided to renovate Vipore, so Mama and Papa went to stay with my aunt Anna and my cousin Paolo, who lived about 15 minutes away. Unexpectedly, this arrangement stretched out for months, and whenever I'd call Italy to see how everyone was doing, Mama would complain, "We're all fat. I'm fat, Papa's fat, even Flick [our dog] is fat." When I finally made it to Pieve Santo Stefano that winter, I saw Mama wasn't exaggerating. Everyone was fat, and soon I knew why.

A few years earlier, Anna had built a small, freestanding kitchen where she could can fruits and vegetables in the summertime. But two kitchens and two sisters in the same house was two too many all the way around. As soon as Anna would head to the big kitchen to cook, Mama would make a beeline for the small kitchen. This went on twice a day, at lunch and dinner, seven days a week. They would both prepare entire meals—antipasto, pasta, meat, vegetable, and dessert. When I sat down for my first dinner, there was so much food on the table, we had to eat with our plates on our laps.

(continued on next page)

Paolo, my cousin, had already figured out the only way to deal with this situation was to eat at home as seldom as possible. He's an only child, like me, and is doted on endlessly by Anna, and he's like a second son to my mother. So, if he refused either, feelings would be hurt. But since I was only visiting for two weeks, I didn't have the option of disappearing at dinnertime. It was like a bad parody of an Italian family meal. *Mangia, mangia,* they'd both insist, pushing their wares toward me. By the time I left, I was just like Mama, Papa, and Flick. Fat.

Crostini al Pomodoro con Erbe Aromatiche

Tomato Toasts with Aromatic Herbs

(SERVES 4–8)

....

2 large ripe tomatoes

2 tablespoons finely chopped scallions

¼ teaspoon finely chopped garlic

1 teaspoon freshly grated ginger

2 teaspoons *each* finely chopped fresh basil, marjoram, dill, and chervil

2 teaspoons finely chopped fresh chives

2 teaspoons red wine vinegar

½ cup extra-virgin olive oil

1 teaspoon salt

5 slices Tuscan bread, toasted

Peel, seed, and dice the tomatoes, placing them in a colander and letting them drain for 30 minutes. Mix in the scallions, garlic, ginger, herbs, and chives and combine well. Add the vinegar, olive oil, and salt and let the mixture rest for an hour at room temperature. Spoon the mixture onto the toasted bread and serve.

Chives

....

The first year I seeded the arometo, I planted chives, which when they sprouted, looked like "cipollina selvatica delle vigne," a wild herb that grew locally, usually in vineyards. My gardener and I methodically weeded out all the "cipollina," using it to feed the chickens and rabbits. But when the plant showed up the second year in a row, I went to see my friend at the local botanical gardens. He told me that what I had was chives, or "erba cipollina," which was very close to the wild herb we found so readily in the country. After that, I stopped planting chives and relied on our own abundant cipollina selvatica. Their edible lavender flowers are lovely in salads and beautiful in bouquets.

Crostini con Peperoni
Red and Yellow Bell Pepper Toasts

We had a lot of peppers in the garden one year and needed to use them up, so Mama and I came up with this recipe. Even though the normal topping for crostini is tomatoes, all our customers loved these and asked for them well into the winter, when there wasn't a pepper to be had in all of Pieve Santo Stefano.

(S E R V E S   4)

....

1/4 cup extra-virgin olive oil

1/3 teaspoon crushed red pepper flakes

3 fresh sage leaves, chopped

1 medium red onion, chopped

2 cloves garlic, chopped

1/3–1/2 cup white wine

1 small to medium red bell pepper, seeded and sliced

1 large yellow bell pepper, seeded and sliced

1/3 cup fresh basil, loosely packed

1 1/3 tablespoons drained capers

2 anchovy fillets, preserved in salt or olive oil, chopped

1 medium tomato, chopped (optional)

3 tablespoons finely chopped fresh Italian parsley

Salt, to taste

8 slices Tuscan bread, toasted

Put the olive oil and red pepper flakes in a medium saucepan and heat over medium. Add the sage, onion, and garlic and sauté for approximately 5 minutes, until the onion starts to color.

Add 1/3 cup white wine and let it reduce completely, about 5 minutes. Add the sliced peppers and half the basil and continue cooking over medium heat for 10 to 12 minutes more. Then add the capers, anchovy fillets, and tomato, if using it. Stir well. If the mixture seems a little dry, add a little more wine at this point, and up to 1/3 cup of water. Continue cooking until the peppers are very soft, another 5 minutes.

Remove the pan from the heat and add the remaining basil and the parsley. Transfer the pepper mixture to a food processor and pulse until it is chunky.

Return the mixture to the saucepan and cook for another 5 minutes over medium heat. It might be necessary to add a little more water at this point. The sauce should be thick and slightly soupy. Add salt, and spoon over the toast.

**PAPA IN THE GARDEN WITH WILD HERBS
AND TOMATOES.**

Riso e Verdure

Rice and Vegetable Soup

You don't need to have all of the vegetables listed, but the more you have, the tastier the dish.

(SERVES 4–6)

2 tablespoons extra-virgin olive oil, plus extra for garnish

1/2 teaspoon crushed red pepper flakes

2 teaspoons chopped fresh rosemary leaves

2 teaspoons chopped fresh thyme leaves

4 tablespoons finely chopped fresh basil

2 teaspoons chopped fresh Italian parsley

1 stalk celery, cut into 1-inch lengths

1 carrot, cut into 1-inch lengths

2 scallions, white part only, chopped

1 small red onion, roughly chopped

1/2 fennel bulb, trimmed and chopped

1 potato, peeled and chopped

1/2 cup (1-inch) pieces of trimmed green beans

1 zucchini, chopped

1 cup well-washed and chopped spinach

1 cup well-washed and chopped broccoli rabe

1 cup well-washed and chopped Swiss chard

9 cups water

1/4 cup frozen or fresh peas

1 plum tomato, quartered

1 cup arborio rice

Salt and fresh ground black pepper, to taste

Freshly grated Parmigiano-Reggiano cheese (optional)

Place the olive oil in a large pot, add the red pepper flakes and heat over medium. Add the rosemary, thyme, 2 tablespoons of the basil, and the parsley. Stir well. After 2 minutes, add the celery, carrot, scallions, onion, fennel, potato, green beans, and zucchini. Cook, stirring occasionally, until the vegetables are softened, about 15 minutes.

Add the spinach, broccoli rabe, Swiss chard, and a cup of the water. Cook for 2 minutes, then stir in the peas and tomato. Add 6 cups more of the water. Bring the soup to a medium boil and let the vegetables cook for 1 hour, covered. Stir occasionally and check the water level. As the mixture becomes thick, add another cup of water.

After 1 hour, remove the vegetables from the heat and puree two thirds of them in a food processor. Return the pureed vegetables to the pot and mix with the whole vegetables.

Return the pot to the stove and bring to a simmer. Add the rice and simmer until it is tender, about 20 minutes. Add salt and pepper and the remaining 2 tablespoons of chopped basil. If necessary, add another $1/2$ cup of water here. Mix well and spoon the soup into bowls. Drizzle a little olive oil into each bowl before serving. A spoonful of Parmigiano-Reggiano is nice as well.

Rovelline

Pan-Fried Veal Scallops in Tomato Sauce

(SERVES 4–6)

1 pound veal scallops (8 scallops),
pounded to ⅛-inch thickness (beef
or chicken scallops can be
substituted for the veal)

2 eggs, beaten with ½ teaspoon salt

1½ cups dried bread crumbs

1 cup plus 2 tablespoons extra-virgin
olive oil

1 tablespoon chopped garlic

3 tablespoons chopped capers

7 tablespoons chopped fresh Italian
parsley

½ cup white wine

3½ cups crushed canned tomatoes

Salt and fresh ground black pepper, to
taste

Dip the veal first in the beaten eggs, then in the bread crumbs, and shake off any excess. In a medium sauté pan, heat the cup of olive oil over medium-high and add the scallops. Quickly brown them, about a minute on each side, and transfer them to paper towels to drain. (For a lower-calorie alternative, broil the scallops for 6 minutes on each side. The meat will be slightly tougher, but waist-watchers might think the sacrifice is worth it.)

Pour the remaining 2 tablespoons of olive oil into a large sauté pan and add the garlic. Sauté over medium heat until the garlic starts to color, about 3 minutes. Add the capers, 1 tablespoon of the parsley, and the wine. When the wine reduces completely, after about 2 minutes, add the crushed tomatoes. Mix well, and add salt and pepper. Let the tomato sauce simmer for 5 minutes, then stir in the remaining 6 tablespoons of parsley. Add the scallops to the sauce, spooning a little sauce on top of each one. Cover the pan and let the scallops absorb a bit of the sauce for 1 minute. Remove the pan from the heat and serve. (Boiled potatoes are a nice complement to this dish.)

Tortino di Ricotta

Country Ricotta Soufflés

This is a rustic dessert, which is typical in the country. I've found that Americans like more sophisticated sweets, but I ate this throughout my childhood, and it's always been one of my favorites.

(MAKES FOUR 4-OUNCE "SOUFFLÉS")

½ stick (¼ cup) sweet butter, cubed

¼ cup plus 2 tablespoons sugar

2 eggs

½ pound fresh ricotta cheese

1¾ tablespoons cornstarch

¾ teaspoon vanilla extract

½ teaspoon baking powder

1½ tablespoons dry Marsala wine

Preheat the oven to 325°. In a bowl, cream together the butter and sugar. Beat in the eggs. Add the ricotta, cornstarch, vanilla, baking powder, and Marsala. Beat until smooth.

Pour the mixture into individual 4-ounce baking cups and bake for 20 to 30 minutes, or until golden brown. Cool and serve.

9

Una Delusione in Pieve Santo Stefano
Deluded in Pieve Santo Stefano

Insalata di Cremini	Cremini Salad
Spaghetti con Pomodoro Fresco	Spaghetti with Fresh Tomatoes
Maialino con Patate Arrosto	Suckling Pig with Roasted Potatoes
Torta di Susina	Plum Tart

SUGGESTED WINES: CHIANTI CASTELLO NIPOZZANO, FRESCOBALDI (GRAPES: SANGIOVESE, CANAIOLO, TREBBIANO, MALVASIA, CABERNET SAUVIGNON); BRUNELLO DI MONTALCINO, MASTROIANNI (GRAPE: SANGIOVESE GROSSO)

I can laugh at this story now, but I have friends who still don't. I've known Benita and Richie—she's an art director and he's a fashion photographer—for years, ever since they started coming to Lucca on vacation. We've spent hours over great bottles of Chianti and Brunello, and the local wines from the hills of Lucca.

One summer, Richie and Benita showed up with a dozen gorgeous, leggy, long-lashed American models to shoot a catalogue for Bergdorf Goodman. They were staying in a rundown villa in Marlia, a few kilometers from Pieve Santo Stefano, and there wasn't a single friend of mine—Mario, Nicola, Brocchini del Patriarca, Piero "il Sarto" (the tailor), Emilio—who didn't fantasize about spending an evening at that villa. Finally, they came up with a plan: I would offer to throw a Vipore-style dinner party for Benita, Richie, and, of course, the models. They would help.

Benita accepted the invitation for herself and her girls. We agreed on a date, borrowed a van, and loaded it up with everything from fresh wildflowers to linens to salt shakers. Once we got to Marlia, the preparations took hours. But by 10:30, we were ready, with a spread so lavish, Catherine de Médicis would have dropped her fork. We had roasted a whole suckling pig; there were mounds of cremini salad and rich garlic-roasted potatoes; bowls of spaghetti with meaty summer tomatoes and basil; a half dozen tarts with the best summer fruits. We knew no English. The models knew no Italian. It didn't matter.

Ma dopo il dolce viene l'amaro. But with the sweet came the bitter. Just before midnight, Benita stood up, clapped her hands, and announced "Bedtime, girls! We've got a 7 A.M. call." We'd barely been sitting for an hour. Our reaction, if verbalized, would hardly be appropriate for a cookbook. Richie diplomatically disappeared. Like I said, I've since forgiven Benita. I can't speak for my friends.

Insalata di Cremini

Cremini Salad

(SERVES 4)

....

2½ tablespoons freshly squeezed lemon
  juice

Salt and fresh ground black pepper, to
  taste

½ cup extra-virgin olive oil

2 teaspoons finely chopped fresh oregano

2 teaspoons finely chopped fresh Italian
  parsley

3 cups cleaned and sliced cremini
  mushrooms

2 cups well-washed arugula

1 cup well-washed curly endive

3 ounces Parmigiano-Reggiano cheese,
  shaved

In a large bowl, whisk together the lemon juice and salt and pepper. Whisk in the
olive oil and the herbs. Add the cremini and toss, coating them with the dressing. Combine the arugula and curly endive, and divide among 4 salad plates. Spoon the cremini on top of the bed of greens, and top each salad with Parmigiano-Reggiano
shavings.

Spaghetti con Pomodoro Fresco

Spaghetti with Fresh Tomatoes

(SERVES 4 AS AN APPETIZER)

3 quarts water

1½ tablespoons salt, plus more to taste

6 tablespoons extra-virgin olive oil

Pinch of crushed red pepper flakes

10 cloves garlic, peeled and crushed

1 cup julienned fresh basil leaves

1 pound very ripe tomatoes, diced

½ pound spaghetti

6 tablespoons freshly grated
    Parmigiano-Reggiano cheese

Bring the water to a boil in a large pot and add 1½ tablespoons of salt. In a large sauté pan, place the olive oil, red pepper flakes, and garlic and heat over medium until the garlic begins to color, about 5 minutes. Add ⅓ cup of the basil and the tomatoes and stir. Add the pasta to the boiling water.

Continue cooking the tomato mixture for 5 minutes, then add salt to taste. When the pasta is *very firm*, drain it, leaving a little of the pasta water with the spaghetti. Add the pasta to the tomatoes and cook for 5 minutes more, until *al dente*. Stir in the Parmigiano-Reggiano and the remaining ⅔ cup of basil leaves and serve.

If you want to conserve basil leaves at their summer peak, you can either cover them with olive oil in a sealed jar, or layer them with sea salt, and keep them in a tightly closed container. (This produces wonderful aromatic oil and salt, both of which can be used for cooking after the basil is used up. Both keep at room temperature.)

Maialino con Patate Arrosto

Suckling Pig with Roasted Potatoes

Usually you make roast suckling pig for a large party. But you can cook half a pig or only the leg with similar results.

(SERVES 8–10)

1 (17–20-pound) baby pig (if you don't want to use a whole pig, you can use half of one)

16 cloves garlic, chopped rough

16 sprigs fresh rosemary, leaves removed and chopped

2 teaspoons fennel seeds

2 tablespoons salt

1 tablespoon fresh ground black pepper

3 cups extra-virgin olive oil

3 cups white wine

2 cups beer

Roasted Potatoes (recipe follows)

For the best-tasting meat, marinate the pig for up to 5 days before you actually cook it. In a bowl, mix together the garlic, rosemary, fennel seeds, salt, and pepper. With the point of a knife, make slits 1½ inches deep and ½ inch long, spaced 2 to 3 inches apart, in the pig. (Put more slits in the meatier parts.) Stuff the herb mixture into the slits. Rub the whole roast with 1½ cups of the olive oil and whatever herbs remain. Wrap the pig in plastic wrap and refrigerate it. Massage and turn it every 2 days. (If you don't have time to do the marinating, the pig will be slightly less flavorful, but still good.)

When you are ready to cook, preheat the oven to 325°. Pour the remaining 1½ cups of olive oil into a roasting pan. Cover the pig's tail and ears with aluminum foil to keep them from burning. Make a small ball of foil and stuff it in the pig's mouth. (Keeping the mouth open lets air escape from the pig while it is cooking. You can also use a potato.) Place the pig in the oven.

After 1½ hours, turn and baste the pig. (Be careful when you turn the pig not to rip the skin.) After another hour, turn the pig again. After another 45 minutes, add the white wine. Raise the heat to 450°, and continue to roast the pig for another hour. The wine will have mostly reduced. Drain off the oil that is in the pan.

Return the pig to the oven for 20 minutes. Pour the beer over the pig and continue to cook it for another 30 minutes. This will make the skin crisp. The pig should be ready. To double check, make a cut in the leg or shoulder. There should be no blood visible. Remove the pig from the oven and let it rest for 20 minutes in a warm place. Cut the pig in chunks and serve it on a platter with the roasted potatoes.

Patate Arrosto
Roasted Potatoes

(SERVES 4)

1½ pounds potatoes (preferably Yukon Gold), peeled and cut into 1-inch dice

1 tablespoon salt

½ tablespoon fresh ground black pepper

1 cup extra-virgin olive oil

4 sprigs fresh rosemary

4 sprigs fresh sage

6 cloves garlic, crushed with papery covering intact

Preheat the oven to 325°. Place all the ingredients in a roasting pan. Mix well to coat all of the potatoes in the olive oil. Roast the potatoes for 20 minutes, then stir them. Return the potatoes to the oven for another 30 minutes, mixing every 10 minutes. The potatoes will be crusty and golden on all sides. Serve with the roast suckling pig.

Torta di Susina

Plum Tart

(S E R V E S U P T O 8)

· ·

$^1/_2$–$^3/_4$ cup pastry cream (see page 87)   2 tablespoons sugar

1 recipe Pastry Crust (page 127)

$1^1/_2$–2 cups tart plums, sliced (do not
   skin)

Preheat the oven to 350°. Spread the pastry cream inside the piecrust, creating a layer $^3/_4$ inch deep. Arrange the plums in overlapping circles on top. Sprinkle the top with sugar and cover the tart with aluminum foil. Bake for 30 minutes. Remove the foil and bake for another 10 to 15 minutes. The tart is ready when the crust is golden brown and the fruit curls slightly at the edges. Serve the tart warm or at room temperature. (You can also substitute other fruits such as peaches and kiwis for the plums, or any combination you like.)

Iacocca, Sirio, Kissinger, e Me

Iacocca, Sirio, Kissinger, and Me

Insalata di Zucchini	Zucchini Salad
Maccheroncini, Pomodori, Pepolino,	Maccheroncini with Tomatoes, Thyme,
* e Pecorino*	and Pecorino
Bistecca alla Fiorentina con Fagioli	Florentine Beefsteak with Beans
"Zuppa" di Ciliege	Cherry "Soup"

SUGGESTED WINES: CANONICO, CASTELLARE (GRAPE: CHARDONNAY); SASSICAIA, SAN GUIDO (GRAPES: CABERNET SAUVIGNON, CABERNET FRANC)
....

When Henry Kissinger visited Vipore, he was no longer Secretary of State, but he still traveled like one. He came from Florence, an hour away, with one police escort out front, and three in the rear. The only time we'd ever seen anything like that in Lucca was when the President of the Republic, Francesco Cossiga, came to town. That night, Kissinger was the guest of Le Cirque owner Sirio Maccioni, who'd also invited Lee Iacocca and a handful of other friends to be his guests at Vipore. Iacocca happened to have a security detail of his own, and between him and Kissinger, there must have been twenty guards at Vipore.

What I remember most about the evening was the thrill of knowing Sirio trusted me to entertain his friends. We'd only just met—he'd come another night with three of Italy's best-known food journalists, Luigi Veronelli and Gianni and Paola Murra—but he'd been my idol since I was in culinary school. To know that he respected me enough to bring Kissinger and Iacocca to Vipore meant the world to me.

My only restriction, he said, was that Mrs. Kissinger had to have fish. Otherwise, I was free to invent any menu I wanted. Since fish wasn't a local product, we'd never

(continued on next page)

made it before at Vipore. I spent a week testing possibilities, finally choosing a baked fish with a potato crust (see page 142). For everyone else, I labored over a more traditional menu. When Kissinger arrived, right away I overheard him telling Sirio he couldn't stay long, but something obviously changed his mind. He stayed and stayed through every course. I like to think he was seduced by my food and our atmosphere. When he and Mrs. Kissinger finally left, after 11 P.M., they were extremely gracious. The party continued until well past midnight, and I spent much of it sitting with my role model, Sirio, Iacocca, and his wife. I think I'll remember that night forever—my first real taste of a life to come in New York.

Insalata di Zucchini

Zucchini Salad

(SERVES 4)

....

2½ tablespoons freshly squeezed lemon
    juice

1 small clove garlic, chopped fine

Salt and fresh ground black pepper, to
    taste

½ cup extra-virgin olive oil

1 tablespoon finely chopped fresh
    oregano

2 large zucchini, ends trimmed, sliced
    into thin, 1-inch-long batons (You
    can also shred the zucchini, but the
    texture of the salad isn't as nice.)

4 large red leaf lettuce leaves, well
    washed

4 ounces Parmigiano-Reggiano cheese,
    shaved into thin sheets

In a small bowl, whisk together the lemon juice, garlic, and salt and pepper. Slowly drizzle in the olive oil, whisking well, then add the oregano. Toss the dressing with the zucchini.

Place a red lettuce leaf on each plate and spoon on the zucchini. Top the salads with slices of the Parmigiano-Reggiano.

Maccheroncini, Pomodori, Pepolino, e Pecorino

Maccheroncini with Tomatoes, Thyme, and Pecorino

(SERVES 4 AS AN APPETIZER)
....

3 quarts water

1½ tablespoons salt

12 ounces fresh egg pasta, cut into
   2-×-2-inch squares

10 ounces *Pommarola* (recipe follows)

1 tablespoon chopped fresh thyme

6 tablespoons grated Tuscan or Romano
   pecorino cheese

3 tablespoons extra-virgin olive oil

Bring the water to boil in a large pot. Add the salt and the pasta squares and cook until very *al dente*. (If you use fresh pasta, it will only take a few minutes.) Drain the pasta and return it to its pot along with the *pommarola*, ³/₄ tablespoon of the thyme and 1½ tablespoons of the pecorino. Mix and cook over medium for 3 minutes. Add the olive oil and stir. Spoon the pasta onto plates and serve with the remaining thyme and pecorino sprinkled on top.

Thyme
....

Thyme changes its characteristics, depending on where it's grown. The thyme I grew up using in Tuscany is called Pepolino, which has a stronger, minty-lemony flavor and smaller, gray-green leaves than most varieties. Because it's difficult to cultivate Pepolino, it's hard to find today, even in Tuscany. In the United States, garden thyme and lemon thyme are the two most common varieties. I still prefer Pepolino to any other type of thyme I've tasted.

Pommarola

Tomato Sauce

(MAKES 5–6 CUPS)

Pommarola is Lucchese for tomato sauce. In the rest of Tuscany, and Italy, it's called *salsa di pomodoro.* I wouldn't admit it at home, but I always thought *pommarola* sounded Neapolitan.

....

6 tablespoons extra-virgin olive oil

6 cloves garlic, peeled and crushed

1 stalk celery, chopped

1 carrot, chopped

½ teaspoon crushed red pepper flakes

1 cup sliced fresh basil

1 cup chopped red onion

3½ pounds ripe plum tomatoes, cut into pieces (or 3 pounds canned Italian tomatoes)

Salt and fresh ground black pepper, to taste

Water, as needed

In a large saucepan, heat the olive oil, garlic, celery, carrot, red pepper, ½ cup of the basil, and the onion over medium until the carrots are soft, about 25 minutes. Add the tomatoes and cook for 40 to 50 minutes. Add the remaining ½ cup of basil, remove from the heat, and puree the mixture in a food processor. Return the sauce to the saucepan and cook for another 30 minutes. Season with salt and pepper. If the sauce seems too thick, add a little water. The *pommarola* is ready.

NOTE: If you want, you can store *pommarola* in the refrigerator for 5 days, or you can freeze it in small containers for up to 3 months. If you freeze it in small containers, you can create serving portions for two or three instead of freezing and unfreezing all of it.

BEPPE DEL CECCHI,
OUR GARDENER,
1979.

Bistecca alla Fiorentina con Fagioli

Florentine Beefsteak with Beans

(S E R V E S   4)

....

1 pound dried cannellini beans

16 cups water

6 cloves garlic, peeled and crushed

4 sprigs fresh sage

1 tablespoon salt, plus extra to taste

2 tablespoons extra-virgin olive oil

1 small tomato, diced

Fresh ground black pepper, to taste

2 (32-ounce) rib-eye, New York strip, or
   porterhouse steaks

Rinse the beans, picking them over to remove any pebbles. In a pot, soak them overnight in 8 cups of cold water. Drain the beans and cover them with 8 cups of fresh water, add half the garlic and 1 sprig of the sage. Bring the beans to a boil, add the tablespoon of salt, and simmer for 40 to 45 minutes, until they are soft.

Prepare your grill or broiler and preheat the oven to 475°. Drain the beans, discard the garlic and sage, and mix the beans with the olive oil, diced tomato, 2 sage sprigs, and the remaining garlic. Season with salt and pepper. Transfer the beans to a baking dish and bake for approximately 15 minutes.

When your grill is very hot, generously season the steaks with salt and pepper on one side only. This will help the steak form a delicious, spicy crust. Place the seasoned side of the steak on the grill. You should move the steaks around, but don't turn them. When the first side is done, about 8 minutes for medium-rare and 11 for medium (this will vary depending on the thickness of the steaks and the heat of the grill), season the uncooked side of the steaks and flip them. Cook the steak a shorter time on the second side to desired doneness. Serve the steaks with a side of beans garnished with leaves from the remaining sage sprig.

"Zuppa" di Ciliege
Cherry "Soup"

If you can't get sour cherries, try using 2 pounds pitted Bing cherries mixed with ½ cup dried cherries or cranberries.

(S E R V E S   4)

2 pounds pitted sour cherries
½ cup water
1 stick cinnamon
½ cup sugar

16 ladyfingers
4–6 tablespoons Grand Marnier or
    kirsch

Place the cherries, water, and cinnamon stick in a medium-size saucepan and heat over medium. When the mixture starts to boil, add the sugar and reduce the heat. Simmer for 5 minutes.

Arrange the ladyfingers in 4 flat bowls and drizzle them with the Grand Marnier or kirsch. Spoon the cherries and their juice on top and serve.

Fall Menus

1. LA VENDEMMIA	**THE GRAPE HARVEST**
Crostoni d'Arselle	Baby Clams on Thick Toast
Fritto Misto di Pesce	Mixed Fried Fish
Cernia Arrosto	Roasted Grouper
La Favosa	Pine Nut Cream Cake
2. LA RACCOLTA DELLE OLIVE	**THE OLIVE HARVEST**
Fettunta	Garlic Toast with Extra-Virgin Olive Oil
Zuppa alla Frantoiuna	Fall Vegetable and Bean Soup
Baccalà Arrostito con Ceci	Roasted Salt Cod with Chick-peas
La Torta di Fernanda	Fernanda's Pie
3. LA LIBERAZIONE DELL'UCCELLI	**LIBERATING THE BIRDS**
Porrata	Leek Tart
Funghi Misti dell'Autunno con Polenta	Mixed Fall Mushrooms with Polenta
Anatra alla Puccini	Duck Puccini
Composta di Pere	Pear Compote
4. MANOVRE MILITARI	**MILITARY MANEUVERS**
Salsiccia con Fagioli	Sausage and Beans
Cozze in Brodetto	Mussels in Broth
Fricassea di Vitello Toscano	Tuscan Veal Fricassee
Pere con Pecorino, Miele, e Noci	Pears with Pecorino, Honey, and Walnuts
5. SULLA STRADA PER IL PIEMONTE	**ROAD TRIP TO PIEDMONT**
Cotechino in Berlina di Tonino	Tonino's Sausage in Puff Pastry
Spaghetti alla Carbonara di Tonino e Claudia alla Monferrina	Tonino and Claudia's Spaghetti Carbonara, Monferrina Style
Controfiletto alle Nocciole di Claudia	Claudia's Rib-eye Steak with Hazelnuts
Bonet	Chocolate Amaretto Custard

JERRY RUOTOLO

LA VENDEMMIA
The Grape Harvest

Crostoni d'Arselle	Baby Clams on Thick Toast
Fritto Misto di Pesce	Mixed Fried Fish
Cernia Arrosto	Roasted Grouper
La Favosa	Pine Nut Cream Cake

SUGGESTED WINES: TREBBIANO DI TOSCANA, CAPEZZANA (GRAPE: TREBBIANO); I SISTRI, FELSINA (GRAPE: CHARDONNAY)

Of all the fall harvests, *la vendemmia*, the grape harvest, is the most festive. Mostly that's because there's more with which to celebrate. In fact, lots of people who come to help out with the *vendemmia* don't have anything to do with the harvest—relatives who've moved away, friends, acquaintances, they all come for some fun, a free dinner, and *il piggello d'uva*, the plump black-red clusters of grapes that are twined together and given away at the end of the day. And, of course, the promise of a *fiasco*, a flask (or two) of the new wine when it's ready in the spring.

I used to help out with the *vendemmia* of Casa Bertolli, the huge farm outside of Lucca that is famous in America for its olive oil. Like everyone else, I'd arrive in the kitchen by 6 A.M. for a *caffé corretto*, espresso spiked with homemade grappa. By 6:15 we were all in the vineyards working. We'd stop briefly at 9 A.M., when a boy would show up with breakfast—snacks of lard, salami, olives, bread, and cheese; and then again at 2 P.M., when there'd be a fast lunch. By the time the sun set, we'd be on our way home to shower and get ready for dinner, usually prepared by Alberto Bertolli himself.

Signor Alberto always served seafood during the *vendemmia* because his farmers rarely got to eat fish of any kind. The old man loved digging near Viareggio for *ar-*

selle, tiny clams, and heaping them onto perfect slices of thick toast, *crostoni*. He would fry endless batches of the most delicate *fritto misto*. He would roast whole grouper and fillet them tableside, and produce vats of the spiciest, most soul-warming spaghetti with mussels I've ever had.

While Alberto, aided by his magical chef, Lidia, labored in the kitchen, we workers, friends, and hangers-on would settle in the tavern next to the cellar, the same spot where hours earlier we'd brought the grapes to be pressed. The musty, pungent aroma of fermenting grapes would be overwhelming, but we sucked it up like wine, warming ourselves in front of the big fireplace and toasting our host endlessly. We would eat ravenously, family style, at long, rough tables, and we always finished the evening playing *carte*, cards, *dama*, checkers, and *scacchi*, chess. In really good years, Alberto would uncork a few bottles of cognac and pass them around.

Yes, it was French, but we drank it just the same.

Crostoni d'Arselle

Baby Clams on Thick Toast

(SERVES 4)

2 tablespoons extra-virgin olive oil

1 sprig fresh thyme

¼ teaspoon crushed red pepper flakes

3 cloves garlic, peeled and crushed

2 tablespoons chopped fresh Italian
   parsley

½–1 cup white wine

1 cup chopped tomatoes

4 pounds of the smallest clams you can
   find, washed well (see page 302)

½ cup chopped fresh basil

Salt and fresh ground black pepper, to
   taste

4 thick slices Tuscan bread, toasted

In a large sauté pan, heat the olive oil, thyme, red pepper flakes, garlic, and parsley until the garlic starts to color, about 5 minutes. Add the wine, tomatoes, and clams and continue cooking until the clam shells open, 3 to 5 minutes, then remove them from the heat. Discard any unopened clams. Shell the clams and return the clam meat to the cooking liquid. Add the basil and salt and pepper. Spoon the clam mixture on top of the toast and serve.

Fritto Misto di Pesce

Mixed Fried Fish

(SERVES 4)

....

½ pound squid, cleaned and sliced into
   rings

⅓ pound white-fleshed fish, such as red
   snapper or grouper, cubed

⅓ pound raw medium shrimp, shelled
   and cleaned

2 *each* medium zucchini, *and* yellow
   squash, cut into 3- or 4-inch
   julienne

1 medium eggplant, cut into 3- or
   4-inch julienne

6 cloves garlic, peeled

1 sprig fresh basil

1 sprig fresh Italian parsley

1 sprig fresh sage

1 quart milk

1 cup flour

Vegetable oil, for frying

Salt and fresh ground black pepper, to
   taste

Lemon wedges, for serving

Place the seafood, vegetables, and herbs in a large bowl and pour in enough milk
to cover, then drain. Sift the flour over the ingredients, mix them well, and shake off
any excess flour.

Fill a large frying pan one third full with the vegetable oil and heat it over high.
When the oil reaches 375°, add the floured ingredients. Fry in batches, stirring so they
cook evenly. When each batch is golden brown, after approximately 3 minutes, remove
it from the oil, and drain it on paper towels. Sprinkle the *fritto misto* with salt and pepper and serve it with lemon wedges.

Cernia Arrosto

Roasted Grouper

(SERVES 8)

....

1 (6½-pound) whole grouper (or
    substitute red snapper or salmon)

Salt and fresh ground black pepper, to
    taste

4 sprigs fresh rosemary

6 cloves garlic, peeled and crushed

2 lemons, thinly sliced

¾ cup extra-virgin olive oil

1 cup white wine

2 medium tomatoes, quartered

2 tablespoons chopped fresh Italian
    parsley

Have your fishmonger clean the grouper but leave the fish whole (you can remove the head and tail if the fish won't fit in your oven). Salt and pepper the cavity of the fish and place 3 sprigs of the rosemary, 4 cloves of the garlic, and the slices of 1½ lemons inside. Moisten the fish with half the olive oil. Pour the other half into a baking dish large enough to hold the fish.

Cut zig-zag lines, about ½ inch deep and 3 to 4 inches long, on both sides of the fish, from 2 inches below the eye toward the tail. Cut the remaining lemon slices in half and stuff the zig zags with the half circles, the remaining rosemary, garlic, and salt and pepper to taste. Put the fish in the baking dish and cover and marinate the fish in the refrigerator, overnight if possible.

Preheat the oven to 350°. Transfer the baking pan to the oven and roast the fish for 10 minutes, then baste. Roast for another 20 minutes, then add the wine and tomatoes and flip the fish. Return it to the oven for 5 minutes. Baste again and roast for 10 minutes more. The fish should be ready. (Remember, cooking times are approximate. You must watch the fish and judge for yourself. Make a small cut near the spine of the fish and see if it cooked to the temperature you like. It will take about 45 minutes in all.)

Fillet the fish, sprinkle it with the parsley, and serve it along with the strained pan juices, garnished with the sliced lemons. (You can also serve this fish at room temperature.)

La Favosa

Pine Nut Cream Cake

(SERVES 8–10)

2 sticks (1 cup) sweet butter, cubed

1 cup plus 1 tablespoon sugar

6 medium eggs

Grated rind of $1/2$ lemon

Grated rind of $1/2$ orange

$1^3/_4$ cups sifted flour

1 teaspoon vanilla extract

$1^1/_2$ teaspoons sifted baking powder

$1^1/_2$ cups Pastry Cream, cooled (page 87)

1 cup golden raisins, soaked overnight in water or sweet wine to cover

$1/2$ cup plus 2 tablespoons pine nuts

Preheat the oven to 350°. Prepare two 8-inch pastry bags with plain tips. Butter a 10-inch cake pan and line it with parchment paper.

In an electric mixer, cream together the butter and sugar. Beat in the eggs, one at a time, until the mixture is pale yellow. Add the lemon and orange rinds, the flour, vanilla, and baking powder. Make sure the ingredients are well combined.

Spoon the batter into one of the pastry bags and the pastry cream into the other. Moving in a circular motion, squeeze the batter from the pastry bag to fill the bottom of the pie plate. This should use about half the batter. (If you don't have pastry bags, use a spoon; it's just a little messier.)

Then, starting about $1/2$ inch in from the side of the pan, use the same circular motion to squeeze out the cream. There should be none left over.

Sprinkle the raisins and $1/2$ cup of the pine nuts on top of the pastry cream.

For the final layer, squeeze out the remaining batter to cover. Garnish with the remaining pine nuts and bake for 40 to 45 minutes, or until the cake is golden brown. It should be firm to the touch, with a spring in it. Cool before serving.

2

La Raccolta delle Olive

The Olive Harvest

Fettunta	Garlic Toast with Extra-Virgin Olive Oil
Zuppa alla Frantoiana	Fall Vegetable and Bean Soup
Baccalà Arrostito con Ceci	Roasted Salt Cod with Chick-peas
La Torta di Fernanda	Fernanda's Pie

SUGGESTED WINES: BATARD, QUERCIABELLA (GRAPES: PINOT BIANCO, CHARDONNAY, PINOT GRIGIO); SUMMUS, BANFI (GRAPES: SANGIOVESE, CABERNET SAUVIGNON, SYRAH)

In the country, for every harvest, whether for olives, grapes, or potatoes, there's *una festa di ringraziamento*, an Italian-style Thanksgiving celebration. My favorite *festa* was always the olive harvest, especially in the years when we had our own olive grove at Vipore and produced oil to use in the restaurant and to sell and give to our friends. Back then, we would close the restaurant for the day, and just like for the *vendemmia*, the grape harvest, a phalanx of friends and family would show up to help—Piero, Emilio, Renzo, Lido di Bueta, Ezio, Renato di Borchino—each armed with his own basket and burlap sheet. After the ritual 6 A.M. *caffé corretto*, we'd fan out through the grove and start plucking the olives. Two or three of us would work a tree together, picking and letting the fruits fall onto the burlap, adding them to the basket only when the tree was whistle clean. Sometime after lunch, Mama, her sisters, and I would quit so we could get to the *frantoio*, the olive press, in Forci to start preparing dinner, traditionally, *zuppa alla Frantoiana*, a hearty vegetable soup, garlic toast, roasted cod with chick-peas, and steak. The *frantoio* itself, dating from the seventeenth century, belonged to a local noblewoman, Diamantina Scola Camerini, who was a friend of ours. We cooked there so that the workers who were working late and couldn't make it home for their own dinners could eat with us.

Baccalà, cod, was the traditional food eaten during the olive harvest, which meant *il fattore*, Armando, the foreman, and all the olive pressmen ate nothing but cod from November to February. To break up the monotony for Armando and his crew, Mama and I would bring some steaks. But me, what I looked forward to, was that first mouthful of new oil. I'd thrust my thick slab of bread right under the spigot, and pop it straight into my mouth, never losing a drop. When I got older, I got another treat, a chaser of the first wine of the season, just a little fizzy and sweet, and the perfect palate cleanser before another shot of oil.

MY CLASS AT
SCUOLA
ALBERGHIERA,
1977. I'M SECOND
FROM THE RIGHT
IN THE LAST ROW.

Fettunta

Garlic Toast with Extra-Virgin Olive Oil

In Italian, *fetta* means "slice" and *unta* means "greasy." To get the best *fettunta*, use the best oil you can find.

(S E R V E S   4)

....

¼ cup extra-virgin olive oil

Salt and fresh ground black pepper, to taste

4 thick slices day-old country bread

4 cloves garlic, peeled and halved

Preheat the oven to 350°. Whisk the olive oil, salt, and pepper together. Place the bread slices on a sheet pan and bake them until they are golden brown and dry, about 15 minutes. When the toast is cool enough to handle, rub it with the cut garlic cloves. Drizzle the oil over the toast and serve.

Zuppa alla Frantoiana
Fall Vegetable and Bean Soup

When an Italian housewife makes *La Frantoiana*, she goes to the *alimentari*, or grocery shop, and asks the deli man if he has a prosciutto bone left over from carving sandwiches for his clients. If he does, she'll use it to flavor her stock, and if she's very lucky, he'll have kept some of the skin, too. That she'll fry in the *soffritto*, the chopped herb, onion, celery, and carrot mixture that gives a base to many Tuscan dishes. I've substituted a ham bone and pancetta for those ingredients, but if you can get a prosciutto bone and skin, you'll love this super-filling soup even more.

(SERVES 10)

2 cups dried cannellini beans

6 cups plus 4 quarts water

2 cloves garlic, peeled and crushed, plus
3 tablespoons chopped garlic

1 tablespoon salt, plus extra to taste

2 sprigs fresh sage

1 ham bone

3 cups peeled and diced potatoes

1/2 cup extra-virgin olive oil, plus
additional for garnish

1 1/2 tablespoons *each* finely chopped
fresh rosemary, basil, thyme, and
oregano

1 cup well-washed and chopped leeks,
white part only

2 cups chopped red onions

1 cup chopped celery

1 cup chopped carrots

4 ounces pancetta, chopped

1/3 cup white wine

1 cup diced fennel

2 cups diced butternut squash

1 (14-ounce) can Italian tomatoes with
their juices

1 cup roughly chopped red cabbage

1 cup roughly chopped Savoy cabbage

4 cups well-washed, roughly chopped
spinach

4 cups well-washed, roughly chopped
broccoli rabe

(continued on next page)

2 cups well-washed, roughly chopped
    Swiss chard

4 cups well-washed, roughly chopped
    collard greens

2 cups quartered Brussels sprouts

1 large zucchini, cut into 1-inch chunks

Fennel fronds, cut in pieces

Fresh ground black pepper, to taste

Tuscan bread, toasted and rubbed with
    garlic

Rinse the beans, picking them over to remove any pebbles. Soak them overnight in the 6 cups of cold water. Drain and place them in a large stockpot with the 4 quarts of fresh water. Bring the beans to a boil, then lower to a simmer and add the crushed garlic, tablespoon of salt, the sage, the ham bone, and 1 cup of the diced potatoes. Cook for 40 to 45 minutes, until the beans are soft. Discard the garlic, sage, and bone. Reserve a third of the cooked beans and potatoes and puree the rest with 3 cups of their cooking liquid. Mix the puree with the whole beans. Reserve and set aside the remaining cooking liquid.

To the stockpot the beans cooked in, add the olive oil, the chopped garlic, herbs, leeks, onions, celery, carrots, and pancetta. Sauté over medium heat, stirring occasionally, until the mixture starts to brown, about 15 minutes. Add the white wine and reduce completely, about 1 minute. Reduce the heat to medium-low and add the fennel, squash, the remaining 2 cups diced potatoes, and the Italian tomatoes and juice. Stir to mix well and cook for 10 minutes.

Add the red and Savoy cabbage, the spinach, broccoli rabe, Swiss chard, collard greens, Brussels sprouts, zucchini, and fennel fronds. Stir to mix well and cook for 10 minutes, then add the pureed beans and 3 cups of the reserved cooking liquid.

Mix well, then reduce the heat to low and simmer for 1½ hours, stirring occasionally and adding more liquid as necessary. Season with salt and pepper. Spoon the soup into bowls, and garnish with a swirl of olive oil. Serve with garlic toast on the side.

Baccalà Arrostito con Ceci
Roasted Salt Cod with Chick-peas

When we used to make salt cod in Pieve Santo Stefano, we'd wash the salt out by leaving the cod in the village fountain for a day. Today, most housewives leave the fish under running water in the kitchen sink, or let it soak for 2 days in the refrigerator, changing the water often—a less colorful, but more hygienic technique.

(S E R V E S   4)

1½ cups dried chick-peas

1 pound dried salt cod

1 tablespoon salt, plus extra to taste

7 tablespoons extra-virgin olive oil

Fresh ground black pepper, to taste

¼ cup white wine

Baccalà Sauce (recipe follows)

Rinse the beans, picking them over to remove any pebbles. Soak them overnight in 5 cups of cold water.

Soak the fish, refrigerated, in 6 cups of cold water for 24 hours, changing the water 3 times during the soaking.

When you are ready to assemble the dish, drain the chick-peas and put them in a pot with 6 cups of fresh water. Bring them to a boil, add the tablespoon of salt, and reduce the heat to a simmer. Cook the beans for 1 hour, until they are soft, then drain and transfer them to a baking dish. Mix the beans with 4 tablespoons of the olive oil and salt and pepper to taste. Set aside.

Preheat the oven to 500°. Drain the refrigerated cod and bring 6 to 8 cups of cold water to a boil in a large stockpot. Add the cod and cook it for 7 to 10 minutes. (If you parboil it too long, it will become cottony.) Drain the fish and pat it dry.

Cut the fish into 4 serving portions. Rub the pieces with 1½ tablespoons of olive

(continued on next page)

oil and a sprinkling of black pepper and place them in a second baking dish. Bake for 3 minutes, then drizzle the fish with the white wine and continue cooking for another minute. Drizzle the cod with the remaining 1½ tablespoons of olive oil and cook for 1 minute more, then remove the fish from the oven and keep it warm while you finish cooking the beans.

Switch the oven to broil and broil the chick-peas for 2 to 3 minutes. Spoon them onto 4 plates. Center a piece of codfish on top, and spoon a generous amount of the *baccalà* sauce over all.

Baccalà Sauce

12 plum tomatoes

½ teaspoon salt, plus extra to taste

Fresh ground black pepper, to taste

1 tablespoon finely minced fresh
   rosemary

1¾ tablespoons chopped garlic

½ tablespoon chopped fresh Italian
   parsley

2 tablespoons red wine vinegar

¾ cup extra-virgin olive oil

Preheat the oven to 375°. Cut the tomatoes in half and place them on a baking pan, sprinkle them with salt and pepper to taste, and bake them for 25 to 35 minutes, until they start to brown at the edges.

Cool the tomatoes, then peel them and place half of them in a food processor along with the juices from the baking pan, the rosemary, garlic, parsley, vinegar, and ½ teaspoon of salt. Puree, adding the olive oil in a slow, steady stream. Chop the remaining tomatoes roughly by hand and mix them into the puree. The sauce is ready.

La Torta di Fernanda

Fernanda's Pie

This unusual pie is Lucca's most famous dessert. Every family has its own secret recipe, and if you go to any country fair or church dinner, there will be as many versions of Fernanda's pie as there are families participating.

(SERVES 8)

. . . .

½ recipe Pastry Crust (page 127)

2 cups water

1½ teaspoons salt

1 pound Swiss chard, well washed

2 cups cubed Tuscan bread, crust removed

Scant ½ cup raisins, soaked overnight in rum or sambuca to cover

1 egg, beaten

½ cup sugar

3 tablespoons finely chopped candied citron

3 tablespoons toasted pine nuts

½ teaspoon fresh ground black pepper

1 teaspoon grated nutmeg

1 tablespoon rum or sambuca

5 tablespoons milk, as needed

Preheat the oven to 325°. Roll out the pastry dough ⅛ inch thick and fit it into a 9-inch pie plate. Tuck under the overhang to form a rim.

In a medium saucepan, bring the water to a low boil. Add 1 teaspoon salt and the Swiss chard. Cook until the greens are tender, about 10 minutes. Drain well, pressing out as much water as possible. Transfer to a food processor and add the bread. Pulse until the greens and bread are well combined, and turn the mixture into a bowl.

Drain the raisins and add them to the Swiss chard along with the remaining ½ teaspoon of salt, the egg, sugar, candied citron, pine nuts, black pepper, nutmeg, and rum. Mix well. If the filling seems dry, you can add up to 5 tablespoons of milk.

Transfer the mixture to the piecrust, and bake for 45 minutes to an hour, until a toothpick inserted in the center comes out clean. Cool and serve.

3

LA LIBERAZIONE DELL'UCCELLI

Liberating the Birds

Porrata	Leek Tart
Funghi Misti dell'Autunno con Polenta	Mixed Fall Mushrooms with Polenta
Anatra alla Puccini	Duck Puccini
Composta di Pere	Pear Compote

SUGGESTED WINES: BARCO REALE, IL POGGIOLO (GRAPES: SANGIOVESE, CABERNET FRANC, CABERNET SAUVIGNON); ANIA, GABBIANO (GRAPE: SANGIOVESE GROSSO)

Growing up, I slept upstairs, right over Vipore's bar. At night it could get pretty noisy, but every morning I woke up to the sound of birds singing. It was fantastic, like a concert. I imagined they were singing for me, to rouse me before Mama did, and it was the best way to start each day.

But as predictable as the birds and their songs were the hunters who came to shoot them down. It was always the same. Shots would fill the air and the singing would evaporate. It stopped my heart every time. I don't have anything against hunters, and I love a good duck or pigeon, but I really hated seeing my little friends getting picked off day after day.

One morning, Emilio and I decided to take action. We got up before dawn, and snuck down to the woods where the *cacciatori* parked their cars. We let all the air out of their tires and dug deep holes in the dirt road, covering them with sticks and twigs. Then we stole through the forest looking for birds caught in traps, and liberated them. We made fake, piercing bird calls and rattled trees to scare away as many birds as possible. I was working on the door of a trap when a hunter spotted us and started yelling. Emilio and I never moved so fast. The hunter had a gun and he chased us for maybe five minutes. At the end, he even shot a few times, but he was too far away. It didn't matter, our mission had been a success. The next morning, the birds were back in full concert.

Porrata

Leek Tart

There's no written proof, but in Tuscany we believe *porrata* was the inspiration for *quiche lorraine*.

(S E R V E S   6)

1 cup all-purpose flour

⅓ cup cubed cold sweet butter

½ teaspoon salt, plus extra to taste

2–3 tablespoons cold water

2 pounds leeks, well washed

4 tablespoons extra-virgin olive oil

Fresh ground black pepper, to taste

3 eggs

1 cup milk

2 tablespoons freshly grated pecorino Romano cheese

2 tablespoons freshly grated Parmigiano-Reggiano cheese

Dried beans or pie weights

3½ ounces pancetta, chopped fine

Preheat the oven to 375°. In a bowl, combine the flour and butter with your fingers to the consistency of coarse crumbs. Add the ½ teaspoon of salt, then mix in the cold water, stirring until a dough is formed. Refrigerate the dough for 15 minutes.

In the meantime, slice the leeks into rounds, using the whites and a little of the green part, if you want. Pour the olive oil into a large frying pan, add the leeks and salt and pepper to taste, and cook over medium heat until the leeks are soft, 5 to 7 minutes. Remove the pan from the heat and let the leeks cool.

In a bowl, beat the eggs with the milk, pecorino, and Parmigiano-Reggiano, and add this mixture to the sautéed leeks, stirring well. On a well-floured surface, roll out the chilled dough and fit it into a 9-inch pie pan, pinching the edges of the

(continued on next page)

dough to form a rim. Prick the dough with a fork and cover with aluminum foil, filling the pan with dried beans or pie weights. Bake the crust for 8 minutes.

Empty out the beans and discard the foil, then bake the crust for another 5 minutes. Lower the oven heat to 350°, arrange the pancetta in the bottom of the piecrust, and pour in the leek mixture. Bake for 50 to 55 minutes, until the *porrata* is golden brown. Let it rest briefly, then slice and serve.

Funghi Misti dell'Autunno con Polenta

Mixed Fall Mushrooms with Polenta

(SERVES 8 AS AN APPETIZER)

3 pounds mixed mushrooms, including portobello, oyster, cremini, porcini, and shiitake

3 tablespoons extra-virgin olive oil

1 tablespoon finely chopped fresh thyme

1 tablespoon finely chopped fresh oregano

1 tablespoon finely chopped fresh tarragon

Salt and fresh ground black pepper, to taste

Polenta (recipe follows)

Truffle oil, for garnish (optional)

Clean and pare the mushrooms, removing the tough stems (these can be saved to make a flavorful stock).

In a bowl, mix the olive oil with the chopped herbs, then toss with the mushrooms. Add salt and pepper, but don't be tempted to add more herbs. The mushrooms should provide the predominant flavor in this dish.

Separate the large mushrooms from the smaller ones. Place the large ones on a sheet pan and set them under the broiler for 5 minutes; remove, stir, then add the smaller ones and return the pan to the broiler.

Broil until all the mushrooms are tender and the moisture they've released has evaporated, about 8 minutes more. (You can also sauté the mushrooms over medium heat, doing the large ones for 5 minutes, then adding the smaller ones for 8 minutes more.) Spoon over the polenta and serve hot. (If you want, you can sprinkle a little truffle oil over the top of the mushrooms before serving.)

Polenta

Cornmeal

....

2 quarts cold water	1 tablespoon salt
14 ounces cornmeal	2½ tablespoons extra-virgin olive oil

Pour the cold water into a 4-quart saucepan and turn the heat to medium. Add the cornmeal, salt, and oil, stirring constantly. When the polenta starts to boil, lower the heat to a simmer and continue cooking for 40 to 45 minutes. It is ready when it's the consistency of Cream of Wheat. If the polenta is too stiff, add a little extra hot water. Spoon it into bowls and top it with the mushrooms.

MIXED FALL MUSHROOMS WITH POLENTA (FUNGHI MISTI DELL'AUTUNNO CON POLENTA).

GUY BOUCHET

Anatra alla Puccini

Duck Puccini

Giacomo Puccini was born in Torre del Lago, about half an hour from Lucca. Though he's revered as a composer, growing up, what I liked best about him was the fact he was a Don Juan, a gourmet, and a great duck hunter. According to locals, Puccini did his most musical work in waders. That way, if looking out his window, the composer spotted ducks on Lake Torre, he'd grab his rifle, run out, and shoot dinner. This recipe was inspired by Puccini. It's simple, but flavorful.

(S E R V E S   4)

1 (5½–6-pound) duck

Salt and fresh ground black pepper, to taste

1 apple, quartered and seeded

1 orange, peeled and quartered

1 sprig fresh rosemary

2 cloves garlic, peeled and crushed

⅓ cup red wine

1 medium red onion, cut into eighths

1 stalk celery, cut into 1-inch lengths

1 carrot, cut into 1-inch lengths

1 cup apple juice

1 cup orange juice

Trim any excess fat from the duck and soak it in cold water for 6 hours.

Preheat the oven to 350°. Pat the bird dry and prick the skin all over with a fork. Rub the cavity and the outer flesh with salt and pepper.

Stuff the duck with the apple, orange, rosemary, and garlic. Place the duck on a roasting rack in a shallow pan and roast for 20 minutes. Splash the duck with the red wine and cook for another 15 minutes.

Drain the fat that has collected in the roasting pan. Add the chopped onion,

(continued on next page)

the celery, and carrot to the roasting pan. Return the duck to the oven for 30 minutes, turn it, and continue cooking for another 30 minutes, basting it once on each side.

Remove the onion, celery, and carrot and reserve. Raise the heat to 500° and roast the duck for 15 minutes more on each side. Remove the orange, apple, rosemary, and garlic from the bird's cavity and let the duck rest for 10 minutes. Cut it into quarters, removing the backbone, and keep warm while you finish the sauce.

Skim the fat from the pan juices. Place the pan juices, orange quarters, apple quarters, and onion, celery, carrots, apple juice, orange juice, and salt and pepper to taste in a food processor and puree. Spoon some of the sauce onto each dinner plate and place a piece of duck on top. Serve at once.

Composta di Pere

Pear Compote

This is a very light dessert mama used to make when someone wasn't feeling well. I liked it best with *gelato* and *biscotti*.

(SERVES 4)

2 pounds Bartlett or Bosc pears

1 teaspoon ground cinnamon

4 tablespoons sugar

1½ cups water

½ cup golden raisins

¼ cup chopped walnuts

Peel, core, and slice the pears. In a medium saucepan, combine the cinnamon, sugar, and water and bring to a simmer. Add the pear slices and the raisins and cook for 10 minutes, or until soft. Spoon the pears and their sauce into small bowls and sprinkle with the chopped walnuts.

4

MANOVRE MILITARI
Military Maneuvers

Salsiccia con Fagioli	Sausage and Beans
Cozze in Brodetto	Mussels in Broth
Fricassea di Vitello Toscano	Tuscan Veal Fricassee
Pere con Pecorino, Miele, e Noci	Pears with Pecorino, Honey, and Walnuts

SUGGESTED WINES: ROSSO DI MONTALCINO, ARGIANO (GRAPE: SANGIOVESE); NEMO, MONSANTO (GRAPE: CABERNET SAUVIGNON)

As the time approached for me to report for my military service, I had one concern: How was I going to endure twelve months of mess-hall dining? It was an impossible problem, and there was only one solution. I had to fortify myself with a final feast, in Paris.

The plan was a little risky since I was scheduled to report for duty two days later and wasn't supposed to leave Italy. But I managed to get through customs in Milan without incident. By late morning, I was in Paris. My only French friends, whom I hadn't called, were, not surprisingly, not at home, so after an expensive taxi ride from Charles de Gaulle airport to their house and back to the center of town, I decided to explore on my own.

At first I just wandered, ten-kilo suitcase in hand, looking at shops and cafés, watching the people. Then I came across Benoit, a bustling bistro that was so French I half expected to see Toulouse-Lautrec in the corner and cancan girls kicking down the aisle. It was perfect for my last lunch. A man, tall, with a beard, led me to my table. I didn't understand what he said and just followed him, suitcase in hand, saying *"oui oui"* to his questions. I made it understood I wanted to eat and drink well. One by one, he brought me all the dishes on the menu, from vegetable and herb pâté to veal tongue. It was classic French country cooking, which unexpectedly reminded me of Vipore. The *soupe de moules* was like my *cozze in brodetto*, the *pot-au-feu* just like our *bollito misto*. Even today when I make sausage and beans, I think of Benoit's cassoulet.

To digest, I took a nap on a bench, with my suitcase as a pillow, then walked to the Isle St. Louis and checked into a hotel. For dinner, I chose Taillevent, then the temple of classic French cuisine, and feasted on mousse of *foies blonds* with walnut oil, *aiguillettes* of bass with lime, Barbary duckling in black currant vinegar, and cassolette of lobster with tarragon. Even if I didn't eat for the next twelve months, I had stored enough calories to last the better part of my military service.

I woke up the next day to news of an air strike and panicked. If I weren't in Italy on Monday to report for my military service, I'd be classified a deserter. I didn't even stop in the station to buy a ticket, I just hopped on the first train to Italy I saw. I got home just in time to change my clothes and kiss Mama good-bye. Papa drove me into Lucca and I caught the train to Casale Monferrato.

P.S. From a gastronomic point of view, the next year was as bad as I had expected. At first, I refused to eat anything but plain pasta, without sauce, and I would only eat the top layer of noodles, not those that had touched the plate. Remembering Paris was of little consolation.

Salsiccia con Fagioli

Sausage and Beans

(SERVES 8)

....

1½ cups dried cannellini beans

10 cups cold water

2 teaspoons salt, plus extra to taste

8 cloves garlic, peeled

2 sprigs fresh sage

3 tablespoons extra-virgin olive oil

1 pound Italian sausage, cut in 1½-inch
  lengths (If you like spicy sausage,
  use hot Italian sausage. If you don't,
  use sweet Italian sausage, or a
  combination of the two.)

⅓ cup white wine

1 cup peeled, chopped tomatoes

Fresh ground black pepper, to taste

Rinse the beans, picking them over to remove any pebbles. Soak them overnight in 5 cups of cold water. When you are ready to cook, drain the beans, add another 5 cups of fresh cold water to the pot, and bring the beans to a boil. Add the 2 teaspoons of salt and reduce the heat to a simmer. Cook until the beans are soft, 40 to 45 minutes. Drain and set them aside.

In a large sauté pan, heat the garlic and the sage in the olive oil over medium heat until the garlic starts to color, about 5 minutes. Add the sausage, stirring occasionally so the pieces brown evenly, and cook all the way through, 15 to 20 minutes. Add the white wine and let it reduce completely, about 5 minutes. Add the tomatoes, the beans, and salt and pepper, and cook for another 10 minutes to heat the beans through. Serve at once.

Cozze in Brodetto

Mussels in Broth

(S E R V E S 4)

1/4 cup extra-virgin olive oil

8 cloves garlic, peeled and sliced

4 dozen mussels, cleaned

1/2 cup white wine

Crushed red pepper flakes, to taste

1 1/2 cups chopped tomatoes

1/2 cup homemade fish stock or water

Salt and fresh ground black pepper, to
taste

4 slices Tuscan bread, toasted, then
rubbed with cut garlic

Place the olive oil and garlic in a large sauté pan and heat over medium. When the garlic starts to color, after 2 or 3 minutes, raise the heat to high, then add the mussels, white wine, red pepper flakes, and tomatoes. Cook until the mussels open, 3 to 5 minutes. Remove any that don't open. Add the fish stock and salt and pepper. Reduce the heat and cook for 5 to 6 minutes more. Serve in bowls with slices of the Tuscan toast.

Fricassea di Vitello Toscano

Tuscan Veal Fricassee

(SERVES 3–4)

1 red onion, cut into 1-inch pieces

2 carrots, cut into ½-inch lengths

1 stalk celery, cut into ½-inch lengths

3 tablespoons sweet butter

2 tablespoons flour, plus extra for veal

Salt and fresh ground black pepper, to taste

1 cup warm homemade beef broth

3 tablespoons olive oil

2 cloves garlic, peeled and crushed

2 tablespoons chopped fresh sage

1 pound veal loin, cut into 1-inch cubes

½ cup white wine

3 ounces dried porcini mushrooms, soaked in 2 cups warm water for 30 minutes, tough stems removed

2 egg yolks

2 teaspoons freshly squeezed lemon juice

Blanch the onion, carrots, and celery for 1 minute and set them aside.

Blend the butter with the 2 tablespoons of flour and place it in a medium saucepan. Heat over medium until the butter melts and the roux is lightly browned, about 2 minutes. Add salt and pepper and remove the pan from the heat, then add the broth. Return the pan to the heat and cook the sauce until it begins to thicken, 8 to 10 minutes. Remove from the heat and set aside.

In a large sauté pan, combine the olive oil, garlic, and sage. Heat over medium until the garlic starts to color, 5 to 7 minutes. Remove the garlic and set it aside with the blanched vegetables.

Raise the heat to high, lightly flour the veal, and add it to the pan. Stir well so the pieces brown evenly, 8 to 10 minutes. Add the white wine, the reserved vegetables, the mushrooms, reserved garlic, and sauce. Bring the mixture to a boil, then lower the heat and cook covered for 40 to 50 minutes, until the veal is tender.

Beat together the egg yolks and the lemon juice and add them to the veal. Taste and adjust the seasonings. Serve the fricassee with mashed potatoes (see page 28).

Pere con Pecorino, Miele, e Noci

Pears with Pecorino, Honey, and Walnuts

Like the Italians, the French often end their meals with fruit and cheese. The combination of pears, pecorino, honey, and walnuts is incredibly delicious. If you can't find pecorino Toscano, try Manchego, or another mild pecorino.

(SERVES 4)

1 pound Bosc pears, cored and cut into
  $1/4$-inch-thick slices

5 ounces pecorino Toscano cheese,
  shaved

3 tablespoons honey

3 tablespoons chopped walnuts

Fresh ground black pepper

Arrange the sliced pears on 4 plates. Top each slice with a sliver of the pecorino. Drizzle the honey over the cheese and the pears and sprinkle each plate with some of the chopped walnuts. Finish each serving with a generous grinding of fresh black pepper.

SULLA STRADA PER IL PIEMONTE
Road Trip to Piedmont

Cotechino in Berlina di Tonino	Tonino's Sausage in Puff Pastry
Spaghetti alla Carbonara di Tonino	Tonino and Claudia's Spaghetti
e Claudia alla Monferrina	Carbonara, Monferrina Style
Controfiletto alle Nocciole di Claudia	Claudia's Rib-eye Steak with Hazelnuts
Bonet	Chocolate Amaretto Custard

SUGGESTED WINES: CHIANTI CLASSICO, RAMPOLLA (GRAPES: SANGIOVESE, CABERNET SAUVIGNON); BRUNO DI ROCCA, MONTEFILI (GRAPES: CABERNET SAUVIGNON, SANGIOVESE)

....

When I reached my late teens, I decided to take my gastronomic education into my own hands in a serious way. Sometimes that involved sacrificing a day of school to explore the cuisine of my native Tuscany. Other times, like when I was invited to cook on a television show shot in Asti, it meant a road trip. Asti, if you're not familiar with it, is famous for two things: truffles and sparkling wine. Need I say more?

Giovanni Goria, the president of the Accademia della Cucina Italiana, who'd invited me up to Asti, gave me a list of the best restaurants in the area and called ahead to each of them to make sure I was taken care of properly. I hit Gener Neuv in Asti, Rododendro in Bovis, Giorgio in Alessandria, "da Beppe" in Cioccaro di Penago (now called Locanda del Sant'Uffizio), da Guido in Costigliole d'Asti, and da Cesare in Alberetto di Torre. Each was remarkable, but the highlight of the trip for me was discovering Contea di Neive (in Neive) and befriending its exuberant owners, Tonino and Claudia Verro.

Though his name in Italian means "Little Antonio," there's very little that's little about Tonino Verro. He's one of the most generous and gluttonous people I know, my perfect match. That day, he fed me dish after dish of culinary wizardry, from *zuppa della regina*, queen's soup—with a lineage worthy of the Savoys'—to *risotto al fiori di Tarassaco*, a variation on *risotto Milanese* made with a type of saffron used by cooks trying to stretch their budgets. He preserved rabbit the way they do tuna in Sicily; he made a ratatouille the French would envy. We were friends for life before dessert arrived—an amazingly creamy *bonet*, a chocolate custard I still savor—and before I knew it, I was spending all my free time in Neive. Tonino's tastes are eclectic, and so is this menu.

MAMA GETTING
WATER TO FEED
THE CHICKENS,
1979.

Cotechino in Berlina di Tonino

Tonino's Sausage in Puff Pastry

A very American version of this dish is pigs in a blanket. Tonino calls his wrapped sausages *"cotechino in berlina"*—a *berlina* is a hat—after anyone who has ever worn a hat to disguise his identity. With the elegant puff pastry on the outside, you'd never guess that what was inside was a sausage.

(SERVES 4)

1 pound cotechino (garlic sausage)

4 whole cloves

1 stick cinnamon

1 sheet frozen puff pastry

1 egg yolk, beaten

1 black truffle (optional)

1/2 recipe Mashed Potatoes (page 28)

Place the sausage, cloves, and cinnamon in a saucepan with water to cover. Bring the water to a boil and cook the sausage for approximately 40 minutes. Let it cool in the cooking liquid, then peel it. You can either cut the sausage in quarters or leave it whole.

Preheat the oven to 425°. Roll out the pastry very thin and cut out rectangles large enough to wrap the whole sausage or sausage quarters. Seal the pastry closed with the beaten egg yolk and bake the sausage for 10 minutes, until it is golden brown.

To jazz this dish up, Tonino suggests grating a little black truffle into the mashed potatoes, then spooning them out onto 4 plates. If you've left the sausage whole, slice it into disks and arrange the disks on top of the potatoes. Serve at once.

Cotechino

A salami made from slightly cured pork, cotechino comes from Modena, and because of its high fat content—it also uses the pig's cheeks and skin—is sometimes thought of as the poor man's salami. It's traditionally poached or steamed and served hot, with potatoes, lentils, and spinach. A traditional Italian New Year's Day dish is cotechino or zampone, pig's hooves, with lentils. It brings good luck and fortune for the year ahead. Ask your butcher for garlic sausage.

Spaghetti alla Carbonara di Tonino e Claudia alla Monferrina

Tonino and Claudia's Spaghetti Carbonara, Monferrina Style

According to Tonino, this quintessential Roman dish became popular in northern Italy only after patriot Giuseppe Garibaldi united the north and the south.

(S E R V E S 4)

3 quarts water

1½ tablespoons salt, plus extra to taste

½ pound spaghetti

3 ounces pancetta, chopped

1 clove garlic, peeled and crushed

2 tablespoons white wine

3 tablespoons heavy cream

2 egg yolks

1 tablespoon freshly grated
    Parmigiano-Reggiano cheese

Fresh ground black pepper, to taste

20 asparagus tips, blanched

In a large pot, bring the water to a boil. Add the 1½ tablespoons of salt and the spaghetti.

In a large sauté pan, place the pancetta, garlic, and white wine and heat over medium to reduce some of the fat, 4 to 5 minutes.

In a small bowl, beat together the cream, egg yolks, Parmigiano-Reggiano, and salt and pepper.

When the spaghetti is very *al dente*, drain it and add it to the sauté pan, along with the asparagus tips. Mix well, cooking for 1 to 2 minutes, then blend in the cream sauce. Continue heating for another 2 minutes. Serve at once.

Controfiletto alle Nocciole di Claudia

Claudia's Rib-eye Steak with Hazelnuts

Tonino suggests pureeing this sauce before serving it. I like it better chunky.

(S E R V E S   4)

1/2 cup finely chopped onion

2 tablespoons toasted, finely chopped
   hazelnuts

2 tablespoons extra-virgin olive oil

1/2 cup homemade beef broth

1 tablespoon chopped fresh Italian
   parsley

Salt and fresh ground black pepper, to
   taste

4 (6-ounce) rib-eye, New York, or strip
   steaks

Preheat your grill or broiler.

Place the onion, hazelnuts, and olive oil in a small frying pan and heat over medium. When the onion starts to brown, after about 15 minutes, add the broth and cook for 2 to 3 minutes to combine the tastes. Add the parsley and mix well. Add salt and pepper

Season both sides of the steaks with salt and pepper. Grill or broil the steaks to desired doneness, 4 or 5 minutes on each side. Spoon the sauce over the steaks and serve.

Bonet

Chocolate Amaretto Custard

(S E R V E S   4)

....

³/₄ cup sugar

3 eggs

2²/₃ tablespoons sifted unsweetened
   cocoa powder

2²/₃ tablespoons crumbled amaretti
   cookies

2 cups milk

Preheat the oven to 325°. In a small, heavy saucepan, heat $\frac{1}{4}$ cup of the sugar over a very low heat, stirring constantly until the sugar melts, about 8 minutes. Remove from the heat and quickly pour a little of the melted sugar into the bottom of each of 4 individual baking cups. Move the cups around so the caramelized sugar spreads out a bit (the sugar doesn't have to cover the bottom perfectly; it will melt again when it's baked). Set the cups aside.

In a bowl, beat the remaining $\frac{1}{2}$ cup of sugar with the eggs, cocoa, and amaretti. Add the milk and mix well.

Pour the custard into the 4 cups and place them on a rack in a pan of hot water about 1 inch deep. Bake for 30 to 40 minutes. To test if the *bonet* is done, insert a knife near the edge of the dish. If the blade comes out clean, the custard will be solid all the way through. Remove the cups from the pan and cool on a rack.

La Mostra dell'Etichette di Romano Levi
A Show of Romano Levi's Labels

Radicchio Trevisano Brasato	Braised Treviso Radicchio
Risotto al Vino	Red Wine Risotto
Fegato Saltato con Salvia	Liver Sautéed with Sage Leaves
Torta di Espresso e Noci con	Espresso Walnut Torte with
Composta di Frutta Autunnale	Fall Fruit Compote

SUGGESTED WINES: CHIANTI CLASSICO, IL POGGERINO (GRAPE: SANGIOVESE); GHIAIE DELL FURBA, CAPEZZANA (GRAPES: CABERNET SAUVIGNON, CABERNET FRANC, MERLOT)

My first encounter with grappa, the fiery *eau de vie* made from grape skins and seeds, was hardly auspicious.

Even worse, it was captured on film by an Italian movie crew.

The occasion was the inauguration of a show of Romano Levi's whimsical, hand-drawn labels at a restaurant in Bergamo. If you've never heard of grappa maker Romano Levi, it's probably because he only produces 7,000 bottles a year and there's never enough to go around Italy, let alone to export. Levi is a legendary curmudgeon who does everything from the bottling to the labeling by hand and only sells to people who come to pick up their own orders—and usually only to people he likes. His labels, often dedicated to *La Donna Selvatica*, "The Wild Woman," are collector's items.

Anyway, I had been invited to the dinner by my friend Tonino, who was also a friend of Levi's. Tonino and I have never done anything in moderation, and the grappa tasting was no exception. I overindulged.

To sober up, I stepped outside for some fresh Bergamo air—and right into a

(continued on next page)

movie that was being shot in the piazza. A member of the film crew came over and asked, politely, if I would stay inside until the scene was done. But with the bravado of grappa in me, I burst out of the restaurant a second, and then a third time. By the fourth, everyone in the restaurant was cheering me on as if I were a toreador in corrida. The last thing I remember is the film crew forming a barricade outside the restaurant door to block my exit. When I woke up, I was in the back seat of their car, and Tonino and Claudia, his wife, were in front. They told me a doctor had made sure I was okay before they carted me off.

What I never found out was the name of the film. I wonder if I made it on screen.

GRANDPA BEPPE, WEARING THE SWEATER, ON VACATION AT TERME BAGNO ROMANO.

Radicchio Trevisano Brasato

Braised Treviso Radicchio

(SERVES 4)

1 pound Treviso radicchio, cleaned and quartered (if you can't find Treviso radicchio, which is long and thin, use the round Verona radicchio)

3 tablespoons balsamic vinegar

Salt and fresh ground black pepper, to taste

3½ tablespoons extra-virgin olive oil

3 tablespoons red wine

3½ tablespoons homemade beef broth

Preheat the oven to 350°. Place the radicchio in a roasting pan and sprinkle it with the remaining ingredients. Cover the pan with aluminum foil and roast the radicchio for 20 to 25 minutes. It should be wilted. Serve immediately.

Risotto al Vino

Red Wine Risotto

This is an easy way to make risotto.

(SERVES 4–6 AS AN APPETIZER)

5 tablespoons finely chopped red onion

3 tablespoons extra-virgin olive oil

12 ounces arborio rice

4 cups good red wine, at a simmer

4 cups homemade beef broth, at a
   simmer

Salt and fresh ground black pepper, to
   taste

6–8 tablespoons freshly grated
   Parmigiano-Reggiano cheese

In a large saucepan, sauté the onion in the olive oil over medium heat until the onion starts to color, about 5 minutes. Add the rice and sauté for 1 to 3 minutes, stirring well, until it is lightly toasted. Add three quarters of the wine and three quarters of the broth, all at once. Bring the mixture to a simmer over medium heat, stirring occasionally, for 12 to 15 minutes. As the liquid evaporates, add the remaining wine and broth, if needed, and salt and pepper to taste. The risotto should be slightly soupy and the rice firm to the bite. Remove it from the heat and stir in the grated cheese. Serve.

Fegato Saltato con Salvia

Liver Sautéed with Sage Leaves

(SERVES 4)

¼ cup extra-virgin olive oil

2 cloves garlic, peeled and crushed

16 sage leaves

4 (6-ounce) slices calf's liver

Flour, for dusting

Salt and fresh ground black pepper, to
taste

In a large frying pan, heat the olive oil, garlic, and sage over medium until the garlic starts to color, about 5 minutes. Lightly dust the liver with the flour and add it to the pan. Cook the liver slices for approximately 3 minutes, then flip them and cook them for 2 minutes on the other side. The meat should be slightly pink when you cut into it. Add salt and pepper and serve. (I like this dish with sautéed spinach, page 99, and mashed potatoes, page 28.)

Sage

You can understand from the look of the leaves why sage is considered a calmante, a calming influence, in Italy. But its taste is so strong, I always thought there weren't very many dishes in which you could use sage. Then one day I saw Mama using it as a base for peperonata, a mix of cooked mixed bell peppers. When cooked for a long time, sage loses its bitterness and adds great flavor. I especially like the minty-mustiness of sage with fish. If you chew the leaves raw, they'll clean your teeth as well as toothpaste.

Torta di Espresso e Noci con Composta di Frutta Autunnale

Espresso Walnut Torte with Fall Fruit Compote

(SERVES 8)

....

3/4 cup plus 2 tablespoons flour

1/4 teaspoon baking powder

1/4 teaspoon ground cinnamon

1/2 teaspoon ground ginger

1/2 teaspoon ground cardamom

1/2 tablespoon unsweetened cocoa
   powder

6 tablespoons sweet butter

1/4 cup granulated sugar

1/4 cup light brown sugar

2 eggs

1/2 tablespoon Kahlúa liqueur

2 tablespoons brewed espresso, cooled

1/4 cup milk

1/2 cup toasted, chopped walnuts

Fall Fruit Compote (recipe follows)

Confectioners' sugar (optional)

Preheat the oven to 350°. Butter an 8-inch cake pan and dust it with flour.

In a bowl, sift together the flour, baking powder, spices, and cocoa powder and set them aside.

In a separate bowl, cream together the butter and the sugars until light and fluffy. Beat in the eggs one at a time. Add the Kahlúa and espresso and mix well. Add half the flour mixture, blend, then add the milk and the remaining flour mixture. Don't overmix. Stir in the walnuts.

Pour the batter into the cake pan and bake the cake for 35 to 40 minutes, or until a toothpick inserted in the center comes out clean. Allow the cake to cool in the pan, then invert it onto a serving platter. Serve it just warm, with the compote, and confectioners' sugar sifted on top, if you wish.

Composta di Frutta Autunnale

Fall Fruit Compote
....

1 tablespoon sweet butter

¼ cup sugar

1 apple, peeled, cored, and cut into
   ½-inch cubes

1 pear, peeled, cored, and cut into
   ½-inch cubes

6 small fresh figs, quartered

6 Italian plums, pitted and cut into
   eighths

Preheat the oven to 350°. In a heavy saucepan over medium heat, melt the butter and 2 tablespoons of the sugar. Add the apple and pear, stirring occasionally until they are cooked but not mushy, 5 to 6 minutes. Place the figs and the plums on a baking sheet and sprinkle them with the remaining 2 tablespoons of sugar. Roast them in the oven for about 15 minutes, or until the edges start to brown slightly. Mix the figs and plums with the apple and pear cubes and serve with the sliced cake.

LA MISSIONE MANGERECCIA

An Epicurean "Mission Impossible"

Tartara di Manzo	Steak Tartare
Fagioli e Caviale	Beans and Caviar
Tagliata di Manzo alle Erbe Aromatiche	Rib-eye Steak with Aromatic Herbs
Torta di Cioccolato	Flourless Chocolate Cake

SUGGESTED WINES: CHIANTI CLASSICO VIGNETO RANCIA, FELSINA (GRAPES: SANGIOVESE, LOCAL VARIETALS); VIGNA L'APPARITA, AMA (GRAPE: MERLOT)

. . . .

One afternoon when we had nothing better to do, Tonino and I started planning *La Missione Mangereccia*, the Epicurean "Mission Impossible." We dubbed it that because it was a trip that involved four lavish feasts at four of the best restaurants in Europe—and in just under two days. We chose carefully: Paul Bocuse in Lyons, Alain Chapel in Mionnay, Georges Blanc in Vonnas, and Pierre Troisgros in Roanne. Our plan consisted of my driving to Neive the following Sunday at midnight. I would nap in one of the hotel Contea di Neive's empty rooms until dawn, wake Tonino, and we would set out together very early Monday morning.

Things started badly when I arrived at Contea at 3 A.M. and all the rooms were unexpectedly occupied. That meant my sleeping on the dining-room floor and our departure delayed by a good three hours. That in turn meant us sacrificing our first lunch, at Troisgros, and heading straight for dinner at Bocuse. By the time we arrived at the French border, it was late afternoon. Tonino was uncharacteristically impatient. As the customs officer approached, he revved the engine. "Where do you think you are—Monza?" the officer asked sourly, referring to one of Italy's best-known racetracks. "No," said Tonino smartly, "Imola," another famous racetrack.

In no time flat, we were strip searching our own car, emptying everything from the glove compartment to our suitcases for the customs officer. It was when he discovered that neither Tonino nor I had the right 15,000 lira bollo (a nine-dollar stamp which technically isn't necessary if you have an identity card) that he smiled. *"Dovete tornare a Bardonecchia,"* he said. You have to go back to Bardonecchia to get the correct stamp. *"Buon Viaggio!"*

Having already relinquished Troisgros, Tonino and I weren't about to lose Bocuse by arguing. We raced to Bardonecchia, then gunned for Lyon. By the time we got to Bocuse, it was 9 P.M. We found a clearing in the woods across from the restaurant, splashed ourselves with stream water, and dressed *al fresco* for dinner.

The meal was as unexpected as we expected. Bocuse paired Perigord foie gras with a sauce made from Gewürztraminer, Bass with lobster mousse, Guinea hen with flower blossoms, and dozens of other outrageously succulent combinations you'd find no where else. Tonino and I tried them all, including three bottles of great Bordeaux. After dinner, we closed down a hundred-year-old wine bar in Lyons.

With only the briefest rest stop in our hotel, we were back on the road the next noon. This time, our destination was Vonnas, about forty miles away, home of Georges Blanc. Georges, without a doubt, is one of my favorite chefs in the world. I'd eaten his food once before, when I spent three days in his *auberge* "la Mere Blanc," with a friend. It is a magical place, especially in the late spring when the flowers are in bloom. The breakfasts I'd had there were the most perfect of my life. That day at lunch with Tonino I remember a blissful haze filled with everything from fatted hen sweetbreads with foie gras and truffle vinaigrette to lobster, prawn, and crayfish in a spicy Sauternes sauce. Dessert, as I recall, was a dreamy praline cake and cold nougat soufflé.

The problem was, we still had another reservation ahead of us, at Alain Chapel's in Mionnay. We decided that a walk, a long one, was the only answer. After an exhausting four-hour foot tour of Mionnay, neither of us was hungry, but we had a mission and intended to accomplish it. At Chapel's, we toasted our chef by cleaning our plates, draining our glasses, and squeezing in a plate of world-class cheeses. We finished just after midnight and started to drive home.

By 6 A.M. we were in Neive. I dropped Tonino off, had a coffee, and by lunch, was in the kitchen at Vipore. My body at any rate. My spirit was in France.

Tartara di Manzo

Steak Tartare

(SERVES 4)

....

¾ pound filet mignon

2 pinches of crushed red pepper flakes

1½ tablespoons finely chopped capers

8 chopped pitted Italian black olives

8 chives, chopped fine

8 fresh basil leaves, chopped fine

1 bunch scallions, white part only, chopped fine

1 teaspoon Worcestershire sauce

1½ tablespoons freshly squeezed lemon juice

4 drops Tabasco sauce

1⅓ tablespoons finely chopped fresh ginger

Salt and fresh ground black pepper, to taste

1 cup arugula, well washed and julienned

16 cherry tomatoes, halved

Paprika

8 slices Tuscan bread, toasted, then cut into small pieces

Dice the filet, then chop it as fine as possible. Mix in the next 10 ingredients and season with salt and pepper.

Divide the meat into 4 portions, and form 4 small balls. Make a small bed of arugula in the center of each plate, and top it with the tartare. Arrange the tomatoes around the arugula, sprinkle the plates with paprika, and serve with the toasted bread.

If you want, you can divide all the ingredients into 4 portions and arrange them on the plate, hollowing out the tomatoes and using them to hold the Tabasco sauce, lemon juice, and Worcestershire sauce. Let each guest then mix his or her own tartare. Traditionally, tartare includes raw egg, which I don't like, but if you do, I suggest using quail eggs.

Ginger

. . . .

*I*n standard Italian, the word for ginger is zenzero, but in Tuscany, zenzero are big hot red peppers, and zenzeri, the tiny, hotter ones. Ten years ago in Lucca, no one had ever even heard of ginger. I remember when I did my first television appearance and one of the production assistants showed me the ingredients he'd gathered. This is zenzero, he said, pointing to a knobby root. No, I insisted, zenzero is a tiny red thing. I wouldn't believe him. He had to show me a dictionary to convince me he was right. It wasn't until a young Japanese chef, Yoshimi, came to Vipore to do an internship that I started using ginger more often. Since coming to the States, I use it in fish marinades, with pork chops and chives, in steak tartare, and in soups and salad dressings.

Fagioli e Caviale

Beans and Caviar

This might seem like a new idea, but Florentine restaurants have been serving beans and caviar since the late 1800s. The precursor to this dish was a mix of boiled beans served with anchovies.

(SERVES 4)

1 scant cup dried cannellini beans

6 cups cold water

1½ teaspoons salt, plus extra to taste

2 ounces caviar

1 teaspoon finely chopped sweet onion

1 teaspoon freshly squeezed lemon juice

3 tablespoons extra-virgin olive oil

Fresh ground black pepper, to taste

4 slices Tuscan bread, toasted (optional)

Rinse the beans, picking them over to remove any pebbles, and soak them in 3 cups of cold water overnight. Drain the beans and place them in a medium saucepan with 3 cups of fresh cold water. Bring the beans to a boil and add the 1½ teaspoons of salt. Lower the heat to a simmer and cook them for 40 to 45 minutes, until they are soft. Drain them.

Place the warm beans in a serving bowl and mix in the caviar and the onion. Stir in the lemon juice, olive oil, and salt to taste. Grind a generous amount of black pepper over the dish. Serve as is, or spoon the beans over Tuscan toast.

Tagliata di Manzo alle Erbe Aromatiche

Rib-eye Steak with Aromatic Herbs

(SERVES 2)

Salt and fresh ground black pepper, to taste

2 (18–20-ounce) shell, rib-eye, T-bone, New York, or strip loin steak with bone

3 tablespoons *arometo* sauce (see page 15)

5 tablespoons homemade beef or vegetable broth

Preheat the broiler. Salt and pepper the steaks on both sides generously. Broil them for about 4 minutes on each side. The meat should be very rare when sliced.

Trim the fat and carve the meat into 1/4-inch-thick slices. Arrange the slices, one touching another, in an ovenproof serving dish. Mix together the *arometo* sauce and the broth. Spoon the sauce over the meat. (If you want, you can prepare the dish up to this step and refrigerate it, saving the final broiling until right before you serve the steak.) Place the meat under the broiler for 1 to 2 minutes, until it is cooked as you like it. Serve immediately.

RIB-EYE STEAK WITH AROMATIC HERBS (TAGLIATA DI MANZO ALLE ERBE AROMATICHE).

Torta di Cioccolato

Flourless Chocolate Cake

(SERVES 8–10)

....

12 ounces bittersweet chocolate	7 eggs, separated
1½ sticks (¾ cup) sweet butter	⅛ teaspoon salt
2 tablespoons brandy	1 cup plus 1 tablespoon sugar

Preheat the oven to 325°. Line a 9-inch springform pan with parchment paper. Melt the chocolate and the butter in the top of a double boiler over simmering water, stirring constantly until the mixture is smooth and creamy, with a glossy finish. Stir in the brandy and set the mixture aside to cool.

In the bowl of an electric mixer, beat the egg whites with the salt at a low speed until the mixture is frothy. With the motor on, add 10 tablespoons of the sugar in a slow, steady stream, slowly increasing the speed to incorporate the sugar. When the sugar has been added, move the mixer to the highest speed and beat until the mixture has tripled in volume and is thick and glossy. Set aside.

Whisk the yolks, then add the remaining 7 tablespoons of sugar, and beat vigorously until the sugar has dissolved and the mixture is pale yellow. Gently fold the yolk mixture into the chocolate and blend well without overbeating. Fold in the beaten egg whites, a third at a time, mixing thoroughly after each addition.

Pour the batter into the springform pan. Center the pan on a baking sheet and bake for 30 to 35 minutes, or until the cake is firm to the touch. Let the cake cool and release the clamp. Serve the cake warm or at room temperature.

La Cena della Chiusura del Campo Bar
The Last Dinner at the Campo Bar

Polpo Affogato	Stewed Baby Octopus
Zuppa di Gran Farro della Garfagnana	Wild Barley Soup, Garfagnana Style
Tonno all'Etrusca	Etruscan Tuna
La Ficata	Fig and Nut Cake

SUGGESTED WINES: CHIANTI CLASSICO, VILLA CAFAGGIO (GRAPES: SANGIOVESE, LOCAL VARIETALS); BRUNELLO DI MONTALCINO, CIACCI PICCOLOMINI (GRAPE: SANGIOVESE)

....

In the spring of 1990, I decided to open Il Campo Bar at Vipore—literally, the bar in Vipore's field. The name referred to the fact that the Campo Bar was in the middle of our herb garden and had a commanding view of the Lucchese countryside. Not unlike the thatched-roofed huts you see in the Caribbean, the Campo Bar looked like it had been tossed up by a strong wind from an island resort and landed on a hill in Tuscany. It was a place where locals could come at the end of the day—and into the wee hours of the morning—to wind down with good wine, cheese, pasta, music, and dancing. The atmosphere was almost more important than the food. This was a place to relax, enjoy, and occasionally, to get into the good kind of trouble.

Faith Willinger, a friend of mine, told me it must be my Etruscan roots that gave me this idea. I think she said this because my nose, which is famously large, looks like the profiles you see on Etruscan vases. At that time, I knew little about the Etruscans, only that they had once roamed Lazio and Tuscany (and gave the region its name), that no one knew exactly where they came from, or what had happened to them. The Etruscans had been the highest civilization in Italy before the Romans, but by the third century B.C., they had disappeared.

I did some research and discovered that the Etruscans loved food and luxury. They

A VIEW OF THE GARDEN AT VIPORE.

left behind records—on pottery, frescoes, and reliefs—of incredibly extravagant banquets, with men and women dining together on recliners, being served by legions of nubile nude slaves. I saw one relief of a banquet where a group of slaves preparing pasta, meat for the grill, and grape focaccia were being serenaded by other slaves playing flutes. Hanging from the ceiling were birds, wild rabbit, and a calf. Except for the clothes, the scene looked like it could have been cut from a contemporary bride's scrapbook recording the events leading up to her wedding dinner. This lifestyle apparently scandalized the Greeks, and Aristotle even condemned the Etruscans as decadent.

That fall, I decided to make an Etruscan feast for my friends at the Campo Bar to celebrate the season's bounty. Except for the tomatoes in some of the dishes—a food that didn't exist in Etruscan times—the menu was faithful to the Etruscan table.

Unfortunately, I had to make a few other concessions to modern times: Everyone ate sitting on chairs, and the waiters and waitresses were completely dressed.

Polpo Affogato
Stewed Baby Octopus

It's sometimes hard to find baby octopus, which can be added raw to this sauce. If you can only get regular octopus, you must cook it before adding it to the tomato sauce.

(SERVES 4–6)

6 cloves garlic, chopped fine

1 cup finely chopped red onion

6 sprigs fresh sage

½ teaspoon crushed red pepper flakes

½ cup finely chopped celery

3 tablespoons finely chopped carrot

¼ cup extra-virgin olive oil

½ cup white wine

1 (28-ounce) can Italian tomatoes, with
   their juice

Salt and fresh ground black pepper, to taste

3 pounds baby octopus, cleaned (see Note)

1 cup water

¼ cup chopped fresh Italian parsley

6 thick slices Tuscan bread, toasted

Place the garlic, onion, sage leaves, red pepper flakes, celery, carrot, and olive oil in a large saucepan and sauté over medium heat until the garlic and onion start to color, about 5 minutes. Add the wine and let it reduce completely, 2 to 3 minutes. Add the tomatoes and their juice. Add salt and pepper.

When the sauce starts to boil, reduce the heat and simmer for 15 minutes. Add the baby octopus and water, cover, and cook for 40 to 45 minutes, until the octopus is firm. Stir in 2 tablespoons of the parsley. Put the toasted bread in bowls, spoon the octopus mixture on top, and sprinkle each serving with some of the remaining parsley.

NOTE: If you are using regular octopus, have your fishmonger clean it. Freeze it overnight, then defrost it before you start to cook. That will help tenderize the meat.

Put the octopus in a large pot and cover it with water. Add 3 tablespoons vinegar; 1 carrot; 2 cloves garlic; and 1 onion, quartered. Bring to a boil and simmer about 30 minutes. The octopus should be very firm to the touch. Quarter the octopus lengthwise and add it to the tomato sauce. Cook as instructed above.

Zuppa di Gran Farro della Garfagnana
Wild Barley Soup, Garfagnana Style

Americans love this soup garnished with grated Parmigiano-Reggiano cheese, but no self-respecting Tuscan would use anything but freshly pressed olive oil.

(SERVES 8)

1½ cups dried mixed pinto, kidney, and cranberry beans

1½ cups *farro* (wild barley); if not available, substitute barley

Fresh ham bone (optional)

2 cups peeled, diced potatoes

2 cloves garlic, peeled and crushed, plus 1 tablespoon chopped fine

1 sprig fresh rosemary, plus 1 tablespoon chopped fine

1 sprig fresh sage, plus 1 tablespoon chopped fine

1 tablespoon salt, plus extra to taste

½ cup extra-virgin olive oil

¼ pound pancetta or unsmoked bacon, chopped

1 small red onion, chopped fine

⅓ cup finely chopped celery

½ cup finely chopped carrot

⅓ cup well-washed and finely chopped leek, white part only

¼ teaspoon crushed red pepper flakes

½ cup white wine

6 tablespoons tomato paste

Fresh ground black pepper, to taste

Rinse the beans, picking them over to remove any pebbles. Soak them overnight in 5 cups cold water.

Rinse the barley, cover it with 3 cups cold water, and set aside. Drain the beans and put them in a large stockpot with 5 quarts fresh, cold water. Add the ham bone, the potato, crushed garlic, the rosemary and sage sprigs.

Bring the beans to a boil, add the tablespoon of salt, and reduce the heat to a simmer. Cover and cook until the beans are soft, 40 to 45 minutes. Drain the beans and potato,

**WILD BARLEY SOUP, GARFAGNANA STYLE
(ZUPPA DI GRAN FARRO DELLA GARFAGNANA).**

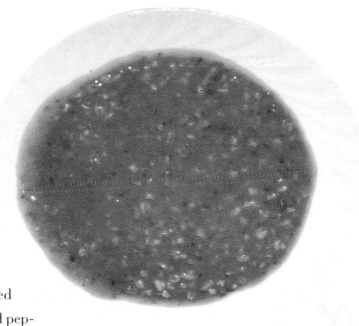

reserving the liquid. Discard the garlic and herbs. Puree half the beans and potato with 2 cups of the cooking liquid. Mix the puree with the remaining drained beans. Reserve the remaining cooking liquid.

In a large stockpot over medium heat, sauté in ¼ cup of the olive oil the pancetta, chopped rosemary, chopped sage, chopped garlic, the onion, celery, carrot, leek, and red pepper flakes. When the mixture starts to color, in 15 to 20 minutes, add the wine, and cook until it reduces, about 1 minute. Add the tomato paste, the beans and puree, and 7 cups of the reserved liquid. Simmer over low for 30 minutes, stirring occasionally.

Drain the barley and add it to the soup. Cook for another 45 minutes, adding the reserved bean broth a little at a time if the soup gets too thick or dry. Taste and adjust for salt. Serve the soup garnished with black pepper and the remaining olive oil. (Don't throw the cooking liquid away. The soup gets very thick overnight and you will need to thin it out if you reheat it. Or you can use water.)

Tonno all'Etrusca

Etruscan Tuna

(SERVES 4)

....

¼ cup extra-virgin olive oil

4 cloves garlic, chopped

1 small red onion, sliced thin

¼ teaspoon crushed red pepper flakes

1 cup crushed canned tomatoes

¾ cup chopped fresh tomato

3 cups homemade fish stock

⅓ cup pitted Italian black olives

¼ cup drained capers

4 (6-ounce) tuna steaks

Salt and fresh ground black pepper, to
    taste

Place the olive oil, garlic, onion, and red pepper flakes in a large sauté pan and sauté over medium heat until the mixture starts to color, about 5 minutes. Add the crushed and fresh tomatoes, the fish stock, olives, and capers. Cook the sauce over medium heat until the sauce is rich and thick, 25 to 30 minutes. Add the tuna steaks, cover the pan, and cook the tuna to the desired doneness, turning it once. Depending on thickness, the steaks will take 2 to 5 minutes per side. Season with salt and pepper and serve the fish with the sauce spooned on top.

La Ficata

Fig and Nut Cake

(SERVES 6–8)

1 cup dried figs

1 cup plus 2 tablespoons sugar

1 stick (¹/₂ cup) sweet butter

4 eggs

6 tablespoons raisins

4 tablespoons sliced almonds

6 tablespoons chopped toasted hazelnuts

6 tablespoons chopped toasted walnuts

2¹/₄ cups flour

1 teaspoon baking powder

2 tablespoons Grand Marnier liqueur

Preheat the oven to 325°. Lightly butter a 10-inch cake pan. In a food processor, grind the dried figs to a smooth paste.

In a bowl, cream together the sugar and butter until light and fluffy. Add the eggs, one at a time, mixing well after each addition. Add the figs, continuing to mix well. Add the raisins, almonds, hazelnuts, and walnuts. Then add the flour and baking powder, mixing well to make sure the dough is well blended. Add the Grand Marnier and mix.

Scrape the dough into the cake pan. Place on a sheet pan and bake for about 45 minutes, or until the cake is golden brown. Serve warm or at room temperature. (*Ficata* goes nicely with zabaglione. See page 114.)

Un Pranzo per Eileen

Eileen's Lunch

Patate Toscane	Tuscan Fries
Penne Gialle	Yellow Bell Pepper Penne
Rosticciana di Maiale con Olive e Rosmarino	Pork Ribs with Olives and Rosemary
Mattonelle, Fichi, e Gorgonzola	Brick Biscotti, Figs, and Gorgonzola

SUGGESTED WINES: CHIANTI CLASSICO, ANTINORI (GRAPES: SANGIOVESE, LOCAL VARIETALS); SOLAIA, ANTINORI (GRAPES: CABERNET SAUVIGNON, SANGIOVESE, CABERNET FRANC)

....

I wouldn't call Francesca Antinori a friend, but I do know her. She has eaten at Vipore many times, with a variety of guests, and Antinori wines are some of my favorites. One September afternoon, *Signora* Antinori showed up with a journalist from *W* magazine. I didn't know what *W* was, and we didn't serve lunch during the week. But I was always cultivating the press and figured if a journalist was accompanied by an Antinori, she must be important. All I had to do, I thought, was charm her just a little and I could add an American magazine clipping to my already thick press file.

The journalist happened to be Eileen Daspin, who would become my co-author on this book. As Eileen tells it, she began the meeting completely uncharmed. She had called ahead, sometime after 11 A.M., to confirm that she and *Signora* Antinori would be arriving for a preliminary interview at lunchtime. But those were the days of the Campo Bar, my late-night club, and I usually worked until 4 A.M. and slept very late. When Eileen phoned, I got up long enough to confirm the confirmation then went back to bed; when she and *Signora* Antinori arrived at 1 P.M., I was still sleeping.

Not surprisingly, Eileen was predisposed against me, especially when I emerged in baggy fluorescent surfer shorts, an oversized Hawaiian shirt, and a tiny braid I wore at the nape of my neck. If I had to bet, I'd say I won her over with my heaping platters of pecorino, and Parmigiano-Reggiano. Or maybe it was the fennel-seed-studded *finocchiona*, the *coppa*, and the lard dotted with fresh rosemary. Or maybe it was the *scalogni sott'aceto*, shallots I had preserved myself.

Whatever it was, I did something right. The next day, she came back with a photographer for a six-hour lunch, an interview, and a photo shoot. I served them my famous Tuscan fries mixed with rosemary, sage, and whole red peppers, capped off with a plate of figs plucked straight from the tree that shaded their table. I knew I'd be getting good press when, after lunch, Eileen started rolling around in the grass next to the herb gardens. She was wearing yolk yellow pants, a bright blue tank top, a cherry red belt, a red bandanna in her hair, and she looked alarmingly like a Playskool *giocattolo* (toy). The story she wrote then, and all the subsequent pieces, have always been very generous, but just in case, I've kept the Polaroids of her rolling in the grass. You never know when they might come in handy.

Patate Toscane

Tuscan Fries

(SERVES 4)

Peanut oil, for frying

4 medium potatoes, peeled and sliced
  into long, thin strips about ¼-inch
  thick

4 sprigs fresh rosemary

4 sprigs fresh sage

2 fresh whole red chili peppers

8 cloves garlic, papery covering intact

Salt, to taste

Fill a large saucepan one third full with the peanut oil and heat it over high. When the oil reaches 375°, add the potatoes, rosemary, sage, chili peppers, and garlic. Fry the potatoes in batches, 3 or 4 minutes per batch, and remove them from the oil with a skimmer. Drain them on paper towels, salt to taste, and serve with the crispy herbs, the peppers, and the garlic. (Caution your guests not to try the chili peppers.)

Penne Gialle
Yellow Bell Pepper Penne
(SERVES 4 AS AN APPETIZER)

3 quarts water

1½ tablespoons salt, plus extra to taste

1 pound yellow bell peppers, halved and
seeded

3 tablespoons extra-virgin olive oil

1 stalk celery, chopped fine

1 large onion, chopped fine

1 small carrot, chopped fine

3 ounces pancetta, cubed

1 cup canned or homemade beef broth
or water, or more as needed

2 tablespoons chopped fresh Italian
parsley

Fresh ground black pepper, to taste

½ pound penne

4 tablespoons freshly grated pecorino
Romano cheese

Bring the water to a boil in a large pot and add the 1½ tablespoons of salt. Pre-heat the broiler. Place the peppers, skin side up, 2 to 3 inches from the heat, and watch them carefully. When the skin blackens, turn them over to blacken on the other side. It will take about ten minutes. Remove the peppers and place them in a plastic bag for 15 minutes, then peel off the skin and chop them.

In a large, heavy saucepan, place the olive oil, the chopped celery, the onion, carrot, and pancetta. Stir to mix well and heat over medium until the vegetables start to color, 15 to 20 minutes. Add the chopped peppers and half the broth to the vegetable mixture and stir. Keep adding broth as the mixture dries out (you might need more than a cup). It should be slightly soupy, like thick vegetable stew. Then add the chopped parsley and salt and pepper to taste.

Add the penne to the boiling water. When it is very *al dente*, drain, add it to the peppers, and cook for another 5 minutes. Mix in the pecorino and serve.

Rosticciana di Maiale con Olive e Rosmarino

Pork Ribs with Olives and Rosemary

(SERVES 4)

4 pounds pork ribs, cut into individual ribs

Salt and fresh ground black pepper, to taste

4 tablespoons extra-virgin olive oil

4 cloves garlic, roughly chopped

4 tablespoons roughly chopped fresh rosemary

½ cup white wine

1 (15-ounce) can Italian tomatoes, drained and cut in pieces

½ cup Italian black olives

Preheat the oven to 400°. Rub the ribs with salt and pepper. Place them in a roasting pan, and roast in the oven for 10 minutes. Drain any liquid the ribs give off.

Add the olive oil, garlic, and rosemary, and stir to coat the ribs. Return the pan to the oven until the garlic starts to soften, about 8 minutes, then add the white wine. When the wine reduces completely, after approximately 15 minutes, turn the ribs and add the tomatoes, distributing them evenly. Taste and adjust the seasoning for salt and pepper. Roast the ribs for another 25 minutes. Just before they are ready, add the olives. Serve immediately.

Mattonelle, Fichi, e Gorgonzola

Brick Biscotti, Figs, and Gorgonzola

Arrange a plate of *mattonelle* with quartered fresh green figs. In the middle of each fig, place a nut-size chunk of sweet Gorgonzola. Gorgonzola isn't a Tuscan cheese, and I never would have thought of pairing it with figs, let alone cookies. In Tuscany we take our biscotti with vin santo. But one night I was at a friend's, who only had sweet gorgonzola, figs, and biscotti in his kitchen. I was so hungry, I ate all three together and was shocked to discover how good they were.

(MAKES 40 BISCOTTI)

3½ cups sifted all-purpose flour

1¼ cups sugar

2 teaspoons baking powder

¼ cup (½ stick) sweet butter, softened

2 eggs

½ cup milk

1 teaspoon vanilla extract

Grated rind of 1 lemon

1 teaspoon salt

1½ cups whole toasted almonds

Preheat the oven to 325°. Line a cookie sheet with parchment paper.

In a large bowl, combine the flour, sugar, and baking powder, then blend in the softened butter.

In a separate bowl, beat the eggs with the milk, vanilla, lemon rind, and salt. Add the flour mixture, stirring well until a dough forms. Incorporate the almonds.

Divide the dough in half. (If you wet your hands with water, it will be easier to handle the dough and it won't stick as much.) Form two logs, about 12 by 2 inches and place them on the cookie sheet. Bake the logs for 30 to 35 minutes, until they are golden brown, then remove and cool for 10 minutes. Lower the heat to 300°.

(continued on next page)

Transfer the logs to a cutting board and, using a long sharp knife, cut them into ³/₄-inch-thick slices. Stand the biscotti up on the cookie sheet and bake for another 10 to 15 minutes. Remove them from the oven and cool them on wire racks.

Serve with the figs and Gorgonzola.

MAMA UNDER A FIG TREE IN MASSA MACINAIA, 1958.

Una Cena da Romano

A Dinner with Romano

Insalata di Calamari e Fagioli di Cesare	Cesare's Squid and Bean Salad
Spaghetti con le Acciughe di Romano	Romano's Spaghetti with Anchovies
Langostine al Guazzetto di Romano	Romano's Prawns in Cognac
Fagottini di Mele con Crema al	Romano's Apple Cream
Calvados di Romano	Crepes with Calvados

SUGGESTED WINES: RIECINE BIANCO, RIECINE (GRAPES: MALVASIA, TREBBIANO); SALAMARTANO, MONTELLORI (GRAPES: CABERNET SAUVIGNON, MERLOT)

Romano and Franca Franceschini, who own Da Romano in Viareggio, are two of my oldest friends, so old in fact, I don't remember how or where or why we met. All I do know, and they would surely agree with this, is that our friendship owes a great deal to their incomparable baby octopus and bean salad, which I only ever ate cold, and loved just the same. Once a week, I would drive the forty-five minutes to Viareggio after work, usually at 1 A.M., to finish my night. There was never a question of going into Lucca to cap off an evening, it was too small and quiet, plus, at that time of the night, nothing would even be open. More importantly, Lucca didn't have Romano himself, a big, warm man with a fierce bear hug, nor the lovely Franca, who keeps both Romano and his kitchen running smoothly all year long.

The first thing I would do when I got to Romano's was head for the refrigerator and the cold baby octopus. I never bothered with a plate or a napkin, though I did use a fork. Either Romano or Franca would appear with a glass of their homemade wine, a Montecarlo Bianco, and we'd be off and gossiping.

(continued on next page)

One night, I remember, Papa had brought some porcini home from the mountains, and I had a case that were tiny and wonderful. Knowing the Franceschinis loved porcini, I packed a box into my car, invited Eileen, who was visiting, to join me, and set off at midnight to deliver my gift.

We arrived at the restaurant around 1 A.M., and through the window spied Romano asleep at a table; Franca was nowhere to be found. I believe Romano smelled the perfume of the mushrooms, because he was up and hugging me before I got through the door. I introduced Eileen, handed over the porcini, and made my usual beeline for the refrigerator and the cold baby octopus. But Romano stopped me.

In all the years I'd known him, I never saw Romano cook. The cook is Franca. But that night, because of Eileen, Romano put on an apron and went to work. While we waited, he filled our glasses with champagne. We were served at 2 A.M., a perfect meal—sautéed langoustine, spaghetti with anchovies, and my favorite, baby octopus with beans, eaten hot for the first time in my life.

Insalata di Calamari e Fagioli di Cesare

Cesare's Squid and Bean Salad

Romano closely guards his baby octopus recipe, so I'm fudging it with my own recipe for squid and bean salad. I don't think you'll be disappointed.

(S E R V E S   4)

2 cups dried cannellini beans

14 cups cold water

3 cloves garlic, peeled and crushed

1 tablespoon salt, plus extra to taste

1¼ pounds squid, cleaned and cut into
    rings

¼ cup extra-virgin olive oil

12 sprigs fresh sage

Fresh ground black pepper, to taste

2 cups crushed canned tomatoes or
    peeled, chopped fresh tomatoes

1 teaspoon crushed red pepper flakes

1 tablespoon chopped fresh herbs
    (thyme, oregano, rosemary)

4 slices Tuscan bread, toasted, then
    rubbed with garlic

Rinse the beans, picking them over to remove any pebbles. Soak them overnight in 6 cups of cold water. When you are ready to cook, drain the beans and put them in a large stockpot with the garlic and 8 cups of fresh cold water. Bring the beans to a boil, add the tablespoon of salt, and let them simmer until they are soft, 40 to 45 minutes.

Remove the garlic, drain the beans, and set them aside. Put the squid, olive oil, and sage in a large frying pan and heat over medium until the squid loses its translucency, about 5 minutes. Add salt and black pepper, the crushed tomatoes, and red pepper flakes. Cook for 10 minutes, stirring occasionally. Add the beans and herbs and cook for another 5 to 6 minutes. Spoon on top of the toast and serve.

Spaghetti con le Acciughe di Romano

Romano's Spaghetti with Anchovies

(SERVES 4 AS AN APPETIZER)

3 quarts water

1½ tablespoons salt, plus extra to taste

½ pound spaghetti

8 ounces anchovies preserved in olive oil

2 tablespoons extra-virgin olive oil

¼ teaspoon crushed red pepper flakes

1 clove garlic, peeled and crushed

Fresh ground black pepper, to taste

½ cup peeled, chopped ripe tomatoes
  (or canned Italian tomatoes)

1 tablespoon finely chopped fresh Italian
  parsley

In a large pot, bring the water to a boil. Add the 1½ tablespoons of salt and the spaghetti.

Rinse the anchovies under running water. Place the olive oil in a large frying pan and add the red pepper flakes, garlic, 6 ounces of the anchovies, and salt and pepper. Cook over medium heat until the garlic turns golden, about 5 minutes. The anchovies will dissolve as they cook. Reduce the heat to low, add the tomatoes, and break them up with the side of a spoon. Add the parsley and continue cooking for 5 minutes more. Leave the heat under the anchovy sauce on low.

When the pasta is very *al dente*, drain it, then add it to the anchovy sauce. Cook for another 2 to 3 minutes. Garnish each dish with some of the remaining whole anchovies, and serve.

Langostine al Guazzetto di Romano

Romano's Prawns in Cognac

(SERVES 4)

16 prawns, cleaned and shelled, leaving the heads intact (if you can't get prawns, use very large shrimp)

Flour, for dredging

2 tablespoons sweet butter

2 tablespoons olive oil

1 clove garlic, peeled and crushed

Pinch of crushed red pepper flakes

Salt and fresh ground black pepper, to taste

3 tablespoons white wine

2 tablespoons finely chopped fresh Italian parsley

1 tablespoon Cognac

1 cup homemade fish stock

Flour the prawns lightly. (If you are using shrimp, shell them, leaving just the tail.) Put the prawns, butter, olive oil, garlic, and red pepper flakes in a pan and sauté them over medium heat. When the prawns start to turn pink, after about 2 minutes, add the salt and pepper and the white wine. When the wine reduces completely, after about 1 minute, add the chopped parsley and Cognac. After a few seconds, add the fish stock. Cook until the stock evaporates, 5 to 10 minutes. Serve immediately.

Fagottini di Mele con Crema al Calvados di Romano

Romano's Apple Cream Crepes with Calvados

(S E R V E S 5)

Il Ripieno

FILLING:

2 apples

7 tablespoons sugar

4 tablespoons sweet butter

4 tablespoons white wine

3 tablespoons Calvados liqueur

¼ teaspoon vanilla extract

1 cup milk

1 egg

1 tablespoon flour

(M A K E S 5 C R E P E S)

Fagottini

CREPES:

2 tablespoons sweet butter

2 eggs

6 tablespoons flour

10 tablespoons milk

Confectioners' sugar

To make the filling: Wash and peel the apples. Place the peel, 2 tablespoons of the sugar, and 1 tablespoon of the butter in a small saucepan and sauté the peel until it softens, about 7 minutes. Add the white wine and let it reduce completely, 5 to 6 minutes. Puree the mixture in a food processor, adding another tablespoon of the butter. Set the puree aside.

Dice the apples and place them in a sauté pan with the remaining 2 tablespoons of butter, 2 tablespoons of sugar, and the Calvados. Heat over medium, stirring the apples occasionally, until the Calvados has reduced, about 10 minutes. Set the chopped apples aside.

Add the vanilla to the milk and bring to a boil in a small saucepan, then remove it from the heat. Beat the egg with the remaining 3 tablespoons of sugar; when the egg is well beaten, add the flour and the hot milk. Stir well, pour back into the saucepan, and heat over medium, stirring constantly, until the pastry cream thickens, 2 or 3 minutes. Do not allow it to boil. Set aside.

To make the crepes: Preheat the oven to 400°. Butter an ovenproof dish.

Clarify the butter by placing it in the top of a double boiler over hot water. Let the butter stand until it melts. When the fat separates from the white foam, skim off the foam. You now have clarified butter.

In a bowl, beat the eggs with the flour until smooth. Slowly add the milk, beating until you have a thin batter.

Brush an 8-inch non-stick skillet with a little of the clarified butter and heat the skillet until it is very hot. Pour in 3 tablespoons of the batter, then quickly tilt the skillet to spread the batter evenly. Cook until lightly brown on the bottom, about 30 seconds, then flip and cook the crepe on the other side for 10 to 15 seconds. (This will take some practice to get right.) Stack the crepes on a plate, separated by wax paper to keep them from sticking.

Fill each crepe with a heaping tablespoon of the pastry cream and the apple filling, then roll them closed. Place the crepes in the baking dish and heat through, about 4 minutes. To serve, transfer the crepes to individual plates, sprinkle each crepe with confectioners' sugar, and dot with a bit of the apple peel puree.

Winter Menus

PHOTOS BY EDUARDO FORNACIARI (ABOVE LEFT); FOTO ALCIDE (ABOVE RIGHT)

Nonna Maria e la Vita di Fattoria

Nonna Maria on the Farm

Frittata di Cipolle	Red Onion Omelet
Pasta Tordellatta	Pasta with Ricotta, Spinach, and Meat Sauce
Coniglio Fritto Nostrano	Fried Rabbit, Our Way
Ricotta al Caffè e Rhum	Ricotta with Coffee and Rum

SUGGESTED WINES: ROSSO DI MONTALCINO, IL POGGIONE (GRAPE: SANGIOVESE);
PARETO, RUFFINO (GRAPE: CABERNET SAUVIGNON)

Translated literally, the Italian word *furbo* means "foxy" or "sly," but those words don't capture the real meaning of *furbo*. *Furbo*, in fact, was my grandmother Maria, Beppe's wife, who would buy shoes a size too big because she thought she was getting more shoe leather for her money, who would skim cream off the top of the milk she sold the local dairyman and who made sure the same dairyman never noticed by serving him a glass of wine, or even two, whenever he'd call. It was Grandma Maria who tutored me about farm life, taught me how to milk the cows, how to make butter and ricotta, how to feed the chickens.

When I slept at Grandma Maria's and Grandpa Beppe's, I was always in the same *camerone*, or big room, where they kept huge closets filled with old clothes, sacks of grain waiting to be sold, old mattresses, and anything that didn't have its own rightful place. Grandma would wake me up early and we'd go to the cow shed. Bianchina, the younger one with the doleful eyes, was my responsibility. I had to wash her teats with warm water before she would give up a drop of *latte*. Grandma tended to Mora, who liked to be sung to.

Later, with the fresh milk, Grandma would make ricotta, which she wrapped in plastic bags from the grocery store and sold to our neighbors. The warm ricotta was delicious. I especially loved it mixed with sugar and rum and ground coffee. It didn't take me long to learn how to open the bags and sneak out a few spoonfuls, a trick that didn't sit well with the customers. They would complain to Grandma that their containers were a few *etti*, ounces, short and she would begin yelling my name. That was my cue to disappear. But I knew she wasn't really angry. If anything, it gave her great satisfaction to know her grandson was trying to be as *furbo* as she was.

Nonna Maria would have prepared this meal with great pleasure, because its only real cost is time. The other ingredients, from the onions to the rabbit, are cheap and plentiful in Tuscany. If only we had Maria to prepare it!

ME WITH
GRANDMA MARIA
IN THE VINEYARD.

Frittata di Cipolle

Red Onion Omelet

(S E R V E S 4)

....

3 tablespoons extra-virgin olive oil

2 cups thinly sliced red onions

1 teaspoon salt

2 tablespoons white wine

4 medium eggs

1 teaspoon finely chopped fresh thyme

1 teaspoon finely chopped fresh Italian
   parsley

$^1/_2$ teaspoon fresh ground black pepper

Place $1^1/_2$ tablespoons of the olive oil, the onions, and $^1/_2$ teaspoon of the salt in a large frying pan. Sauté over medium heat until the onions are brown, 10 to 12 minutes. Add the white wine and continue cooking for 10 minutes. Remove the pan from the heat and let the onions cool.

In a bowl, beat the eggs with the herbs, the remaining $^1/_2$ teaspoon of salt, and the pepper. Then add the onions. Pour the remaining $1^1/_2$ tablespoons of olive oil into a frying pan. When it is well heated, pour in the egg mixture, stirring it with a fork for 1 to 2 minutes. When the under side of the omelet is lightly browned, in about 2 minutes, flip it. (An easy way to do this is to hold a pot lid with no lip over the frying pan. Turn the frying pan upside down, so the omelet falls into the lid. From the lid, you can slide the *frittata*, upside down, back into the frying pan.) Cook until the second side is lightly browned. Cut in wedges and serve.

Pasta Tordellatta

Pasta with Ricotta, Spinach, and Meat Sauce

(SERVES 4 AS AN APPETIZER)

....

3 quarts water

1½ tablespoons salt

10 ounces fresh pasta (I prefer 3-×-1-
   inch rectangles, but any size will do)

1 cup Meat Sauce (page 97)

1 cup Sautéed Spinach (page 99)

1 cup fresh ricotta cheese

6 tablespoons freshly grated
   Parmigiano-Reggiano cheese

In a large pot, bring the water to a boil. Add the salt, then the pasta (fresh pasta cooks very quickly, check it after 2 minutes). In a bowl, combine the meat sauce, spinach, and ricotta. When the pasta is very *al dente*, drain it, return it to the pot, add the ricotta mixture, and combine well. Cook over low heat for another 5 minutes. Stir in the Parmigiano-Reggiano and serve.

Coniglio Fritto Nostrano

Fried Rabbit, Our Way

At Vipore, we almost always serve rabbit on a big platter. It becomes a festive communal dish, and more fun to eat.

(SERVES 4)

1 (3–4-pound) rabbit, cut into serving pieces

Salt and fresh ground black pepper, to taste

Juice of 1–2 lemons, plus 1 lemon, quartered

Peanut or vegetable oil, for frying

2 cups flour

2 eggs, lightly beaten

Wash the rabbit and dry it with paper towels. Season the pieces with salt and pepper. Squeeze the juice of 1 or 2 lemons over the rabbit and rub the juice into the flesh. Cover the rabbit with plastic wrap and let it sit for 1½ to 2 hours on the counter.

When you are ready to eat the rabbit, pour the peanut oil into a large sauté pan until it is a third full. Using a thermometer, heat the oil to 375° degrees. It should not smoke.

Mix the flour with salt and pepper. Dredge the rabbit pieces in the flour, then dip them in the beaten eggs. Add the rabbit to the oil, being careful not to splash yourself with hot oil. Cook at a simmer for 10 to 15 minutes, depending on the size of the pieces, turning them every few minutes to keep them cooking evenly. Remove the pieces from the oil and drain them on paper towels. Serve the rabbit with lemon wedges.

Ricotta al Caffè e Rhum

Ricotta with Coffee and Rum

For anyone who might have done one too many shots of grappa last night, I recommend a good dose of this ricotta with your morning coffee. It's easier on your stomach than a Bloody Mary, and—take it from one who's tried both—more effective. It's also a wonderfully easy dessert. Serve it with biscotti.

(SERVES 4)

2 cups fresh ricotta cheese

3½ tablespoons sugar

2 teaspoons finely ground coffee beans

2 tablespoons rum

Mix all the ingredients together in a bowl and spoon into individual serving dishes. Serve immediately.

SALARE LA SCUOLA
Playing Hooky

Insalata di Gran Farro	Wild Barley Salad
Spaghetti con Salsiccia	Spaghetti with Sausage
Pollo alla Diavola	Grilled Chicken, Devil's Style
Zuppa Lucchese	Lucchese "Soup"

SUGGESTED WINES: CHIANTI CLASSICO, FONTERUTOLI (GRAPES: SANGIOVESE AND LOCAL VARIETALS); ELIGIA, POLIZIANO (GRAPES: PRUGNOLO GENTILE AND SANGIOVETO)

When I was fifteen, I enrolled in Scuola Alberghiera, the hotel and restaurant academy in Montecatini. Fifteen sounds young to be taking classes in a specialized institution, but in Italy, it's normal. Mama and Papa wanted me to be a doctor or lawyer, but nothing bored me more than studying. I wanted to be a chef, not a *dottore*, the name we give anyone with a degree. When I heard about Scuola Alberghiera, where they taught courses on food preparation, I thought I had the solution. No math, no science, no French. This was my kind of curriculum. But Montecatini was still a school, and one that complied with Italian educational regulations. It was business as usual—calculus, geography, and so on. I'd been had!

But not for long. On days I knew I'd be in the kitchen, I was always punctual. But on days when I had French or math or anything else, I'd somehow forget to get off the train. By the time I realized it, I was in Florence or some small village far from school. It was uncanny. My favorite way to spend these missed days was trying new restaurants. Once, on my seventeenth birthday, I even treated myself to lunch at Pinchiorri, a restaurant in Florence sacred to Italian gourmets.

Usually I'd manage to miss my stop with Emilio, who didn't even go to Scuola Alberghiera, but nevertheless found himself on the same train. Often we'd get off at Lunata because Emilio had a friend who had some older friends there with an empty house. They used it after dates as a bachelor pad, but since we were only fifteen and not yet interested in girls, we liked it for its well-stocked bar and kitchen. My contribution was always a jar of the wild barley salad I loved making. Emilio, who had a *pollaio*, a chicken coop, would bring our *secondo*. For dessert, we always had *buccellato*, the typical sweet from Lucca, which we'd buy from Taddeucci, a 200-year-old shop in Piazza San Michele, before we got on the train in the morning. This might not have been the way most kids would choose to play hooky. Too bad for them.

SCUOLA ALBERGHIERA, 1978. THAT'S ME WITH THE AFRO, SECOND FROM THE LEFT IN THE MIDDLE ROW.

Insalata di Gran Farro

Wild Barley Salad

(SERVES 4–6)

4 cups cooked farro (wild barley, or regular barley if you can't find farro)

1 tomato, diced

Peel of 1 zucchini, chopped

1/2 *each* red, yellow, and green bell pepper, seeded and diced

1/4 cup finely chopped red onion

1/4 cup chopped fresh basil

3 tablespoons drained capers

1/4 cup halved Italian black olives

2 tablespoons red wine vinegar

Salt and fresh ground black pepper, to taste

1/3 cup extra-virgin olive oil

1/2 pound mozzarella, cut into 1/2-inch cubes (optional)

1 1/2 cups tuna, canned in oil, drained, and flaked (optional) (if you can't get tuna in oil, water is okay)

In a large bowl, combine the barley with all of the vegetables, the basil, capers, and olives.

In a small bowl, whisk together the vinegar and salt and pepper. Whisk in the olive oil. Pour the dressing over the salad and mix well. If you want mozzarella and tuna, add them here. Serve the salad at room temperature.

Spaghetti con Salsiccia
Spaghetti with Sausage
(SERVES 8 AS AN APPETIZER)

¼ cup extra-virgin olive oil

6 cloves garlic, chopped

1 medium onion, chopped

¼ cup chopped celery

1 tablespoon chopped fresh rosemary

1 cup (about ½ pound) sweet Italian
sausage, removed from its casing

1 cup (about ½ pound) hot Italian
sausage, removed from its casing

1½ cups red or white wine

1½ cups peeled and chopped tomatoes
(or canned Italian tomatoes)

1–2 cups water, plus 6 quarts

3 tablespoons salt, plus extra to taste

Fresh ground black pepper, to taste

Pinch *each* of grated nutmeg, ground
cinnamon, ground cloves

1 pound spaghetti

6 tablespoons freshly grated
Parmigiano-Reggiano cheese

In a large frying pan, place the oil, the garlic, onion, celery, and rosemary and cook over medium heat, stirring well. When the mixture begins to color, after 5 to 7 minutes, add the sausage to the pan. Brown the sausage, breaking it into small pieces with the back of a spoon. Stir in the wine. When the wine has reduced completely, after about 5 minutes, add the tomatoes. Cook for 30 minutes. Add 1 or 2 cups water, depending how dry the mixture is, salt and pepper to taste, and the spices. Reduce the heat to low and cook the sauce for another hour.

Meanwhile, in a large pot, bring the 6 quarts of water to boil. Add the 3 tablespoons of salt and the spaghetti. Stir. When the pasta is very *al dente*, drain it, and add it to the sauce. Cook the pasta with the sauce for 5 minutes. Stir in the Parmigiano-Reggiano and serve.

Pollo alla Diavola

Grilled Chicken, Devil's Style

(SERVES 4)

This recipe comes out best if the chicken is grilled over coals or in a wood-burning oven, otherwise, what kind of devil is at work? At Vipore, we'd split the chicken open, weigh it down with a brick, and cook it over a hot fire. On a busy night, if there wasn't room on the grill, we'd place the flattened bird between 2 bricks and bake it in the oven. If neither of these options is available to you, you can simply broil the chicken.

. . . .

2 (2-pound) chickens, cleaned

4 cloves garlic, chopped fine

4 tablespoons chopped fresh sage

4 tablespoons chopped fresh rosemary

Juice of 4 lemons

$2/3$ cup extra-virgin olive oil

Salt and fresh ground black pepper, to taste

Split the chicken open along the backbone, opening it like a book. With your hands, flatten the bird as much as possible.

In a bowl, mix together the remaining ingredients. Coat the chicken with the mixture and let it marinate for 2 hours (or overnight) in the refrigerator, turning it often.

Remove the chicken from the marinade and place it on a hot grill or under the broiler, skin side down. Broil the bird for 20 minutes, turn skin side up, and broil for about another 10 minutes. The chicken is done when the skin is dark and crispy. Serve at once.

Zuppa Lucchese
Lucchese "Soup"

Traditional zuppa Inglese, or English "soup," is a variation on trifle—ladyfingers soaked in liqueur and layered with pastry cream and chocolate. Zuppa Lucchese, or Lucchese "Soup," brings the dessert completely into Tuscany. It uses *buccellato*—one of Lucca's trademark sweets, which dates back to Roman times—Vin Santo, strawberries, and pastry cream. *Buccellato* is wonderful on its own, toasted, or in our "soup."

(S E R V E S 6)

12 slices *Buccellato* (recipe follows)

Vin Santo or dry Marsala

6 tablespoons granulated sugar

3 cups chopped fresh strawberries

1 recipe Pastry Cream (page 87)

Confectioners' sugar, for dusting

Place 3 or 4 slices of *buccellato* in the bottom of a serving bowl. Splash them generously with Vin Santo. Sprinkle on a little granulated sugar, spoon a layer of strawberries on top, then a layer of pastry cream. Repeat the layers until all the ingredients have been used. Finish with a layer of the pastry cream. Dust the top with confectioners' sugar and serve.

Buccellato
Lucchese Sweet Bread
(MAKES 1 LOAF)

1 package active dry yeast

¼ cup warm water

1 teaspoon plus ½ cup sugar

2 to 2¼ cups flour

½ teaspoon salt

⅓ cup milk

3 tablespoons butter

2 medium eggs

Vegetable oil, for the bowl and pan

3 tablespoons raisins

3 tablespoons finely chopped mixed
candied fruit (optional)

1 tablespoon aniseed

In a small bowl, combine the yeast with the warm water and 1 teaspoon of the sugar. Let the mixture stand until it starts to foam, 5 to 10 minutes.

In a large bowl, combine the smaller quantity of flour, the ½ cup of sugar, and the salt. Set aside.

In a pan, scald the milk. Add the butter, and allow the mixture to cool. Beat in 1 egg.

Make a well in the flour mixture and stir in the yeast and the egg mixture (it must be cooler than the yeast). Mix until a dough forms, then let it rest for 10 minutes. On a lightly floured surface, slowly add the remaining flour, kneading the dough until it doesn't stick to your hands, about 10 minutes.

Lightly oil a large bowl. Place the dough in the bowl and turn to coat it with oil. Cover the bowl loosely with a towel and let the dough rise in a warm place for about 8 hours. Punch it down. Work in the raisins, the candied fruit, and the aniseed. Shape the dough into a loaf and place it on an oiled baking sheet. Make a shallow cut the length of the top of the bread. Cover it, and allow it to rise for another 2 hours.

Meanwhile, preheat the oven to 350°. Beat the remaining egg and brush it over the dough. Bake the loaf for 45 minutes, until the top is browned. The bread is done when its internal temperature is between 200 and 210° F. Do not overbake. Cool and slice.

GIOCHI DELLA GIOVENTÙ
Youth Games

Insalata Uova e Carne Secca del Pontormo	Pontormo's Warm Salad with Egg and Pancetta
Bucatini all'Amatriciana	Bucatini with Tomatoes, Bacon, and Onion
Spezzatino Classico Toscano	Classic Tuscan Veal Stew
Torta di San Marcello	San Marcello Cake

**SUGGESTED WINES: CABREO VIGNETO LA PIETRA, RUFFINO (GRAPE: CHARDONNAY);
SAFFREDI, PUPILLE (GRAPES: CABERNET SAUVIGNON, MERLOT, ALICANTE)**

....

I never liked high school, least of all literature, history, or anything that involved reading and studying. Math and technical subjects, I didn't mind because I was good at them. But still, if I had to tally up the hours, I'd bet I spent more time getting excused from classes than I did attending them.

The only period I looked forward to, besides cooking, was physical education. That wasn't because I was physically fit or a natural athlete, but because my second year at the Scuola Alberghiera coincided with the *Giochi della Gioventù*. The *Giochi*, which ended with national finals in Rome, was a series of Olympic-style games for high school students. For me, that meant sanctioned school-skipping: The more events I entered and won, the more school I could skip. After researching which sports were least popular—and least competitive, increasing my chances of winning and advancing to Rome—I signed up for the 16-pound hammer throw, the 110-meter hurdles, the marathon, the javelin, and the 3,000-meter run.

(continued on next page)

My coach knew I wasn't a great athlete, but he was a regular customer of Vipore, and very patient with me. With his help, I actually made it to the provincial competitions in three events and to the regionals in one, the hammer throw. With every new heat, I got to travel to a different city and, best of all, try new restaurants and dishes. In Pistoia, I discovered *torta di San Marcello*, a cake made with bitter almonds; in Florence, I had great *spezzatino*, a traditional veal stew. When I returned to Montecatini, I'd discuss these meals with my cooking teacher. He joked that the *Giochi* weren't doing much for my athletic ability, but they were contributing enormously to my gastronomic education. That's exactly how I saw it.

The ruse wore thin at the end, however. In Rome for the hammer-throwing finals, I couldn't bring myself to go to the stadium. Even though it was what I had worked toward for months, I was too afraid of making a fool of myself. I was no more a hammer thrower than a prime minister. I withdrew at the last minute, then headed for Piazza Navona, where I had one of the best *bucatini all'Amatriciana* of my life. It was just as gratifying as a blue ribbon.

TRAINING FOR THE GIOCHI DELLA GIOVENTÙ 3,000-METER RACE, 1976. I'M ON THE LEFT.

Insalata Uova e Carne Secca del Pontormo

Pontormo's Warm Salad with Egg and Pancetta

Pontormo was a reclusive sixteenth-century painter who lived in Florence. He and Il Rosso Fiorentino are credited with being the first artists to break away from the High Renaissance. I can't offer art criticism, but I do know that Pontormo and Rosso were great gourmands. This dish, a warm salad of eggs mixed with greens, was one of Pontormo's favorites. I started toying with the recipe years ago, after reading about Pontormo in an historical cookbook. It's become one of my most requested dishes, both at Vipore and in New York.

(SERVES 4)

2 tablespoons extra-virgin olive oil

1 tablespoon mixed dried herbs (use any combination of dried rosemary, thyme, basil, savory, chives, oregano, and mint that you like)

3½ ounces Italian pancetta, sliced and cut into strips (if not available, use blanched bacon)

6 eggs

Salt and fresh ground black pepper, to taste

4 cups washed, mixed salad greens, torn into bite-size pieces

3 tablespoons Pontormo Dressing (recipe follows)

Place the olive oil, herbs, and pancetta in a large frying pan and cook over medium heat. When the pancetta is transparent, after 5 to 7 minutes, beat together the eggs, salt, and pepper and scramble them in the pan. They shouldn't be too dry. If you see they are drying, take them off the heat and continue stirring. Dress the greens with the Pontormo dressing and mix with the eggs. Serve immediately. (If you want a bit of crunch, croutons are a nice touch.)

(continued on next page)

Condimento del Pontormo
Pontormo Dressing

This dressing can be used for any salad.

....

1 tablespoon red wine vinegar

1 tablespoon balsamic vinegar

1 tablespoon red wine

³/₄ teaspoon salt

¹/₂ teaspoon fresh ground black pepper

¹/₄ cup extra-virgin olive oil

In a small bowl, whisk together the vinegars and the wine. Whisk in the salt and pepper, then the olive oil.

Pancetta

....

Little belly" is the literal translation, and you'll get one if you eat too much of this unsmoked bacon (sometimes called pork belly in America). Pancetta is delicious cut thin onto crusty bread and topped with wafer-thin red onion slices, ground pepper, and olive oil. Or, for a treat, you can cook it like bacon. Pancetta gives depth to spaghetti alla carbonara and many soups and sauces. If you can't find pancetta, use unsmoked bacon, or blanche and drain smoked bacon.

**PONTORMO'S WARM SALAD WITH EGG AND PANCETTA
(INSALATA UOVA E CARNE SECCA DEL PONTORMO)**

Bucatini all'Amatriciana

Bucatini with Tomatoes, Bacon, and Onion

(SERVES 4 AS AN APPETIZER)

1 tablespoon extra-virgin olive oil

2 teaspoons finely chopped garlic

1/8–1/4 teaspoon crushed red pepper flakes

2/3 cup chopped red onion

2 teaspoons chopped fresh rosemary

2 teaspoons chopped fresh sage

5 ounces pancetta, chopped

2 slices prosciutto, chopped

1/3 cup white wine

1 (28-ounce) can Italian tomatoes

1 1/2 tablespoons salt, plus extra to taste

Fresh ground black pepper, to taste

3 quarts water

1/2 pound bucatini

4 tablespoons freshly grated pecorino Romano cheese

Put the oil, the garlic, red pepper flakes, and onion in a large saucepan and sauté over medium heat until the garlic starts to color, about 5 minutes. Lower the heat, add the rosemary and sage, and continue cooking until the onion softens, another 3 to 5 minutes. Then add the pancetta and the prosciutto. Cook, stirring occasionally, until the meat is translucent, about 7 minutes. Stir in the white wine and let it reduce completely, another 2 minutes, then add the tomatoes and salt and pepper to taste. When the sauce starts to boil, lower it to a simmer and cook it uncovered for 30 to 40 minutes.

In a large pot, bring the water to a boil and add the 1 1/2 tablespoons of salt and the bucatini. When the pasta is *al dente*, drain it and toss it with the Amatriciana sauce and the grated pecorino Romano. Serve immediately.

Spezzatino Classico Toscano
Classic Tuscan Veal Stew

You can also use beef shank or beef shoulder for this stew.

(SERVES 4)

½ cup extra-virgin olive oil

3 tablespoons chopped garlic

⅓ cup chopped fresh sage

1½ pounds boneless veal shank or shoulder, cut into 1-inch cubes

Flour, for dusting

½ cup red or white wine

Salt and fresh ground black pepper, to taste

1 cup crushed canned tomatoes

1 cup homemade beef broth or warm water, as needed

1½ pounds potatoes, peeled and cut in ¾-inch cubes

In a large sauté pan, place the oil, garlic, and sage and cook over medium heat until the garlic starts to color, about 5 minutes. Dust the veal cubes with flour, turn the heat to medium high, and add the veal to the pan, stirring so the pieces cook evenly. When the meat has browned, after about 3 minutes, add the wine. Let it boil for 30 seconds and scrape the bottom of the pan to loosen the residue. Add salt and pepper and the tomatoes.

Bring the *spezzatino* to a boil again, then reduce the heat to low and cover the pan. Continue cooking, stirring occasionally, for about an hour. If the *spezzatino* begins to dry out, add a little beef broth or warm water. Thirty minutes before the *spezzatino* is done, add the cubed potatoes. When the potatoes are tender, remove the *spezzatino* from the heat and serve.

Torta di San Marcello

San Marcello Cake

This is Pistoia's favorite dessert. The Pistoiese use bitter almonds, but they're illegal in the States, so I substituted apricot pits, which are available in health food stores. If you can't find them, just use more toasted almonds.

(SERVES 8)

½ cup sugar

6 tablespoons sweet butter, plus
  additional for the pan

2 eggs

¼ teaspoon vanilla extract

2½ tablespoons rum

Grated rind of ½ lemon

2 cups flour

½ teaspoon baking powder

¼ teaspoon salt

5 tablespoons chopped toasted almonds

2 tablespoon chopped apricot pits

Preheat the oven to 325°. Butter a 9-inch cake pan and lightly dust it with flour.

In a bowl, cream together the sugar and the 6 tablespoons of butter. Beat in the eggs, vanilla, rum, and lemon rind. Sift together the flour, baking powder, and salt and add them to the batter. Mix well, then add the toasted almonds and apricot pits.

Pat the batter into the pan and bake for 40 minutes, or until a toothpick inserted in the center comes out clean. This cake is very nice served warm, with a scoop of vanilla ice cream.

LADRI DI ALBERI
The Tree Thieves

Crostini di Fegatini	Liver Toasts
Lasagna con Salsiccia e Radicchio	Lasagna with Sausage and Radicchio
Stracotto alla Toscana	Chianti Braised Beef
Panforte	Spicy Sienese Fruit Cake

SUGGESTED WINES: CHIANTI CLASSICO, BADIA A COLTIBUONO (GRAPES: SANGIOVESE, CANAIOLO, AND LOCAL VARIETALS); BRUNELLO DI MONTALCINO, ARGIANO (GRAPE: SANGIOVESE)

....

A Tuscan Christmas dinner is something to behold. Preparations start days ahead, with every last *zia*, aunt, and *cugina*, cousin, slaving over regional favorites: *crostini* of every sort, marinated tongue, lentil soup, tortellini in broth, lasagna, boiled beef, braised beef, veal and hen served with a mustard-flavored fruit sauce, roasted rabbit, roasted chicken, roasted turkey, sautéed greens, roasted potatoes, *panforte*, panettone, and towering plates of *ricciarelli*.

At Vipore, we never celebrated Christmas; we worked. But one year, we closed the restaurant and invited all the Casellas, Papa's family, and Polidoris, Mama's family, from all over Tuscany. On Christmas Eve, the kitchen, with everyone dropping by with their contributions, was as busy as if we were working. *Zia* Beppa, Mama's twin, brought over the turkey. Anna, her other sister, roasted chickens. My Aunt, *La Spezina*, braised a roast. Papa went to the butcher and got a side of beef and veal to make *bollito misto*. Beppe brought his own wine, and, as usual, less than great. But we all tipped a glass, or took a *caffè* or *un corretto* (espresso with grappa), played cards, and waited to go to midnight mass.

It was over a not-too-interesting hand of *briscola* that my cousin Paolo and I decided the tree Papa had brought in was too small for the importance of the day, our first family Christmas. What we really needed was an enormous tree, an *alberone*. Promising to be back in time for mass, we set off for the woods of a cranky neighbor, Aldo, who was known to shoo away trespassers with a beebee gun. But it was icy and damp, and it took an hour of wandering just to spot our prize, a great twelve-foot spruce. Keeping an eye out for Aldo and whizzing beebees, we started to saw and hack at the tree. It took forever to cut it down, and twice as long to drag it home. We didn't have gloves or proper coats, and only Totó, my favorite comic, could have made the scene more preposterous.

Well past one o'clock, Paolo and I arrived, half frozen, matted in sap and pine needles. Mama and Papa, having come back from church, were already in bed. No one was even up to see our prize. We propped up the tree and huddled, deflated, around the fireplace. That's when *Zia* Anna's chicken, sitting on the counter, and even Beppe's bad wine, started to look good. Finally, our just rewards. With all that food, who'd miss one chicken?

Luckily, we were right. Anna couldn't have been prouder. We chose *her* chicken above Beppa's turkey *and La Spezina*'s rabbit. Both aunts had had their feelings hurt and they let us know it. Mama, meanwhile, kept quiet, but Papa couldn't. He insisted on a truce, then sealed it by making Anna, Beppa, and *La Spezina* baptize the tree. With what else? A glass of Beppe's red wine.

Crostini di Fegatini
Liver Toasts

(SERVES 4–5)

....

1 pound chicken livers

2 tablespoons extra-virgin olive oil

1 small onion, chopped

3 cloves garlic, sliced

1 tablespoon flour

1 tablespoon drained capers

½ cup Vin Santo or dry Marsala

Salt and fresh ground black pepper, to taste

1 loaf Tuscan bread, sliced thick

Clean the livers well and place them in a large frying pan with the olive oil, onion, and garlic. Cook the mixture over medium heat until it is browned and the liquid given off by the livers has almost evaporated, about 15 to 16 minutes, then add the flour, capers, and Vin Santo or Marsala. When the wine has completely reduced, about 3 minutes, add salt and pepper.

Remove the mixture from the heat and let it cool. Transfer it to a chopping board and chop well. Transfer to a serving dish. Toast the bread, spread it with the liver mixture, and serve.

Lasagna con Salsiccia e Radicchio
Lasagna with Sausage and Radicchio

The proportions of filling to lasagna might seem off to you, but this is the way Italians eat lasagna, not overstuffed the way Americans like it. If you insist, you can always increase the amount of sausage sauce, radicchio, Béchamel, and Parmigiano-Reggiano cheese.

(SERVES 8 AS AN APPETIZER)

$6^3/_4$ quarts water

3 tablespoons plus 1 teaspoon salt

9 lasagna noodles

1 large head radicchio, shredded

2 cloves garlic, peeled and crushed, plus
   2 tablespoons finely chopped

6 tablespoons extra-virgin olive oil

2 tablespoons finely chopped red onion

2 tablespoons finely chopped fresh
   rosemary

1 pound Italian sausage, hot or sweet or
   a mixture of the two, removed from
   its casing

$^1/_2$ teaspoon fresh ground black pepper

$^1/_2$ teaspoon crushed red pepper flakes

$^1/_2$ cup white wine

$1^1/_2$ cups crushed canned tomatoes

1 recipe Béchamel Sauce (page 326)

1 cup freshly grated Parmigiano-
   Reggiano cheese

Preheat the oven to 350°. Bring 6 quarts of the water to a boil in a large pot. Add 3 tablespoons of the salt and the lasagna. Cook the noodles until they are *al dente*, then plunge them into cold water to stop the cooking. Drain the lasagna on dish towels and set aside.

Place the radicchio in a roasting pan and mix in the $^3/_4$ cup of water, the 2 cloves crushed garlic, and 1 tablespoon of the olive oil. Braise the radicchio in the oven for 10 to 12 minutes, until the leaves are wilted. Remove the radicchio from the oven, discard the garlic, and drain any remaining water. Set aside. Keep the oven on.

In a large saucepan, place 4 tablespoons of the olive oil, the chopped garlic, chopped onion, and rosemary, and sauté over medium heat until the garlic starts to color, about 5 minutes. Then add the sausage, breaking it up with the back of a spoon. Add the remaining teaspoon of salt, the black pepper, and red pepper flakes. Cook for 10 minutes more and add the white wine. When the wine reduces completely, in about 5 minutes, add the crushed tomatoes and cook for 15 minutes. The sauce is ready; set it aside.

To assemble the dish, grease a $7\frac{1}{2}$-by-$11\frac{3}{4}$-inch roasting pan with the remaining tablespoon of olive oil. Arrange a layer of lasagna noodles on the bottom. Spoon on a layer of the meat sauce, a layer of the radicchio, a layer of Béchamel, and sprinkle with the cheese. (As I said in my headnote, these will be scant layers. Think of the layers as sauce for a pasta, not mortar for a wall of lasagna.) Repeat this process until you have used all the ingredients. The top layer of sauce, radicchio, Béchamel, and cheese should be the thickest. Finish with the cheese on top. Bake for 30 minutes, or until the cheese is golden brown, and serve immediately.

Stracotto alla Toscana

Chianti Braised Beef

This dish is even better after sitting for 1 or 2 days in the refrigerator.

(SERVES 4)

2 pounds eye round beef roast

6 whole cloves

1 stick cinnamon

6 juniper berries

2 red onions, cut into eighths

2 carrots, cut into 1-inch lengths

2 stalks celery, cut into 1-inch lengths

1 bottle Chianti

2 tablespoons chopped garlic

2 tablespoons chopped fresh rosemary

Salt and fresh ground black pepper, to taste

4 tablespoons extra-virgin olive oil

2 ounces pancetta, chopped

2 ounces dried porcini mushrooms soaked in 2 cups warm water for 30 minutes

1¼ cups crushed canned tomatoes

Homemade beef broth or water, as needed

Place the roast, the cloves, cinnamon stick, juniper berries, onions, carrots, and celery in a 5-quart casserole. Pour in the Chianti. The meat should be completed submerged. Cover and marinate overnight in the refrigerator.

Preheat the oven to 350°. Remove the meat from the marinade, strain the marinade, and reserve the wine and vegetables separately. Cut 10 deep slits in the roast. Mix together the garlic, rosemary, and salt and pepper, and stuff the slits with this mixture. Rub any extra into the flesh of the meat. Rub 2 tablespoons of olive oil into the flesh.

Pour the remaining 2 tablespoons of oil into the casserole and add the roast. Return it to the oven for 10 minutes and add the chopped pancetta. Turn the roast and cook for another 15 minutes. Add 2 cups of the reserved Chianti and return the roast to the oven for 20 minutes. Add the reserved vegetables, then drain the porcini (reserving the liquid) and add them, too. After 15 minutes, add the tomatoes and the mushroom liquid. If there isn't enough liquid to completely cover the roast, add a little beef broth or water. Cover the casserole and return the roast to the oven for $1^{1}/_{2}$ to 2 hours. The meat is ready when it feels very tender when touched with a knife.

Remove the roast from the liquid. Transfer the juices and the vegetables to a food processor, and puree them. Return the puree to the casserole. Slice the meat $^{1}/_{4}$ inch thick and add the slices to the puree. Cover the casserole and return it to the oven for another 2 to 4 minutes. Spoon the meat and the sauce onto plates and serve.

Panforte
Spicy Sienese Fruit Cake

This fruit cake, Siena's trademark dessert, is called *panforte* or "strong bread," because it is made with lots of fresh ground pepper. It is a direct descendant of a medieval spiced sweetened bread.

(SERVES 20)

Butter, for the pan

1½ cups granulated sugar (see Note)

6 tablespoons water

2½ cups chopped mixed candied fruit

½ cup chopped candied citron

¾ cup whole almonds

¼ cup whole hazelnuts

1 cup flour

½ teaspoon grated nutmeg

½ teaspoon ground cloves

Pinch of salt

¼–½ teaspoon fresh ground black pepper

1 teaspoon crushed coriander seeds

1–2 teaspoons ground cinnamon

Confectioners' sugar, for dusting

Preheat the oven to 350°. Butter a piece of parchment paper on both sides and use it to line the bottom and sides of a 9-inch springform pan. (Using parchment paper is very important. Otherwise, you will never get the cake out of the pan.)

In a medium saucepan, combine the granulated sugar and the water over medium heat until the sugar is completely dissolved and you have a thick, clear syrup, about 7 minutes. Remove the pan from the heat and mix in the candied fruit, citron, almonds, hazelnuts, flour, nutmeg, cloves, salt, and black pepper.

Spoon the mixture into the baking pan and spread evenly. Sprinkle the top with the coriander seeds and the cinnamon. Bake until the *panforte* is set, 50 to 60 minutes. It should be soft to the touch, not runny.

When the cake is cooled, release the sides and peel off the parchment paper. Dust the *panforte* generously with the confectioners' sugar. Cut into small wedges on a cutting board with a good chef's knife. (It will be difficult to slice.)

NOTE: If you like the flavor of honey, you can substitute a syrup made from ¾ cup honey and ¾ cup sugar for the sugar/water syrup. Mix them together in a medium saucepan and bring the mixture to a boil over medium heat. Reduce the syrup to a simmer. When it reaches 234° on a candy thermometer, remove the syrup from the heat and proceed with the recipe as written.

C'É UNA OSTRICA NELLA SUA TASCA?

Is That an Oyster in Your Pocket?

Ostriche alla Fiorentina	Florentine Oysters
Fusilli al Gorgonzola	Fusilli with Gorgonzola
Filetto di Pesce al Forno con Timballo di Patate	Baked Fish Fillets with Potato Timbale
Non Brutti, Ma Buoni	Not Ugly, But Good Cookies

SUGGESTED WINES: CHARDONNAY, MONSANTO (GRAPE: CHARDONNAY); PINOT NERO, MARCHESE PANCRAZI (GRAPE: PINOT NERO)

. . . .

Raw oysters are one food I've never understood. I was twenty the first time I had them, during a trip to Monte Carlo with my friend Giovanni. If it had just been the two of us, we never would have thought of going to an oyster bar. But the afternoon we arrived, Giovanni and I ran into a client from Vipore, Alberto, who was traveling alone and who insisted on treating us to oysters and champagne at the San Raphael, a nearby restaurant.

Alberto started by ordering a bottle of champagne and a dozen oysters for each of us. Out of fear of seeming provincial, I didn't mention that these were my first raw oysters, and I almost gagged on the first one. It was so slippery, I had to chug the champagne to get it down. I couldn't imagine how I was going to get through a dozen.

With oyster number two, inspiration struck. I made a sandwich with a roll from the bar, using the bread to sort of dry off the oyster. Then I surreptitiously dropped the oyster itself into my jacket pocket. The strategy got me through the whole platter. An hour later, I had six oysters in my pocket and six in my stomach, along with six rolls and eight glasses of champagne. Bless Dom Pérignon. The champagne was so good, I forgot the oysters altogether.

But after I'd been back at Vipore a week, I started to smell a smell. Mama and I cleaned my room, but it didn't go away. Then we moved all the furniture outside and scrubbed everything furiously. Still no results. Then Mama opened the armoire. What a stink. The jacket was where I'd hung it, but the right pocket was gone. Something in the oysters had eaten through the fabric. I couldn't imagine what they did to my stomach. I'm still not much of an oyster fan, though I can deal with the smaller ones, like Olympia and Malpeque. I like them best lightly cooked.

ENTERING VIPORE.

Winter
Menus
283

Ostriche alla Fiorentina

Florentine Oysters

(SERVES 4)

1½ pounds spinach, well washed, tough
    stems removed

3 tablespoons extra-virgin olive oil

2 cloves garlic, sliced

Salt and fresh ground black pepper, to
    taste

3 tablespoons freshly grated
    Parmigiano-Reggiano cheese

3 tablespoons dried bread crumbs

Pinch of grated nutmeg

16 oysters

2 tablespoons chopped fresh chives

Place the spinach, with the water still clinging to its leaves, in a pot large enough to hold it. Cook it, covered, over medium heat, stirring occasionally, until the spinach just wilts, about 7 minutes. Drain the spinach in a colander, pressing out the excess water with the back of a spoon, then transfer it to a cutting board and chop it roughly.

Put the olive oil and garlic in a medium sauté pan and heat. When the garlic begins to color, after about 5 minutes, add the spinach and cook it briefly, about 2 minutes, adding salt and pepper. Keep the spinach warm.

In a bowl, mix together the Parmigiano-Reggiano, bread crumbs, and nutmeg. Set it aside.

Preheat your broiler. Shuck the oysters. Wash and dry half the shells and discard the rest. Spoon some of the spinach into each shell, then top it with an oyster. Sprinkle each shell with some of the Parmigiano-Reggiano/bread crumb mixture and a little of the chopped chives. Place the oysters on a baking sheet and broil them until the crumbs are lightly browned, about 3 minutes. Serve.

Fusilli al Gorgonzola
Fusilli with Gorgonzola
(SERVES 4 AS AN APPETIZER)

3 quarts water

1½ tablespoons salt

½ pound fusilli

2 cloves garlic, chopped fine

1 tablespoon extra-virgin olive oil

6 ounces sweet Gorgonzola cheese

6 tablespoons homemade beef broth or
   water

5 tablespoons freshly grated
   Parmigiano-Reggiano cheese

1 tablespoon finely chopped fresh Italian
   parsley

Fresh ground black pepper, to taste

In a large pot, bring the water to a boil and add the salt and fusilli. In a saucepan, sauté the garlic in the olive oil over medium heat until the garlic starts to soften, 3 or 4 minutes. Reduce the heat to medium-low and add the Gorgonzola, and the broth, stirring until the cheese is melted.

When the fusilli is *al dente*, drain and mix it with the Gorgonzola sauce. Stir in 3 tablespoons of the Parmigiano-Reggiano, the parsley, and black pepper. Sprinkle each dish with a little of the remaining Parmigiano-Reggiano and serve.

Gorgonzola Dolce and *Naturale*

....

The first time I thought I had Gorgonzola, it wasn't Gorgonzola at all, but blue cheese, prepackaged in aluminum foil. Thinking this was the exalted Gorgonzola, I didn't understand what the fuss was about. That changed when I joined Linea Italia in Cucina, a chef and restaurateur's association dedicated to using natural ingredients. One of our members was Franco Colombani, who owned the restaurant Sole di Maleo, near the town of Gorgonzola. For every meeting, Franco would bring a sample of spectacular Gorgonzola, usually an artisan production that wasn't available on the market. One of my favorite ways to eat Gorgonzola Naturale is to layer it with mascarpone in a terrine and spread it on warm toast. Gorgonzola Dolce, which is younger and creamier is incredible stuffed into ripe, quartered figs. If you can't find Gorgonzola Naturale, Saga Blue or Stilton are good substitutes.

Filetto di Pesce al Forno con Timballo di Patate

Baked Fish Fillets with Potato Timbale

(SERVES 4)

5 tablespoons extra-virgin olive oil

3 tablespoons chopped fresh rosemary

2 tablespoons chopped fresh thyme

2 teaspoons fresh grated ginger

Salt and fresh ground black pepper, to
taste

4 (6-ounce) fillets of monkfish, salmon,
or red snapper

½ cup white wine

Potato Timbale (recipe follows)

4 cups mixed greens, washed and lightly
dressed

Mix together the olive oil, chopped herbs, ginger, and salt and pepper. Coat the fish fillets with this mixture, then cover and refrigerate them for 24 hours. The fish can be marinated for as few as three hours, but it will be less flavorful.

Preheat the oven to 375°. Drain the olive oil from the fish into an ovenproof sauté pan large enough to hold all the fish. (If there isn't enough oil to coat the bottom, add a little more.) Heat the olive oil over medium high, then add the fish, skin side down, and cook for 2 to 3 minutes.

Transfer the pan to the oven. After 5 minutes, add the white wine and flip the fish. Return the pan to the oven for another 4 or 5 minutes, depending on the thickness of the fish. To test if the fish is done, insert a toothpick near the spine and see if it is the temperature you wish. Remove the pan from the oven and serve the fillets with the timbale and a spray of salad.

Timballo di Patate

Potato Timbale

(SERVES 4–6)

8 tablespoons extra-virgin olive oil

½ cup chopped onion

½ cup cleaned shiitake mushrooms

⅓ cup *each* chopped red, green, and
   yellow bell pepper

¼ teaspoon chopped fresh thyme

2 teaspoons chopped garlic

1 pound (2 medium) potatoes, peeled
   and cut into 1-inch chunks

Salt and fresh ground black pepper, to
   taste

¼ teaspoon chopped fresh Italian
   parsley

¼ teaspoon chopped fresh rosemary

Preheat the oven to 400°. In an ovenproof sauté pan, heat 4 tablespoons of the olive oil for 1 minute, then add the vegetables and thyme and sauté over medium high for 1 minute. Add the garlic and sauté for another minute. Transfer the mixture to a plate and set it aside.

To the same pan, add the remaining 4 tablespoons of the olive oil and heat it over medium-high until hot, then add the potatoes and sauté until they are brown on all sides, about 5 minutes. Add the onion mixture. Add salt and pepper to taste, the parsley, and the rosemary, and sauté for another minute.

Place the pan in the oven for 15 to 20 minutes, until the potatoes are cooked through. Remove them and mash them with a fork. Fill a 9-inch quiche dish with the potatoes, lower the oven heat to 375°, and heat the timbale all the way through, about 5 minutes. Serve with the fish and the salad.

Non Brutti, Ma Buoni

Not Ugly, But Good Cookies

"Brutti ma buoni" (ugly but good) were cookies imported to Tuscany from Piedmont when Florence reigned briefly as Italy's capital. The town of Prato, which is between Lucca and Florence, calls them "the sister cookies" to their famous *cantuccini*. Usually *brutti ma buoni* are made with large pieces of almond and hazelnuts, but when Eileen was testing this recipe, she ground the nuts very fine. I liked the results and dubbed the cookies *"non brutti, ma buoni,"* Not ugly, but good. Serve them with almond ice cream.

(M A K E S   3 0   C O O K I E S)

....

3 egg whites

⅛ teaspoon cream of tartar

⅛ teaspoon salt

1 cup plus 2 tablespoons sugar

¾ cup blanched, toasted almonds, ground

¾ cup blanched, toasted hazelnuts, ground

Preheat the oven to 300°. Line a sheet pan with parchment paper. In an electric mixer, beat the egg whites on medium-low until frothy. Add the cream of tartar and the salt and beat well. Continue beating while adding the sugar in a steady, slow stream. When the sugar has been incorporated, turn the speed to high and mix for 5 minutes, until the mixture has become quite stiff, dense, and glossy. Fold in the ground nuts.

Drop spoonfuls of the dough, 2 inches apart, onto the sheet pan. Bake for 15 to 20 minutes, until the cookies are light brown. Let the cookies cool and store them in an airtight container.

Qualcosa di Crudo
Some Like It Raw

Carpaccio di Tonno	Tuna Carpaccio
Zuppa di Ceci	Chick-pea Soup
Branzino al Forno con Vegetali	Oven-Baked Sea Bass with Vegetables
Crostata con Pere al Vino Rosso	Wine-Poached Pears in a Cornmeal Crust

SUGGESTED WINES: IL VASARIO, BUONAMICO (GRAPE: PINOT BIANCO); CHARDONNAY
VIGNA REGIS, MONTEFILI (GRAPES: CHARDONNAY, SAUVIGNON BLANC, TRAMINER)

If you've ever spent time with Italians, you will know just how seriously we take food. Our pasta must be *al dente;* our olive oil, extra *vergine;* our *caffè, ristretto.* The best *sughi,* sauces, are made by *mamma, nonna,* or, best of all, *bisnonna* (great-grandmother): If you can't get your meals homemade, the next best thing is from a neighborhood trattoria. This is one of the dozens of reasons why I think Italian cooking is very tied to place. We never order risotto with saffron, the typical Milanese pasta, when we are in Naples; never order pesto in Florence; or spaghetti carbonara in Venice. Likewise, the only tuna we eat in Lucca is tinned, what we call *"sott'olio,"* "under oil," because the sea is sixty miles away, quite a distance when you were traveling the old way, by horse.

Having grown up in Lucca, at age thirty I had never tried raw fish, until a trip to New York, where some friends took me out for sushi. Stefano, who had been living in New York, ordered for the table, and, as a guest, I went along. But I was a little worried when the first thing set in front of me were garnet red strips of what appeared to be raw fish. I was told it was tuna, and not wanting to be difficult, I took a bite. It was very strange for me, bland. What it needed I thought was a little bread, but there was none.

As the meal went on, the fish, abetted by sake, went down a little easier. What amazed me most of all, was how much everyone else was enjoying their meal. A few days later, on my own, I tried another sushi restaurant, so I could taste the fish in a more professional way. Over the years, I tried lots of different raw fish dishes, and even tried to adapt a few for Vipore. To tell you the truth, they were never among the restaurant's best sellers, and eventually I gave up attempting to convince customers to try *pesce crudo*. However, when I moved to New York, I found a city gripped by raw fish mania, so I put a Tuscan spin on the fad.

Carpaccio di Tonno

Tuna Carpaccio

(S E R V E S   4)

½ pound sushi-quality tuna (4 pieces, 2 ounces each)

10 tablespoons extra-virgin olive oil

Juice of 1 lemon

2 cups washed mixed salad greens

Salt and fresh ground black pepper, to taste

½ cup finely chopped tomatoes

2 tablespoons finely chopped scallions (or fresh chives)

4 fresh basil leaves, chopped very fine

Grating of fresh ginger

Place each piece of tuna between 2 sheets of wax paper or plastic wrap and, with a flat mallet, pound each piece as thin as possible without tearing the paper. (This is a lot of work, and it will take you a while to get the hang of it.)

In a bowl, mix together 2 tablespoons of the olive oil and half the lemon juice. Mix with the salad greens. Scatter the greens over 4 plates. Lay a piece of tuna on top of each salad.

In a separate bowl, whisk together the remaining lemon juice with salt and pepper. Then beat in the remaining 8 tablespoons of olive oil and stir in the tomatoes, scallions, basil, and grated ginger. Spoon the sauce over the tuna and serve.

Zuppa di Ceci
Chick-pea Soup
(SERVES 6)

1 pound dried chick-peas

16 cups cold water

1 tablespoon salt, plus extra to taste

¼ cup chopped pancetta

1 cup chopped onion

2 tablespoons chopped garlic

½ cup chopped celery

1 cup chopped carrots

¼ cup extra-virgin olive oil

1 ounce dried porcini mushrooms
    soaked for ½ hour in ½ cup warm
    water

2 large tomatoes, or 2 cups crushed
    canned tomatoes

4 leaves Swiss chard, well-washed,
    leaves and stalks finely chopped

Fresh ground black pepper, to taste

4 slices Tuscan bread, toasted then
    rubbed with garlic

Rinse the chick-peas, picking them over to remove any pebbles. Soak them overnight in 8 cups of cold water. Drain the chick-peas, then add them to a large stockpot with 8 cups of fresh cold water. Bring the water to a boil and add the tablespoon of salt. Cover the pot and reduce the heat to very low. You will cook the beans for 3 hours.

Place the pancetta, onion, garlic, celery, and carrots in a large sauté pan with the olive oil. Heat over medium until the mixture starts to color, about 20 minutes. Add the mixture to the chick-peas after they have been cooking for 1½ hours. After 20 minutes, drain and add the reconstituted porcini. Strain the soaking liquid and add that, too. Puree the tomatoes in a food processor and add them to the soup. Add the Swiss chard, and salt and pepper to taste. Continue cooking the soup, covered, approximately 1 hour more.

(continued on next page)

When the soup has cooked for 3 hours, use a slotted spoon to remove 2 cups of the chick-peas. (If there is too much liquid, drain it off and reserve it. If you want a more liquid soup, you can add it back, later.) Transfer the remaining soup to a food processor and puree. Return the puree and the reserved chick-peas to the stockpot and mix. Cook for another 5 minutes. Spoon the soup over the slices of Tuscan toast and serve.

**MAMA PICKING
PLUMS IN THE
ORCHARD.**

Branzino al Forno con Vegetali

Oven-Baked Sea Bass with Vegetables

(SERVES 4)

Salt and fresh ground black pepper, to taste

4 (1¼-pound) whole sea bass, cleaned (you can use other whole fish such as red snapper)

4 sprigs fresh rosemary

4 sprigs fresh thyme

2 lemons, 1 cut into eight wedges, plus juice of ½ lemon (optional)

1 cup extra-virgin olive oil

½ cup white wine

Bowl of ice water

½ cup cauliflower florets

1 carrot, peeled and sliced thin

⅓ pound snow peas

1 stalk celery, sliced thin

4 cabbage leaves, chopped

3 cloves garlic, peeled and crushed

2 tomatoes, chopped

Salt and pepper the cavity of each fish and stuff each with a sprig of rosemary, a sprig of thyme, and a lemon wedge. Place the bass in a platter with ¾ cup of the olive oil and salt and pepper to taste, and marinate for at least 2 hours, refrigerated. (It's best if you can marinate it overnight.) Preheat the oven to 375°. Transfer the fish and its marinade to a baking dish and roast it for 10 minutes. Add the wine and return the fish to the oven. When the wine has evaporated, after about 10 minutes, the fish is ready.

While the fish cooks, prepare a bowl of ice water.

In a pot, steam the cauliflower, the carrot, the snow peas, the celery, and the cabbage for 3 or 4 minutes, then plunge them into the ice water. To a large sauté pan, add the remaining ¼ cup of olive oil and the garlic and cook over medium heat until the garlic is golden, about 5 minutes. Add the chopped tomatoes and cook less than a minute, then add the steamed vegetables, salt and cook for about 3 minutes. Remove the sea bass from the oven. Serve each portion with the vegetables and a wedge of lemon. You can squeeze the juice of ½ lemon over the vegetables if you want.

Crostata con Pere al Vino Rosso
Wine-Poached Pears in a Cornmeal Crust
(SERVES 8)

3 pounds pears

Juice and peel of 1 lemon

1 tablespoon whole black peppercorns

½ tablespoon whole cloves

1 tablespoon whole allspice berries

6 cups red wine

1¼ cups granulated sugar

2 sticks cinnamon

½ cup dried cranberries

1½ sticks (¾ cup) plus 1 tablespoon
    sweet butter, at room temperature

2 egg yolks

¼ teaspoon salt

1¼ cups flour

10 tablespoons finely ground cornmeal

2 tablespoons light brown sugar

Peel and core the pears, then cut them into large chunks. There should be about 6 cups. Rub them with the lemon juice so they don't turn brown.

Tie the peppercorns, cloves, and allspice berries in a piece of cheesecloth and place them in a large saucepan with the wine, 1 cup of the granulated sugar, the cinnamon, and lemon peel. Bring the wine to a boil and stir it to dissolve the sugar. Reduce the heat to a simmer and add the chunks of pear, poaching them until they are tender, 10 to 20 minutes, depending on the firmness of the pears.

One minute before you remove the pears, add the dried cranberries to the wine. Remove the cranberries and the pears with a slotted spoon. Reduce the syrup by half, another 5 minutes. Remove the cheesecloth with the spices, the cinnamon sticks, and the lemon peel and pour the syrup over the pears. Refrigerate the fruit in the syrup overnight.

When you are ready to bake, preheat the oven to 350°. Cream together the remaining ¼ cup of granulated sugar and ¾ cup of the butter. Beat in the egg yolks and the salt.

In a bowl, blend the flour and the cornmeal together and add it, mixing and pressing until a dough is formed. Refrigerate the dough for 10 minutes.

Divide the dough in two, one part slightly larger than the other and on a well-floured surface, roll out the larger part to $\frac{1}{8}$ inch thick. (The dough breaks easily, but it can be pinched back together with a little effort.) Fit the dough into a 9-inch pie plate. Roll out the remaining portion of the dough to $\frac{1}{8}$ inch thick. Arrange a layer of the pears in the pie shell, then sprinkle with the cranberries, a tablespoon of the brown sugar, and $\frac{1}{2}$ tablespoon of the remaining butter. Repeat the layers, then add the top crust, pinching together the edges to form a rim. Bake for 30 minutes, until golden brown. Let the pie cool completely before serving.

Casa Dolce Casa
Home Sweet Home

Peperoni Ripieni con Acciughe e Capperi	Peppers Stuffed with Anchovies and Capers
Spaghetti con Vongole	Spaghetti with Clams
Polletto con Mosto d'Uva	Baby Chicken in Grape Sauce
Torta Pinolata	Pine-nutty Cake

SUGGESTED WINES: TREBIANCO, RAMPOLLA (GRAPES: CHARDONNAY, TRAMINER, SAUVIGNON BLANC); CONCERTO, FONTERUTOLI (GRAPES: SANGIOVESE, CABERNET SAUVIGNON)

. . . .

During the Gulf War, it was lonely and miserable at Vipore. The weather was worse than it had been in years, and there were no clients. On one of those days that seemed like it would never end, my friends Gary and Julie Wagner called with an invitation. Why didn't I come visit them in Napa Valley?

I had met the Wagners through my friend, the writer Faith Willinger. They were great food lovers and, over the years, had visited Vipore a number of times. Their offer couldn't have been better timed. I couldn't wait to escape the tedium of Tuscany in that moment. Because of the war, the jumbo jet from London was practically empty. In all, I think we were twenty-three passengers. I stopped in New York to pick up my friend Annie Brody, and by Thursday midafternoon, the four of us were driving around Napa Valley together.

If I didn't know for sure that I had just spent almost thirteen hours flying, I would have sworn I had never left home. Napa Valley was incredibly beautiful and so much like Tuscany, I was doing double-takes left and right. The lush, rolling hills, the vineyards, the shimmering silver-green of the olive trees, the light, it was all amazingly familiar. As I listened to Gary and Julie explaining the sights, I thought I could blink and find myself going up the road to Emilio's house, or down the valley to Camay's. Everywhere we went it was the same. When we visited Beringer Vineyards, it was like Le Cantine del Marchese Antinori; as we pulled into the Grace Family Vineyards, I could have been at Lido di Bueta's.

There were some differences, of course. The one that impressed me most was the way the Grace Family Vineyards aged its Cabernet Sauvignon. Proprietor Richard Grace told me that after bottling his harvest, he called clients on a waiting list. If the client wanted the wine, he could come and pick it up and age it in his own cellar. Otherwise, Grace would call the next name on the list.

I had a few other entirely American experiences: The Wagners hosted a pot-luck dinner at their house; I took my first whirlpool bath; and one night, had a few too many Sangrita's—shots of tequila chased by peppery orange juice. I also visited the School for American Chefs, which was more impressive and efficient than any Italian cooking institute could hope to be. Even my own alma mater, Scuola Alberghiera in Montecatini couldn't compare, and I was secretly disappointed when they told me only American chefs were allowed to conduct classes at the school. I would have loved to teach a pasta course. On my last night, I reciprocated the California hospitality by bringing a little of Vipore to Napa: I cooked a fundraising dinner at the Joseph Phelps winery to benefit the Napa Valley museum.

As wonderful as my week had been, and as bored as I'd been at Vipore before the trip, I wasn't sorry when it came time to go home. Napa Valley was gorgeous, and the people gracious. But I couldn't get over the sense of *déja vù*. Everywhere I went in Napa, I saw Tuscany, I couldn't help it. As a Tuscan, I loved the Napa Valley, but what it made me long for was the real thing. As someone else once said, "There's no place like home."

Peperoni Ripieni con Acciughe e Capperi
Peppers Stuffed with Anchovies and Capers

The first stuffed peppers I ever ate were the handiwork of my friend Giacomo Bologna. This recipe is a tribute to him.

(MAKES 24 PEPPERS)

6 cups water

2 tablespoons salt

¼ cup red wine vinegar

24 cherry peppers, sweet or hot, as
desired

Extra-virgin olive oil, as needed

50 capers, drained

24–36 anchovy fillets, preserved in salt
or olive oil (if in salt, they need to
be rinsed)

In a large saucepan, bring the water to a boil and add the salt and vinegar. Add the peppers and boil for 5 to 7 minutes, depending on their size. They should soften only slightly. Drain the peppers and let them cool for 30 minutes.

With a sharp knife, carefully cut out the peppers' stems and with a small spoon, scoop out their seeds. Pour a little olive oil into each pepper and then pour it out onto a plate.

Roll 1, 2, or 3 capers inside an anchovy fillet (depending on the size of the peppers) and stuff them into the peppers. Place the peppers into a bowl or container and cover them with olive oil, including the olive oil you poured out onto the plate. Let the peppers sit for 2 to 3 days before serving. They will keep for 6 months in the refrigerator.

Spaghetti con Vongole
Spaghetti with Clams

For people I like, I shell the clams before finishing the pasta, since it's easier to eat that way. Make the sauce up to the point where you put the pasta on to cook. Instead of dropping the pasta in, let the sauce cool enough so you can handle the clams. Shell them, then proceed with the rest of the recipe.

(SERVES 4)

3 quarts water

1½ tablespoons salt, plus extra to taste

4 tablespoons extra-virgin olive oil

4 cloves garlic, peeled and crushed

¼ teaspoon crushed red pepper flakes

4 tablespoons chopped fresh Italian
    parsley

3 pounds baby clams, well washed
    (see Note page 302)

3 tablespoons dry white wine

½ pound spaghetti

Fresh ground black pepper, to taste

In a large pot, bring the water to a boil and add the 1½ tablespoons of salt.

Meanwhile, put the olive oil, garlic, red pepper flakes, and 2 tablespoons of the parsley in a pot large enough to hold all the clams, and heat over medium-high. Stir until the oil is well heated and the garlic starts to color, about 5 minutes, then add the clams. (If the oil gets too hot and the garlic starts to stick to the pan, add a splash of wine.) To help the clams open faster, cover the pot.

Meanwhile, drop the pasta into the boiling water. Add the wine to the clams, and shake the pan and stir until the wine reduces completely, about 4 minutes. When the pasta is very *al dente*, drain it, and add it to the pan with the clams. Continue to cook for 5 minutes. Add the remaining 2 tablespoons of parsley, and salt and pepper to taste, and serve.

(continued on next page)

NOTE: When you buy the clams, they should be alive. Rap on a shell with your knuckle and the clam should move. When you get the clams home, first rinse them well. Then place an inverted plate on the bottom of a very large bowl. Fill the bowl with the clams, then add water to cover and about two tablespoons of sea salt. Let the clams soak for 2 to 3 hours, stirring the water occasionally with a long spoon. The clams will spit out the sand in their shells and the sand will get trapped under the plate. When you remove the clams, be careful not to jostle the plate or the sand will be released.

MAMA MAKING PEAS AND POTATOES AT VIPORE.

Polletto con Mosto d'Uva

Baby Chicken in Grape Sauce

(SERVES 4)

4 (22-ounce) baby chickens (or Cornish
    hens)

4 sprigs fresh thyme, leaves stripped
    and chopped

4 sprigs fresh rosemary, leaves stripped
    and chopped

8 fresh sage leaves, chopped

4 sprigs fresh oregano, leaves stripped
    and chopped

4 cloves garlic, chopped

1 teaspoon crushed red pepper flakes

Salt and fresh ground black pepper, to
    taste

1½ cups red wine

1 tablespoon sugar

1 tablespoon red wine vinegar

Large bunch seedless red grapes,
    removed from the stem

2–3 tablespoons extra-virgin olive oil

½ cup flour

Cut the chickens open along their backbones and flatten them out on your kitchen counter. Cover the chickens with a kitchen towel, then pound them lightly with a meat mallet. Wash and pat the birds dry.

In a small bowl, mix together the chopped herbs, garlic, and red pepper flakes. Season the chickens on both sides with salt and pepper. With your fingertips, rub the herb mixture into the flesh. Place the chickens in a bowl, cover them, and let them marinate in the refrigerator overnight. (If you don't have time, you don't have to marinate. The chicken will be good, but a little less flavorful.)

When you are ready to cook, pour the red wine into a medium saucepan and add the sugar, red wine vinegar, and grapes and bring to a simmer over medium heat. Cook the grapes for approximately 30 minutes, then set them aside.

Preheat the oven to 400°. In a large, ovenproof sauté pan, heat the olive oil

(continued on next page)

over medium-high until it becomes very hot. Flour the skin side of the chickens, shaking off any excess. Slide the chickens, skin side down, into the pan. Be careful, the oil may splatter. Shake the pan to keep the chickens from sticking to the bottom. When the skin is browned, after 4 or 5 minutes, turn the chickens and brown the other side, another 5 minutes. Turn off the heat, flip the chickens again, and pour the grape sauce over them. Transfer the pan to the oven and bake the chickens for 35 to 40 minutes. Test to make sure they're cooked through (when pricked with a fork, the juices should run clear). Place the chickens on a plate, skin side up, then pour the sauce over and around them.

**A LOCAL BUTCHER
SHOP.**

Torta Pinolata

Pine-nutty Cake

(SERVES 8)

....

¾ cup sugar

6 tablespoons sweet butter

1 egg plus 4 egg yolks

2 tablespoons freshly grated lemon zest

1 cup plus 2 tablespoons flour

½ teaspoon salt

½ cup pine nuts

Preheat the oven to 350°. Butter an 8-inch cake pan.

In a bowl, cream together the sugar and butter until the mixture is light and fluffy. Beat in the egg and the yolks, one at a time, blending well after each addition. Add the grated lemon zest, flour, and the salt and blend well.

Pour the mixture into the cake pan and sprinkle the pine nuts uniformly over the top. Bake the cake for approximately 35 minutes, until golden brown. Cool, slice, and serve.

8

L'Arrivo a New York
Arriving in New York

Insalata di Ceci e Porri	Chick-pea and Leek Salad
Pasta con Funghi Trifolati	Pasta with Mushroom Sauce
Coniglio alla Cacciatora	Rabbit, Hunter's Style
Crostata di Mele	Country Apple Tart

SUGGESTED WINES: CHARDONNAY, ISOLE OLENA (GRAPE: CHARDONNAY); BRUNELLO DI MONTALCINO, LA PIEVE DI SANTA RESTITUITA (GRAPE: SANGIOVESE)

Coming from a small town in the Italian countryside, I had a lot to adjust to in New York, and nowhere as much as in the kitchen. In my thirty-three years in Pieve Santo Stefano, I was always aware of the season. Spring meant I could get artichokes and zucchini. Summer meant tomatoes; fall, pears and apples. In New York, I felt disoriented. No matter what the month, I could get any vegetable known—broccoli, green beans, bell peppers. Tomatoes in January! I knew they came from places where they were in season, like Chile or New Zealand, but it seemed incredible. Winter in Tuscany essentially meant cooking without vegetables. For example, starting in November, I used mostly potatoes and dried legumes like chick-peas and lentils. When I wanted tomatoes, I used the ones I had put up in late August. (Like my mother, I took batches of perfectly ripe tomatoes, cut them in half, and put them, with some fresh basil, in a heatproof jar that sealed hermetically. Then I immersed the jar in cold water, brought it to a boil, and heated it for 40 minutes. When I opened the jar in mid-February, I was treated to a whiff of summer.)

Even the seasonal produce I got in New York wasn't the same. I found American fruits and vegetables larger and less flavorful than Italian fruits and vegetables. Basil

MY FIRST TRIP TO NEW YORK.

here had huge leaves, and a slightly minty flavor; spinach and zucchini had a higher water content; artichokes were bigger and tougher. To get the same results with recipes I'd used for years at home, I had to experiment and adjust constantly. At the same time, I started to use a lot of produce, spices, and herbs that I had never tried before. Two of my favorites became ginger and lemongrass, which I added generously to many dishes for an unexpected twist. I also grew to love yucca, which I served fried like a potato, or as a complement to fish. In fact, almost every obstacle turned into a way for me to keep expanding and innovating in the kitchen.

Insalata di Ceci e Porri

Chick-pea and Leek Salad

(SERVES 4–5)

. . . .

2 cups dried chick-peas

12 cups cold water

4 cloves garlic, peeled

4 sprigs fresh oregano

1 tablespoon salt, plus extra to taste

2 leeks, well washed and sliced thin
(you can use the white and half the
green part of the leek)

2 plum tomatoes, seeded and diced

6 tablespoons finely chopped fresh
Italian parsley

6 tablespoons extra-virgin olive oil

1 tablespoon red wine vinegar

Fresh ground black pepper, to taste

Rinse the chick-peas, picking them over to remove any pebbles. Soak them overnight in 6 cups of cold water, then drain them and place them in a large saucepan with 6 cups of fresh cold water, the garlic, and the oregano. When the water boils, add the tablespoon of salt and reduce to a simmer. Cook the chick-peas until they are soft, about 1 hour. Drain them, discarding the garlic and the oregano.

Put the chick-peas in a large bowl and toss them gently with the leeks, tomatoes, parsley, olive oil, vinegar, and salt and pepper to taste. Serve at once.

. . . .

Ninety percent of the oregano that gets used in Tuscany is dried, and it's rarely added to anything but pizza sauce. I like fresh oregano. Tastewise, it is very similar to marjoram, which is in the same botanical family. Marjoram is more delicate and sweet (you should add it toward the end of cooking so it doesn't disintegrate), oregano, more hardy and pungent. Both are nice in tomato-based dishes, and I always use a stalk of one or the other when simmering chick-peas; they give the beans more flavor.

Pasta con Funghi Trifolati

Pasta with Mushroom Sauce

(SERVES 4)

3 quarts water

1½ tablespoons salt, plus extra to taste

¼ cup extra-virgin olive oil

1½ tablespoons *each* finely chopped
   garlic, fresh oregano, and fresh
   Italian parsley

4 cups mixed mushrooms (cremini,
   shiitake, oyster, portobello), cleaned
   and chopped into medium pieces

1 cup homemade vegetable broth or
   water

½ pound spaghetti or other pasta

1 cup peeled and seeded fresh plum
   tomatoes

Fresh ground black pepper, to taste

4 tablespoons freshly grated
   Parmigiano-Reggiano cheese

In a large pot, bring the water to a boil. Add the 1½ tablespoons of salt.

In a frying pan large enough to hold all the ingredients, heat the olive oil and garlic over medium. When the garlic begins to color, after 5 minutes, add the oregano and parsley. Cook for 1 minute, then add the mushrooms. Cook for 7 minutes, then add the vegetable broth.

Add the spaghetti to the boiling water. Add the tomatoes and salt and pepper to taste to the mushroom mixture. Cook for 8 to 12 minutes, until the mushrooms are soft and cooked brown. The mixture should not be too wet or too dry.

When the spaghetti is *al dente*, drain it and mix it with the mushrooms and grated cheese. Serve immediately.

Coniglio alla Cacciatora
Rabbit, Hunter's Style

Eat this dish the way we do in Italy, with your hands.

(S E R V E S   3   T O   4)

10 cloves garlic, peeled

6 tablespoons extra virgin olive oil

1 (3-pound) rabbit, cut in pieces

2 tablespoons chopped fresh sage

2 tablespoons chopped fresh rosemary

1 cup white wine

3 cups crushed canned tomatoes

½ cup pitted black olives

Salt and fresh ground black pepper to
taste

In a large sauté pan, sauté the garlic in the olive oil until the cloves turn golden, about 5 minutes. Add the rabbit, sage, and rosemary. Cook approximately 15 minutes, stirring well so the rabbit browns evenly. Add the white wine and let it reduce completely, about 10 minutes, then remove the rabbit from the pan with a slotted spoon.

To the same pan, add the tomatoes and cook them for 8 to 10 minutes. Return the rabbit to the pan, mix well with the sauce, reduce the heat to low, and simmer, covered, for 10 minutes. Uncover the pan, add the olives, and return the heat to medium. Simmer another 5 to 10 minutes, until the meat is cooked and tender and the tomato sauce is thick, not watery. Season with salt and pepper to taste. Serve.

Crostata di Mele

Country Apple Tart

(S E R V E S 8)

....

1 recipe Pastry Crust (page 127)

2–3 slightly tart apples, such as
 Macintosh or Granny Smith
 (1½–2 cups sliced)

1 recipe Pastry Cream (page 87)

2 tablespoons sugar

Preheat the oven to 350°. Bake the piecrust as directed, leaving the oven on while the crust cools.

To assemble the tart, peel and slice the apples. Spread the pastry cream inside the pastry shell to make a layer ¾ inch deep. Arrange the sliced apples on top of the cream filling and sprinkle them with the sugar. Cover the tart with aluminum foil and bake for 30 minutes. Remove the foil and bake for another 10 to 15 minutes. The tart is ready when lightly browned on top. Serve the tart warm or at room temperature.

CERCANDO CASA

Apartment Hunting

Uova con Tartufo Bianco	Eggs with White Truffle
Tagliatelle con Zucca, Tartufo Nero,	Tagliatelle with Butternut Squash,
e Prosciutto	Black Truffle, and Prosciutto
Faraona con Funghi e Polenta	Guinea Hen with Wild Mushrooms and
	Polenta
Bigné al Cioccolato	Beignets with Chocolate Sauce

SUGGESTED WINES: CHIANTI CLASSICO, FONTODI (GRAPE: SANGIOVESE);
MAESTRO RARO, FELSINA (GRAPE: CABERNET SAUVIGNON)

··················

When I first started working in New York, I was spending a week a month in Italy, and often put in eighty-hour weeks, both here and when I was home at Vipore. I barely had time to apartment hunt in New York's famously tight housing market, but I knew I couldn't live out of a suitcase forever. So one morning, after a long flight from Rome, I went straight from the airport to my real estate agent. I was in his office maybe three minutes when he began looking at me strangely. I didn't understand why, but said nothing.

He ushered me into a cab—I paid the fare—and we headed to the first apartment, off Lexington Avenue. The landlady, a friendly blonde named Sandra, showed us a spacious studio, which I liked. But Sandra got that same strange look on her face as the real estate agent. She began checking in corners, closets, cabinets, and then her friendliness wore off. I felt my lease evaporating. This scenario repeated itself at the next address. Finally, at our third appointment, in front of the building manager, the agent turned to me and, rather hesitantly, said, "I'm sorry to ask, but do you have a strange odor?"

I looked down. I looked normal. The building manager broke into a smile and tapped his nose. "That's not strange, it's truffle. I got a nose like a *trifülao.*" His grandfather was Italian, he explained, an avid truffle hunter from Alba. I laughed. Before I left Italy, I'd wrapped a truffle in a paper towel and put it in my pocket to bring to a friend. I'd completely forgotten about it. I must have radiated funk.

Unfortunately, the apartment the *trifülao's* grandson had was on an airshaft, because I could have had it for a song. Luckily I found something later in the week—after I took my pants to the dry cleaner.

PLUCKING THRUSHES FOR VIPORE.

Uova con Tartufo Bianco

Eggs with White Truffle

(SERVES 4)

4 tablespoons extra-virgin olive oil

8 eggs

Salt and fresh ground black pepper, to taste

2 ounces white truffle, cleaned (this depends on how much money you've got: in season, white truffles go for about $80 an ounce; you can get by with 1 ounce)

In a large non-stick frying pan, heat the olive oil over high. Break the eggs into a bowl but do not scramble them. When the olive oil is hot, remove the pan from the heat and pour in the eggs. Return the pan to low heat.

With a fork, carefully scramble the whites to ensure more uniform cooking. Do not break the yolks. (Or do this in small pans if you can coordinate.) Add salt to the whites and pepper to the yolks. Slide the eggs onto a large platter. If you want a participatory meal, let everyone break the yolks together and shave the truffles over them. If you've fried the eggs separately, give everyone his or her own dish.

Tagliatelle con Zucca, Tartufo Nero, e Prosciutto

Tagliatelle with Butternut Squash, Black Truffle, and Prosciutto

(SERVES 4 AS AN APPETIZER)

1 butternut squash, cut into 3 to 4
   pieces and seeded

1 tablespoon chopped garlic

1/2 cup extra-virgin olive oil

2 tablespoons chopped fresh sage leaves

5 tablespoons thinly sliced strips of
   prosciutto

Fresh ground black pepper, to taste

3 quarts water

1 1/2 tablespoons salt, plus extra to taste

1/2 pound tagliatelle or fettuccine

1 medium black truffle, cleaned and
   shaved into slices

3 tablespoons chopped fresh Italian
   parsley

4 tablespoons freshly grated
   Parmigiano-Reggiano cheese

1 small white truffle, cleaned, or 1
   tablespoon truffle oil (optional)

Preheat the oven to 375°. Place the squash on an oiled baking dish, cut side down, and bake it until it is tender, at least 35 minutes. When the squash has cooled, scoop out the flesh and cut it into 1/2 inch cubes.

In a large frying pan over medium heat, sauté the garlic in the olive oil until the garlic starts to color, about 5 minutes.

To the garlic, add the sage, squash, prosciutto, and salt and pepper to taste and cook until the prosciutto is no longer translucent, about 5 minutes. In a large pot, bring the water to a boil. Add the 1 1/2 tablespoons of salt and the tagliatelle. When the pasta is very *al dente*, drain and add to the sauce. Add the black truffle and 1 1/2 tablespoons of the parsley, and cook for 3 to 4 minutes. Add the Parmigiano-Reggiano and the remaining 1 1/2 tablespoons of parsley and mix well.

If you want, you can shave white truffle slices on top or drizzle each plate with a tiny bit of truffle oil, but it's not necessary. Serve immediately.

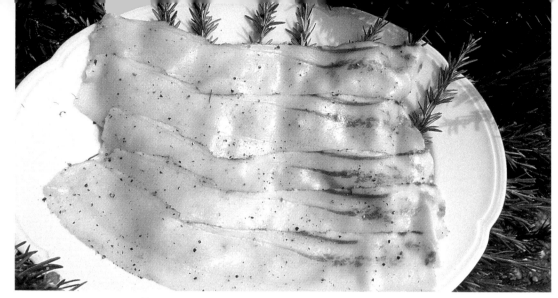

TUSCAN LARD. I CALL THIS "WHITE PROSCIUTTO."

Prosciutto

*T*his most famous of the Italian cured meats, made from the fresh ham of the pig's hindquarters, dates back to Roman times. While prosciutto is popular all over Italy, it figures most prominently in the cooking of three areas: San Daniele in Friuli, which produces what many consider the best prosciutto; in Parma and Langhirano, both in Emilia Romagna; and in Norcia in Umbria, historically, the center of sausage making in Italy. (The Norcia-style prosciutto became so popular that today, the butcher who makes sausage in Italy is called a "norcino.") We also make prosciutto in Tuscany, usually in the Norcia style. One of my favorite ways to eat it is on a slice of fettunta, or garlic bread. Usually the prosciutto found in America is prosciutto di Parma, which is sweet and mild.

Alternately, you can use speck, a deboned prosciutto that is spiced with garlic, salt, pepper, and aromatic herbs, pressed for a month, then smoked at a low temperature. It is a favorite cold-weather snack in Alto Adige. I like it on bread, sprinkled with chopped fresh rosemary.

Faraona con Funghi e Polenta

Guinea Hen with Wild Mushrooms and Polenta

(S E R V E S 4)

....

11 tablespoons extra-virgin olive oil

2 tablespoons finely chopped garlic, plus
    10 whole cloves, peeled and crushed

3 tablespoons finely chopped fresh
    oregano

3 tablespoons finely chopped fresh
    Italian parsley

6 cups mixed mushrooms (cremini,
    shiitake, oyster, portobello), cleaned
    and chopped into medium pieces

1½ cups homemade vegetable broth or
    water

1½ cups peeled and seeded fresh
    tomatoes

Salt and fresh ground black pepper, to
    taste

Flour, for dusting

1 (3½–4-pound) Guinea hen, cut into
    pieces

3 tablespoons chopped fresh sage

3 tablespoons chopped fresh rosemary

½ cup white wine

3 cups polenta (page 198)

Preheat the oven to 325°. In a large sauté pan, heat 5 tablespoons of the olive oil over medium. When the olive oil is hot, add the chopped garlic. When the garlic begins to color, after 1 minute, add the oregano and parsley. Cook for 1 minute, then add the mushrooms. Cook until all the mushrooms have started to brown, about 7 minutes, then add the vegetable broth or water and mix. Turn the heat to medium-high and cook for 5 minutes, then add the tomatoes and salt and pepper. Stirring occasionally, cook for 15 to 20 minutes, until the mushrooms are soft and cooked brown, and the mixture is not too wet or too dry. Set aside.

Lightly flour the Guinea hen pieces. Place the remaining 6 tablespoons of the oil, the 10 cloves of crushed garlic, the sage, and rosemary in a large ovenproof sauté pan and heat over medium. When the garlic starts to color, after 5 minutes, add the Guinea

(continued on next page)

hen pieces, skin side down. Brown for about 5 minutes, then flip, and brown the other side, also 5 minutes. Remove the pan from the heat, add the white wine, return to the heat, and reduce completely, about 1 minute. Pour the mushroom mixture over the hen, making sure the sauce is evenly distributed.

Cover the pan and transfer it to the oven. Bake for 30 minutes, or until the hen is cooked through. Transfer the hen and the mushrooms to dinner plates and serve with the polenta.

Bigné al Cioccolato

Beignets with Chocolate Sauce

Beignets are considered French, but they were actually invented in Florence and exported to France by a Florentine chef in the court of Catherine de Médicis. Back then, *bigné* were called *pasta siringa* (syringe pastry) because chefs used a syringe to shoot the cream into the puff pastry. I also like the puffs sliced in half and filled with good *gelato* instead of pastry cream.

(MAKES 32 PASTRY PUFFS)

1 cup water

1½ sticks (¾ cup) butter, cut into
    1-inch cubes

¼ teaspoon salt

1½ cups plus 2 tablespoons flour

2 tablespoons sugar (optional)

6 eggs, at room temperature

1 recipe Pastry Cream (page 87)

1 recipe Chocolate Sauce (page 320)

Preheat the oven to 400°. Butter a baking sheet.

Place the water and butter in a medium saucepan and heat over medium until the water boils and the butter melts, about 5 minutes. Remove the pan from the heat and add the salt and the flour all at once, stirring until a dough ball forms. Return to the heat for 1 minute, stirring, to dry out the dough. If you want a sweeter dough, add the sugar here and blend well. Let the mixture cool slightly, while stirring 2 to 3 minutes.

Beat in the eggs, one at a time, until the dough is shiny and smooth. Drop the dough by the tablespoon, 2 inches apart, on the baking sheet. Place a pan of water on the bottom rack of the oven. Bake the puffs on the middle rack of the oven for 5 minutes, then reduce the heat to 350°. Continue baking until the puffs are firm and golden, about 15 minutes. Let them cool completely on a rack.

(continued on next page)

If you have a pastry bag, fill it with the pastry cream. With a knife, make a small slit in the bottom of a puff and pipe in a little of the cream. (If you don't have a pastry bag, you can use a serrated knife to cut the puffs in half and spoon a little of the cream between the halves. Replace the tops and arrange the puffs on a plate.) If you do this too long before you serve them, the puffs will get soggy. It's best to fill them right before you serve them. When you are ready to bring the plate to the table, spoon the chocolate sauce over the filled puffs.

Salsa di Cioccolato
Chocolate Sauce

2½ ounces unsweetened chocolate, chopped

2½ tablespoons unsweetened cocoa powder

Up to ¼ cup water

½ cup sugar

⅝ cup heavy cream

In the top of a double boiler set over simmering water, mix the chocolate, the cocoa powder, and water stirring constantly as the chocolate melts. The sauce will become thick and difficult to stir. Remove it from the heat and continue stirring, then add the sugar. Return the sauce to the heat and stir until the sugar dissolves, making sure to get all the lumps out. Add the cream and combine until smooth.

Remove the chocolate from the heat and let it cool a few minutes before spooning it over the *semifreddo*.

La Squadra di Calcio
The Soccer Team

Piccolo Cibreo	Tuscan-Style Chicken Livers
Lasagna di Vegetali	Vegetable Lasagna
Pollo, Tacchino, Agnello, e Manzo Arrosto con Insalata di Rinforzo	Mixed Grill of Chicken, Turkey, Lamb and Beef with Make-You-Strong Salad
Semifreddo con Granella e Salsa di Cioccolato	Semifreddo with Ground Nut Brittle and Chocolate Sauce

SUGGESTED WINES: TRAPPOLINE, BADIA A COLTIBUONO (GRAPES: PINOT BIANCO, TREBBIANO, AND MALVASIA); ORNELLAIA, LODOVICO ANTINORI (GRAPES: CABERNET SAUVIGNON, MERLOT CABERNET FRANC)

When Papa and Mama were growing up, the small town rivalries in and around Garfagnana, Mama's village, and Monte San Quirico, Papa's, were very intense. The locals fought about everything, from who had the best rabbits to who had the juiciest tomatoes. Occasionally, things got out of hand, especially before the Santa Croce agriculture fair. Once, I'm told, old Guido was lured away from his farm for an afternoon by a mysterious woman. When he returned, he discovered that his 600-pound prize-winning boar had been just as mysteriously replaced with a 500-pound sow. Another time, Marco woke up to find his whole pumpkin crop uprooted. Even young kids could be mean-spirited in their rivalries. Papa tells me he and his friends used to ambush boys from other villages who came to San Quirico to *far' l'amore* (what they called dating) with local girls. They pelted them with stones and rotten fruit until they turned back. I suppose you could say it was small-time chauvinism run amok, but I know the old-timers had fun.

(continued on next page)

By the time I got to be a teenager, the rivalries played themselves out in a less agrarian way, usually on a soccer field. The teams—there were twelve in our area—were sponsored by local bars, and the bars themselves doubled as commando centers. During the week we'd hold meetings, strategy, and practice sessions, then on Sunday afternoons, when everyone from the surrounding villages was free, we'd have tournaments.

The games were raucous and high spirited, sometimes even a little violent. Many a game was broken up by a referee ejecting players for fouls, foul language, or both. I personally never finished a game, but then again, I wasn't very good. They only put up with me because Papa was the president of the Vipore team. Once, after the coach pulled me from the field for blowing a play, I got so angry, I jumped the coach and was kicked off the field.

Vipore was the sponsor of the Pieve Santo Stefano team. Because everyone loved the restaurant, our team was very popular. We even had a few semi-pros and pros from national teams like Juventus and Torino. Adding to our allure was the victory party Mama and Papa would throw after every game, win or lose. Sometimes up to a hundred people showed up. The parties were the greatest. We'd have them on the hill behind the restaurant, and they always lasted well into the night. There'd be lasagna by the meter, enough grilled ribs, chicken, steak, and lamb chops to feed a Roman army, and enough *vino*, *rosso* and *bianco*, red and white wine, to erase any simmering rivalries. At least until the pregame warm-up the following Sunday.

AN EARLY VIPORE SOCCER TEAM. I'M THE LITTLE GUY HOLDING THE CUP.

Piccolo Cibreo
Tuscan-Style Chicken Livers

Cibreo is what we call *un piatto tipico Toscano*, a typical Tuscan dish. Out in the country, a farmer's wife would make it with rooster crest and giblets, but since rooster innards (much less the crests) aren't readily available in the United States, I invented an American variation, which is why this *cibreo* is *piccolo*, or small.

(S E R V E S 4)

1 pound chicken livers

5 tablespoons flour

3 tablespoons extra-virgin olive oil

½ cup chopped red onion

2 tablespoons chopped fresh sage

¼ teaspoon crushed red pepper flakes

1 tablespoon chopped garlic

Salt and fresh ground black pepper, to taste

2 tablespoons drained capers

6 anchovy fillets, chopped

¾ cup Vin Santo (or dry Marsala)

1 small tomato, chopped

4 slices Tuscan bread, toasted and
   rubbed with cut garlic

3 tablespoons chopped fresh Italian
   parsley

Wash the chicken livers, dry well and dust them with flour. Pour the olive oil into a large sauté pan and add the onion, sage, red pepper flakes, and garlic, and sauté over medium heat. When the onion is golden, after 6 to 8 minutes, add the chicken livers. Cook for 7 to 8 minutes, stirring so they brown evenly. Season them with salt and pepper, then add the capers, anchovies, and Vin Santo. Cook for another 6 to 8 minutes. Add the chopped tomato and cook for 8 to 10 minutes more.

The dish should be slightly soupy. If it starts to dry out, add a little bit of water. Spoon the livers over the toast, sprinkle with the chopped parsley, and serve.

Lasagna di Vegetali

Vegetable Lasagna

(SERVES 12 AS AN APPETIZER)

4 tablespoons extra-virgin olive oil

2 tablespoon chopped garlic

1 teaspoon crushed red pepper flakes

3 tablespoons dry white wine

1 cup thinly sliced onion

1 cup sliced celery

1 cup thinly sliced carrots

1 cup well washed and sliced leeks, white part only

1 cup trimmed and sliced zucchini

1 cup salted, rinsed, dried, and sliced eggplant

¼ cup seeded and sliced red bell peppers

¼ cup seeded and sliced yellow bell peppers

Fresh ground black pepper, to taste

4 tablespoons salt

2 tablespoons finely chopped fresh basil

1 tablespoon chopped fresh oregano

1 tablespoon chopped fresh thyme

3 cups *Pommarola* (see page 174) or drained, canned Italian tomatoes

6 quarts water

1 pound lasagna noodles

2½ cups Béchamel (recipe follows)

1 cup freshly grated Parmigiano-Reggiano cheese

Make sure all of the vegetables are cut to a uniform thickness. In a heavy sauté pan large enough to hold all the vegetables, heat 3 tablespoons of the olive oil over medium until it gets hazy. Add the garlic and sauté until it starts to color, about 5 minutes. Add the red pepper flakes and the white wine (be careful, it may flame up for a brief moment until the alcohol evaporates). When the wine reduces, after about 2 minutes, add the following vegetables, in order: the onion, celery, carrots, leeks, zucchini, eggplant, and the bell peppers. Cook each vegetable for approximately 1 minute before adding the next. Add the black pepper and a tablespoon of the salt. Cook the mixture for 5 minutes more. Then add the basil, oregano, and thyme and cook for 5 minutes. Add the *pommarola* and cook for another 5 minutes. Set aside.

Bring the water to a boil in a large pot, add the remaining 3 tablespoons of salt and drop in the lasagna noodles. When the noodles are very *al dente*, drain them, and plunge them into an ice water bath to stop them from cooking. Lay them out on kitchen towels to drain.

Preheat the oven to 350°. Oil a 13-x-9-inch baking dish with the remaining tablespoon of olive oil. Spoon a little Béchamel sauce on the bottom of the pan. Cover the bottom with sheets of pasta, side by side, draping it up the sides, and over the edge of the pan. Trim the pasta to the size of the pan. Spread a layer of Béchamel over the pasta. Add a layer of the vegetable/tomato mixture, and sprinkle with Parmigiano-Reggiano. Repeat the process until all the ingredients have been used up. The top layer should be pasta, a very thick layer of Béchamel, and Parmigiano-Reggiano. (You can prepare the lasagna up to this point, then refrigerate it, and cook it when you are ready to serve, a day later if you like. An alternative is that after it is cooked, you can cut it into individual portions, wrap in foil, and freeze it. The pieces can be placed directly into the oven to reheat.) Bake for approximately 30 minutes, until the lasagna is heated through and the top begins to turn golden.

Besciamella
Béchamel

(MAKES 2 ¹/₂ CUPS)

6 tablespoons sweet butter

4¹/₂ tablespoons all-purpose flour

3 cups milk

Pinch of grated nutmeg

Pinch of ground cinnamon

Pinch of white pepper

Pinch of salt

In a heavy-bottomed medium saucepan, melt the butter over low heat. Add the flour, stirring constantly to incorporate it well and prevent lumps. Do not let the flour brown, otherwise your sauce will be pasty tasting. In another pan, heat the milk, but do not let it boil. While stirring the butter and flour mixture, add the hot milk all at once. Add the nutmeg, cinnamon, white pepper, and salt. Turn the heat to medium-high and whisk constantly until the mixture boils, then thickens. Cook at a simmer for 5 minutes, then remove from the heat.

For almost three hundred years, the world has called the popular white sauce of French cuisine, Béchamel, after Louis de Bechameil, a butler to Louis XIV. But Bechameil had nothing to do with the invention of this versatile white sauce. According to Italian cooking books from the renaissance period, biancomangiare or "white food," already existed in the 1300s. One recipe, by Anonimo Toscano, an "anonymous Tuscan," calls for combining rice flour with goat, sheep, or almond milk. Legend has it that Catherine de Médicis, when she moved to France to marry Henry II, brought the recipe with her and taught her chef how to make a sauce she called Colla—in modern Italian, "glue."

Pollo, Tacchino, Agnello, e Manzo Arrosto con Insalata di Rinforzo

Mixed Grill of Chicken, Turkey, Lamb, and Beef with Make-You-Strong Salad

(SERVES 4 TO 5)

4 lamb chops (loin or rib), trimmed of fat

1 pound boneless shell steak, cut into 4 pieces

Salt and fresh ground black pepper, to taste

2 tablespoons extra-virgin olive oil

8 cloves garlic, chopped

4 sprigs fresh rosemary, chopped

4 sprigs fresh thyme, chopped

1 can beer

4 chicken thighs

4 turkey wings

Make-You-Strong Salad (recipe follows)

Rub the lamb chops and steaks with salt and pepper and drizzle them with olive oil. Mix together the garlic and the herbs and rub half the mixture into the lamb chops and steaks.

Pour the beer into a large bowl and add the chicken and turkey, the remaining garlic-herb mixture, and salt and pepper. Let all the meat marinate for 2 hours in the refrigerator.

Heat the grill or broiler and cook the meat to desired doneness—approximately 4 minutes per side for the lamb chops (for medium-rare), 4 to 5 minutes per side for the strip steak (for medium-rare), and 15 minutes per side for the chicken. (If you broil the meat, it will take slightly less time than on the grill.) Serve with the salad.

Insalata di Rinforzo
Make-You-Strong Salad
. . . .

1 quart water

8 shallots, peeled

1 head cauliflower, broken into florets

2 small zucchini, cut into 3-x-1/2-inch
   lengths

1 yellow bell pepper, halved and seeded

1 red bell pepper, halved and seeded

3 tablespoons pitted, halved, green
   olives

3 tablespoons pitted, halved Italian
   black olives

10 cornichons, cut in half

2 tablespoons drained capers

4 anchovy fillets, chopped

3 tablespoons red wine vinegar

Salt and fresh ground black pepper, to
   taste

6 tablespoons extra-virgin olive oil

2 tablespoons chopped fresh Italian
   parsley

Bring the water to boil in a saucepan and add the shallots. Cook them until tender, 15 to 20 minutes, depending on their size. Mix together the cauliflower and zucchini and steam them until they are tender-crisp, about 5 minutes.

Preheat the broiler. Place the peppers, skinside up, 2 to 3 inches from the heat and watch carefully. When the skin blackens, turn them over and blacken on the other side. Place the peppers in a closed plastic bag for 15 minutes. Peel off the skin and cut the peppers into chunks.

Toss all the vegetables, olives, cornichons, capers, and anchovies together in a large bowl. In a small bowl, whisk the red wine vinegar with salt and pepper. Whisk in the olive oil in a thin, steady stream. Add the parsley, and pour the dressing over the salad. Toss well and serve warm or at room temperature, with the mixed grill.

Semifreddo con Granella e Salsa di Cioccolato

Semifreddo with Ground Nut Brittle and Chocolate Sauce

Semifreddo, which means "almost frozen," unites the creamy coldness of gelato with the airy lightness of mousse. I grew up on it, and it's added more than a handful around my midriff. The *granella*, a ground-up nut brittle, gives this *semifreddo* a tasty candy-bar crunch. (If you don't want to make your own *granella*, you can buy a bar of peanut brittle and a bar of almond brittle, break them up, and grind them in a food processor.) For a really decadent flourish, serve the *semifreddo* with warm chocolate sauce and strawberries.

(SERVES 8)

3 medium eggs, separated
6½ tablespoons sugar
½ cup *Granella* (recipe follows)
1½ cups heavy cream

⅓ cup water
Chocolate Sauce (page 320)
3 cups fresh washed strawberries
(optional)

In a bowl, beat the egg yolks with 2½ tablespoons of the sugar until they are pale. Add the *granella* and mix well. In the bowl of an electric mixer, whip the heavy cream on medium-high speed until it begins to thicken, then lower the speed and continue beating until the cream is stiff and glossy. Fold the whipped cream into the egg yolk mixture. Beat the egg whites until they are stiff and smooth.

In a saucepan, bring the remaining 4 tablespoons of sugar and the water to a lively bubble and let it cook for 3 minutes, or until the syrup is clear. Remove it from the heat. Turn your mixer to high, and slowly pour the syrup into the egg whites, beating the 2 ingredients together for about 3 minutes. The mixture should triple in volume. Turn the mixer down to medium and beat until the whites cool to room temperature, about 5

(continued on next page)

minutes. Fold the whites into the yolk mixture. Combine well but do not overmix, or the batter will fall.

Spoon the mixture into individual custard cups and freeze for about 6 hours, or until frozen completely like ice cream. Serve with the chocolate sauce and strawberries, if you wish.

Granella

Ground Nut Brittle

. . . .

³/₄ cup sugar   Sweet butter, for the pan

1 generous cup nuts (hazelnuts,

    almonds, peanuts), toasted and

    cooled

Melt the sugar in a medium saucepan over low heat, stirring constantly, then remove it from the heat, add the toasted nuts, and stir to coat all the nuts well.

Transfer the mixture to a well-buttered sheet pan and spread to cover the bottom of the pan. Let this cool, then place it in the freezer until it becomes brittle.

Break the *granella* into chunks that will fit into a food-processing bowl. Process the *granella* until it is coarse and crumbly. *Granella* can be used for garnishing many sweets. Store these ground nuts in a container wrapped with plastic in a cool, dry place. They will keep for a month.

Index

Index
331